Sea Kayaking Guide
Brittany
60 paddles

Every effort has been made to ensure that the information in this guide is correct and up to date. However, conditions can change from day to day. Neither the authors nor the publisher are responsible for decisions made by kayakers in choosing or undertaking the paddles in this book. Weather and sea conditions can turn even an "easy paddle" into a serious undertaking.

Sea Kayaking Guide
Brittany
60 paddles

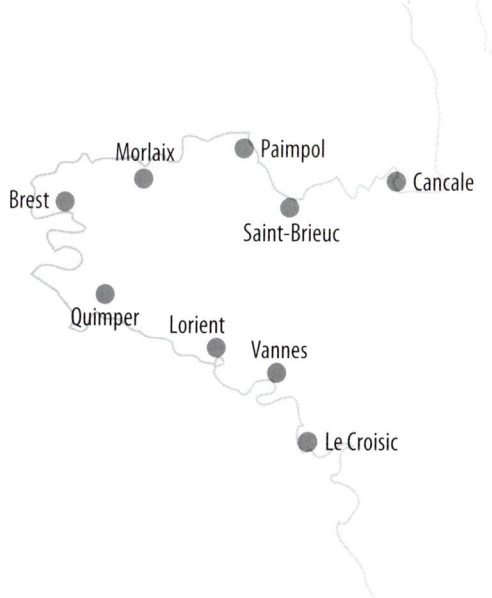

Sea Kayaking Guide
Brittany
paddles

60

Véronique Olivier and Guy Lecointre
translated by Peter Bisset

Photographs

All photos by Guy Lecointre or Véronique Olivier, except where noted. These were contributed by;
Christian Magré, Peter Bisset, Liz Bisset, Yann Dodard, Ivan Leguérinel, Laurent Malthieux, Richard Bate, Dominique Hottois, Éric Julé, Erwan Louet, Pascal Mallard, Artur Antúnez Vitales, Hervé Le Flohic, Robert Mc Lennan, Steve Earl, Christophe Meyer, Éric Ollivier, Françoise de Ravel, Jean-Pierre Van Obbergen, and by Aurélien Audevard and Didier Collin from www.oiseaux.net

Layout Pierre Villecourt, maps Thierry Puyfoulhoux.
Translation Peter Bisset.
Publication ©Le Canotier.

First published in France in 2012 by Le Canotier as *Guide Kayak de Mer, Bretagne 60 itinéraires*. ISBN 978-2-910197-29-2.
English translation published in 2013 by Le Canotier as *Sea Kayaking Guide Brittany 60 paddles*. ISBN 978-2-910197-32-2.

The Authors assert the moral right to be identified as the authors of this work. All rights reserved. No part of this publication may be reproduced, stored in a retrieval system, or transmitted in any form by any means, electronic, mechanical, photocopying, recording or otherwise, without prior written permission of the Publisher.

Dépôt légal Bibliothèque Nationale de France: April 2013.
Le Canotier
206 rue du Moulin à vent – 76760 Yerville – France
tel. 33 (0)2 35 96 61 31 – www.canotier.com

For all those who enjoy the freedom of the sea from their kayak.

Contents

The Authors 12
Paddling in France, the attraction of Brittany 15
How to use the guide 17
Charts 19
Paddle with the Tide 20
Tidal flows and currents 23
Rules and Regulations 24
Weather Forecasts 25
Coastguard Bulletins 26
Safe Paddling 28
Some hazards 31
The Bivouac or Over-night stop 32
Respect the Environment 33

The Paddles

From the Loire to the Vilaine
- **01** The Wild Coast of Le Croisic **/*** 34
- **02** The Island of Dumet ** 38
- **03** The Gold Mine ** 42

The Gulf of Morbihan and surrounding area
- *The Gulf of Morbihan* 46
- **04** The Islands of Boëd and Boëdig * 50
- **05** A Tour of the Gulf of Morbihan ** 54
- **06** Towards the Island of Ilur * 58
- **07** The Mouth of the Gulf of Morbihan *** 62
- **08** Up and down the Auray estuary ** 66
- **09** The Crac'h Tidal River * 70
- **10** Belle-Île *** 74
- *Cliff Birds* 80
- **11** Houat and Hoëdic *** 82
- *Food for Free* 87
- **12** The Quiberon Peninsula **/*** 88

Around Lorient
- 13 The Ria d'Étel (North) * 92
- *Salt Marsh and Mudflat* 97
- 14 The Ria d'Étel (South) **/*** 98
- 15 The Blavet */** 102
- *Brittany's maritime vocation* 106
- 16 The Island of Groix **/*** 108
- 17 The Laïta * 112

The Quimper area
- 18 The Cliffs of Clohars-Carnoët ** 116
- 19 The Aven and the Belon ** 120
- 20 Concarneau Bay ** 124
- 21 Glénan Islands *** 128
- *The Abris du Marin* 133
- 22 The Odet * 134
- 23 Towards Pont-l'Abbé ** 138
- 24 The Étocs **/*** 142

Around Douarnenez
- 25 The Pointe du Raz *** 146
- 26 The Bird Cliffs of Cap Sizun *** 150
- 27 Douarnenez * 154

The Crozon peninsula
- 28 The Caves of Morgat ** 158
- 29 The Tas de Pois **/*** 162
- 30 Islands of L'île des Morts and Trébéron **/*** 166
- *Breton lighthouses* 171

Around Brest
- 31 Brest Harbour–The Aulne */** 172
- 32 The Headland of Saint-Mathieu *** 176
- 33 Molène Archipelago *** 180
- *The Formation of the Abers* 185
- 34 Aber Ildut to Portsall **/*** 186
- 35 The Aber Benoît and the Island of Guénioc ** 190
- 36 Aber Wrac'h and Île Vierge * 194
- *The Goémoniers* 198
- 37 The Pagan Coast ** 200
- 38 The Dunes of Keremma ** 204

Contents

The Morlaix area
- **39** The Island of Siec **/***...208
- **40** The Island of Batz ***..212
- **41** The Bay of Morlaix */**..216
- **42** Primel and the Heather Coast **/***....................................220

The Pink Granite Coast
- **43** Trébeurden and Île Grande **/***.......................................224
- **44** Trégastel */**..228
- **45** The Pink Granite Coast */**..232
- **46** Les Sept Îles–The Seven Islands **/***..............................236

Around Paimpol
- **47** The Islands of Port-Blanc **...240
- **48** The Island of Er **..244
- **49** The Sillon de Talbert and Les Héaux * or **/***................248
- *The Bréhat Archipelago*..252
- **50** The Rocky South West of Bréhat */**................................254
- **51** Circumnavigating Bréhat **/***...258
- **52** The Trieux Estuary **..262
- **53** Porz Even and the Island of Saint-Rion */**......................266
- **54** The Cliffs of Bréhec **...270
- **55** The Islands of Saint-Quay **...274
- *Kayak Fishing*..278

The Emerald Coast
- **56** Cape Fréhel **/***..280
- **57** Saint-Briac and Les Hébihens Island **............................284
- **58** The Tidal Rance */**..288
- **59** The Forts of Saint-Malo **..292
- **60** The Emerald Coast **/***...296

Epilogue—60 paddles… and your own..300
Beaufort Scale..302
Useful Addresses..303
Useful Websites..315
Lexicon...316

Contents

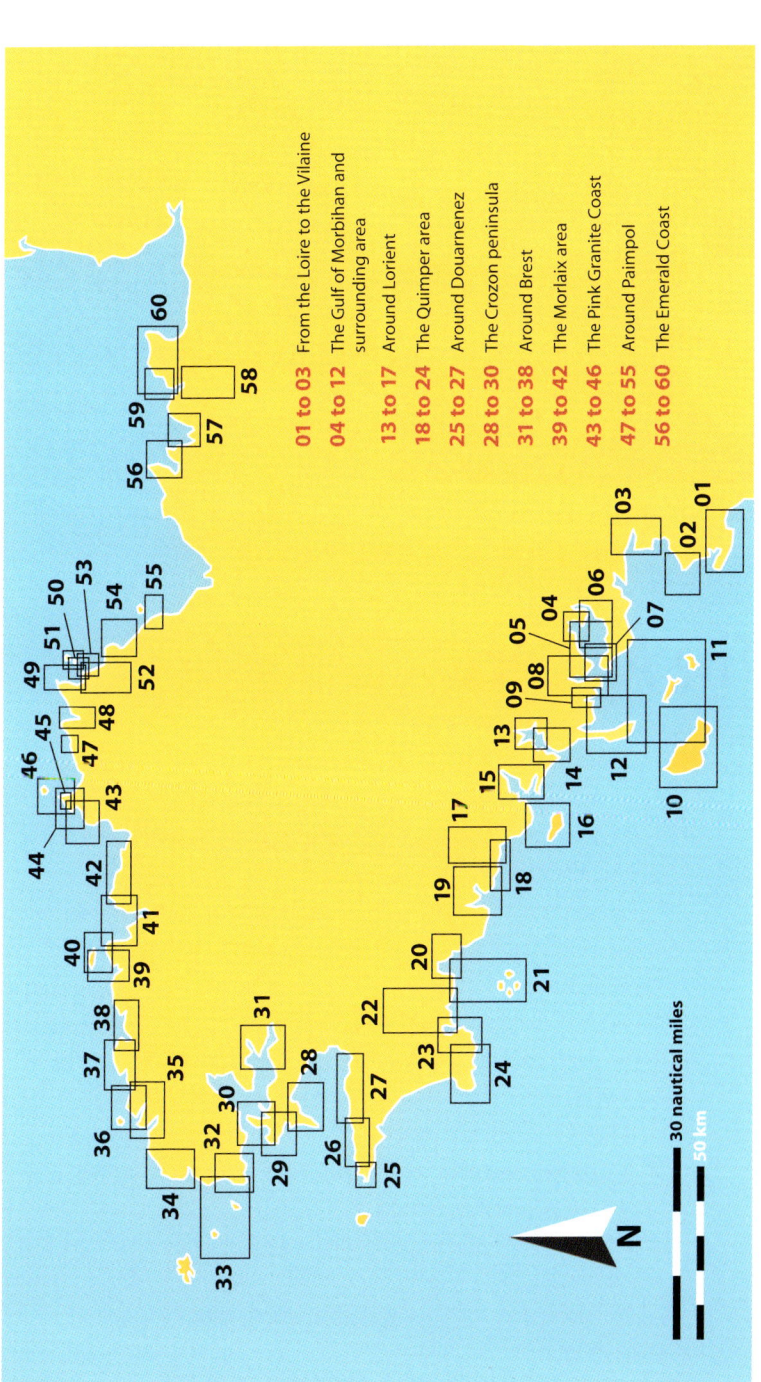

01 to 03	From the Loire to the Vilaine
04 to 12	The Gulf of Morbihan and surrounding area
13 to 17	Around Lorient
18 to 24	The Quimper area
25 to 27	Around Douarnenez
28 to 30	The Crozon peninsula
31 to 38	Around Brest
39 to 42	The Morlaix area
43 to 46	The Pink Granite Coast
47 to 55	Around Paimpol
56 to 60	The Emerald Coast

Guy. Photo V. Olivier

Véro. Photo Y. Dodard

The Authors

TEACHER AND CAMERAMAN, Guy and Véro tried out various outdoor activities: long distance walking, sailing, paragliding... before looking for a sea based activity, using minimum equipment and offering maximum freedom: this was sea kayaking, which they started in 1993.

After starting off in the Gulf of Morbihan, they found the Youth Hostel at Paimpol and the Bréhat archipelago, which at that time was a centre for sea kayakers. Here they learned the essential skills. This approach, based not on competition, but on self sufficiency and being responsible for oneself and the group, became a basis for their paddling. As well as many many paddles in Brittany, they have also made enjoyable sea kayaking trips to Norway, Ireland, Scotland, Croatia, Alaska...

The urge to pass on their experiences made them; write (him and her), film (him), draw (her), lead groups (him and her), organise meets (him and her); as volunteers in diverse sea kayak associations and clubs.

This guide is a natural progression: we hope you enjoy reading it!

Our thanks go to the fellow long distance paddlers who checked some of the paddles in this guide: Christian Magré, Patrick Lemoine, Ivan Leguérinel, Henri Gabolde, Eric Ollivier, Yann Guillou, Eric Julé, Guy Van Achter, Olivier Friconneau; and

The Authors

also Alain Corre (geology) and Yann Dodard (fishing) for their expert input.

All those who accompanied us on the paddles to develop this guide and who let us use their photographs, especially: France Hallaire and Dominique Hottois, Gaëlle Lefeuvre, Louis Le Bégat, Alain Caffiau, Carole Beaudouin, Dominique Calderon and our friends from Pagaia, Stéphanie Long, Annick Le Moigne, Gilles Cadier, Brice Mathelier, Yves Denizeau, Ivan Leguérinel, Paul Couillandeau, Franck Clavaud, Hervé Nédellec, Yann Guillou, Anne-Gaëlle Ryo, Sandie Desbois, Jean-François Tribot and the club RKM from Larmor-Baden, Béatrice Le Galès and David Viguier, Erwan Louët, Claude Boyer, and all the others…to all the talented photographers who contributed their pictures.

To all those who helped us in other ways with the preparation of this book: Michel Bazile, Fanch Rault and Michelle Bougeard, Anne and Michel Jollivet, Marie-France Le Bégat, Joël Cavy, Marif and Yann Prigent, Christophe and Frédérique Claeys, Guénolé Diguet and Manon Faillenet, Thierry and Max Edet, Erwan, Nathalie, Mathis and Rose Noury.

To François Demont for vital help with information technology.

To Yvette Olivier who proved an attentive listener and Michel Olivier with whom we shared our first paddle strokes on the sea.

To Laurent Demai and Pascal Paoli for introducing us to this collection of sea kayaking guide books.

To Thierry Puyfoulhoux who drew the maps for this guide, for his patience and professionalism.

To Peter Bisset for the quality of his translation and the apposite nature of his suggestions. His knowledge of Brittany proved very valuable. To Liz for her proof reading and advice on the English text.

To Patrice de Ravel, our editor, who helped us all the way through the work.

And especially to Guy Cloarec who, from the Youth Hostel of Paimpol from 1980 to 2000, inspired an entire generation of sea-kayakers, including ourselves, with his passion for sea kayaking. ■

The Translator

Peter is a recreational sea kayaker, who has explored many sections of the UK coast and also paddled in France, Norway, Sweden, around Elba and ¾ of the way around Corsica. Most of his paddling is in the Solent with the Portsmouth and District Canoe Club.

However, his main love must be extended trips in wild places. He spends several weeks in April-June each year paddling in Scotland, sometimes with his wife, sometimes alone, from Sandwood down to Kyle. Another annual destination is Brittany. He has paddled all of the areas, and many of the individual paddles in this book. Having learnt French for his work in francophone Africa and paddled with the authors, he was well placed to work on the translation.

Translator's Note

by Peter Bisset

Brittany has a lot to offer the sea kayaker, just look at the statistics, a coastline of 2,700km with about 800 islands, and then there is the Breton culture. Over the years I've kayaked much of the coast, from the warm waters of Quiberon and Morbihan, to the cooler, but still warmer than UK, Channel coast. From the white water of the Raz de Sein and the mouth of the Gulf of Morbihan, to the placid estuaries and tidal rivers, the *Abers*, far from the open sea. Sometimes on our own, having researched tides and put-ins very carefully; but often with local paddlers. Two of these are the authors of the French version of this book. You will see me with my yellow *Anas acuta* in the oasis of Port Saint-Nicolas on Île de Groix (see paddle 16). The contrast that day between the peaceful scene in the photo and the open sea -only 100m away-; surf surging up the cliffs, with the choice of death defying rock-hopping or an exciting but safe paddle 50m offshore, typified paddling in Brittany for me.

Peter floating waiting for the others to launch, Île Tomé (paddle 47). Photo Liz Bisset

When Guy and Véro brought out their book, I thought that I knew the region well. However, I soon realised that even in places I'd visited several times and even though I'd visited them with local paddlers, I'd missed out on some lovely trips. This translation will get you, the English speaker, started, but there is so much to see and do, always an excuse to go back again next year! French sea kayakers are a friendly bunch, so say hello to people on the water, maybe it will turn out to be Guy and Véro.

In their book, Guy and Véro, not only express their enthusiasm for sea kayaking in the region, but also their love of the French language. This translation does not attempt to follow word for word, but rather to cover all of the practical detail of the 60 paddles and as much as possible of their enthusiasm. Extra paragraphs have been added at the translator's whim to make things clearer for the non-French reader. French place names are maintained as it is those you will find on the map. A short French-English lexicon of kayaking words and expressions has been added. ∎

Exploring the nature reserve of Cap Sizun.

Introduction

YOU MAY HAVE HEARD of draconian laws inhibiting sea kayaking in France.

Paddling in France

In the past, kayaks were regarded as beach toys and forbidden to go more than a few hundred metres offshore. However, lobbying by sea kayaking bodies has had the sport and its practitioners recognised as serious sea goers. The limit is now 6nm offshore provided basic safety equipment is carried (see Regulations), these are all the items that a prudent sea kayaker would be carrying with them anyway. French kayakers must register their kayaks, but this rule does not apply to foreigners. Unless you are behaving in a dangerous or stupid way there is nothing to fear from the authorities.

Other water users tend to have less confidence in the seamanship of kayakers than is the case in Britain, not expecting kayakers to know or follow collision regulations or, for example, to keep to starboard in narrow channels. The average pleasure boat in Brittany goes out to sea less than 11 times a year, so taking account of regular boaters, most are rarely or never used. Seamanship may be haphazard and summer kayakers are tarred with the same brush. However, good seamanship, like everywhere else in the world, rapidly wins friends amongst fishermen, serious sailors and professional skippers, so it is worth being a good ambassador for the sport.

Paddling amongst the rocks and swell.

The attraction of Brittany

The Brittany coast is not remote and wild in the same way as the Highlands of Scotland, although long stretches are protected by nature reserves. Brittany is one of the more densely populated areas of France and over the last 30 years there has been sprawling development of holiday homes along the coast. In the south and east of Brittany the summer population of holiday makers leads to crowds at honey-pot sandy beaches. In Finistère, even in summer, the neat holiday villages with their white walls and slate roofs, are mainly empty. On foot or by bike, it is a succession of eerie ghost villages, building them no doubt seemed a good idea at the time. However, for the kayaker, this matters not a jot.

Access and parking by the sea is a lot easier then in most parts of Britain. Holiday makers start their day late and finish early, arrive somewhere at 10 a.m. and the parking spots will be empty, leave at 6 p.m. and they will be empty again, but park considerately, if it is near a sandy beach and the sun is shining, it may have been chock-a-block at 3 p.m. Once on the sea, the coastal development can only be seen for a short period around high water. Most of the time it is hidden behind the rock wall exposed by the tide and might as well be a thousand miles away.

The coast is as unchanging and wild as it was 50 years ago, or even 1,500 years ago when the Britons, displaced by the Saxon invasion of Great Britain, arrived.

The weather is definitely better and the sea warmer than further north, the food tastier, campsites and gites, toilets, and taps for rinsing kit, in better supply. Breton culture is alive and well, as you will see when they come down from their inland villages for a Fest-Noz by the sea.

Wild rocky coasts are interspersed with sheltered inlets, guaranteeing that from any base, whatever the conditions, there will be a paddle available within a short drive away. ■

Introduction

How to use the guide

THIS GUIDE WILL HELP you choose and prepare for paddles. However, it cannot make decisions as to whether it is safe or wise to undertake any particular paddle. It is up to you to decide. It is not necessary to be an expert, but it is necessary to know, bearing in mind your experience, the strength of the group, the weather, sea conditions, your mood etc. when to go and when not to go. Assess your capacity with modesty. Make sure you are well equipped. This guide will not replace learning the techniques of navigation and trip planning, rescue and, if you are on your own, self rescue, necessary for safe paddling.

Sea and weather conditions in Brittany can change rapidly, listen to weather and swell forecasts, but also keep a weather-eye open during the paddle. For each paddle, especially those venturing offshore, think of a plan B, and a plan C, in case plan A fails and you have to cut the paddle short or are unable to return to the starting point. Have a bivi bag and warm spare clothing with you in case of a forced bivouac.

All of the paddles in this book were undertaken in a sea kayak with waterproof bulkheads and the necessary equipment to legally paddle up to 6nm offshore. (see Regulations). All of the planning is based on a cruising speed of 3kt (5.5km/hr). A reasonable day's paddle is taken as 15nm (28km) and will probably take 5-6 hours including halts. Many of the inshore paddles could be undertaken in general purpose kayaks, but in that case, plan on 1-1.5kt over the water; in these boats, paddling against even a moderate tide might not be possible so the planning has to be taken even more seriously.

Planning your paddle

In Brittany, the tide is everything, the shoreline changes from one hour to the next. This is why, as well as the description of the paddle, we have included departure times relative to tide times and the impact the tide will have on the paddle. Sometimes various alternatives are given and the timings needed to do the paddle in the opposite direction.

The difficulty of the paddles has been assessed assuming good conditions. Bad conditions can turn even apparently simple and easy places into danger spots. The paddles are divided into three categories, these take into account the exposure of the paddle.

Exploring the Odet by sit-on-top.

✘ These are in more or less protected water, often in estuaries or in the flooded valleys called *abers* or *rias* (the Cornish "ria") in Brittany. Some of them are quite long, but could be cut short or done in two sections. Tidal flow weak or medium. Would equal BCU 2-3 star paddling.

✘✘ Paddles with sections exposed to the open sea or stronger tidal flows. Strong winds and swell may be encountered. Some sections of coast may preclude any landing. There may be open water crossings up to 1nm from shelter. Equivalent to BCU 3-4 star.

✘✘✘ Committing paddles which should only be attempted in good conditions. Good paddling skills are required and the ability to manage paddling in strong tidal flows and possibly large swell. They often include long stretches of open water and inhospitable coastline. They are often longer than 12nm. Equivalent to BCU 4-5 star.

All of these paddles have been undertaken by the authors themselves, but are described in good conditions. In many cases escape options for if it all goes wrong are mentioned. However, especially for exposed sections, bad conditions could make paddling very difficult and escape impossible.

All of the bearings given in this guide are "true". Magnetic declination should be taken into account where necessary and estimates of lee way due to tide and wind added or subtracted. The tidal flows given are the maximum that can be expected during mean spring tides, neap flows are likely to be around half of this.

In the estuaries and tidal rivers the terms right and left bank correspond to "river right" and "river left". If you don't do any river paddling you might not be aware that these terms always refer to the banks as if you were looking downstream. ■

Where to launch?

More details including, maps, photos and GPS co-ordinates, for all the launch points in this guide, and many more at: **www.kayakalo.fr**

Introduction

Learn more

Doing the chart-work before leaving Rosmeur harbour, Douarnenez.

Charts

There is a reference to the appropriate SHOM and Navicarte charts and IGN maps at the head of each paddle as these are the most commonly used. However, other mapping may be available in your country. Whichever charts you choose, get used to them and be able to estimate timings and distances at that scale. Carrying a marine chart of the area is one of the requirements for going more than 2nm offshore.

For coastal paddling, the French IGN maps at 1:25,000 are very useful. Excellent for finding landing spots, they also give considerable detail on marine features and many buoys and navigation marks are marked. Numerous spot heights on rocks give a good idea as to which will appear prominent. On these maps the zero height contour, traced in light brown, corresponds to mid-tide whether it is springs or neaps. It is very useful for getting an idea of how far out the tide will be and how easy it will be to access the shore.

Except at high water, it may be difficult to see the shoreline, it is hidden behind the rocks. Landmarks on high ground, often far inland, are all that you have to go on. Identifying church spires, water towers and villages etc. on the map before you set off will make it much easier to find your way to that hidden beach.

Important: The sketch maps in this guide are designed to give a general idea of the trip; they are not a substitute for charts or maps. ∎

The rocks of Bréhat at low water.

Paddle with the Tide

THE SEA KAYAKER in Brittany lives with the rhythm of the tides. These determine the launch and landing, where to go and when, avoiding, or not, being caught in the mud or the oyster beds. Short cuts or interesting passages amongst the rocks become possible or not, finding good spots for lunch or a short break, avoiding long portages, all these depend upon the tide. Brittany does have large tides and, even with good planning, having at least one trolley within the group may prove useful to avoid long portages.

Tides result from the gravitational attraction of the moon and sun on the masses of water on the planet. In Brittany there are two high waters and two low waters per day, about 6hrs 12 minutes separate one high water and one low water. High water, *Pleine mer* in French (so HW=PM). Low water, *Basse mer* in French (LW=BM). Succeeding high waters are on average 52 minutes later each day.

The "Service Hydrographique et Océanographique de la Marine" (SHOM), publishes annual tide tables for the principal ports, these give high and low water times and the coefficients. The coefficient indicates the predicted height of the tide. Once you get used to them, coefficients are easy to use, SHOM also predicts the actual heights for each port, like the Admiralty system in the UK, but these are less readily available. The coefficient for any tide is the same for all of the Atlantic and Channel coasts. Coefficients vary between 20 and 120, the larger the coefficient the larger the amplitude of the tide. A coefficient of about 50 equals a mean neap tide and 80 a mean spring tide. A coefficient of less than 50 is a very small tide, a coefficient of 100 or more corresponds to exceptional spring tides where the LW will be very low and the HW very high. The French term for springs; *vives-eaux* (lively tides) and for neaps; *mortes-eaux* (dead tides) are very expressive for those kayakers who like to play in tide races.

The tidal range, the actual difference in height between a LW and the corresponding HW (*marnage* in French) varies from 6m at Saint-Nazaire, to 7m at Brest, and 13m at Saint-Malo. The latter stretch of coast has the second largest tidal range in the World after the Bay of Fundy. The often quoted line that the tide comes in faster than a horse can gallop in the Bay of Saint-Malo is said by local people to be untrue. However, kayakers have found that it does go out faster than you can portage a kayak towards it! This tidal range has permitted the development of a very rich inter-tidal fauna and flora.

The tide does not rise and fall at a constant rate. An estimate of the rise and fall can be made by the "Rule of 12ths"; a rise or fall of 1/12 in the first hour, 2/12 in the second hour, 3/12 in the third hour, 3/12 in the fourth hour, 2/12 in the fifth hour and 1/12 in the sixth hour. Beware, this does not hold for all places.

Launching at fort Duguesclin at mid-tide. The long portage home at low-water.

Tell-tale signs of the tide

Numerous strand lines: neap tides.

Floating sand grains...the tide has turned.

Zonation on the rocks, south Brittany.

The wave of tide runs onto the Atlantic face of France at about the same time for all of the reference ports; Brest, Saint-Nazaire, Port Tudy. Along the Channel coast, the north coast of Brittany, it is constrained by the narrowing sea and arrives progressively later. At Roscoff it arrives about 1hr 10 minutes after Brest, Paimpol 2hr 15 later and 2hr 30 later at Saint-Malo, the difference is less on neap tides.

Almanacs and online sources will give tide tables as well as the predictions from SHOM, which are often displayed at harbour masters offices and alongside quays. Although most tide tables are now corrected for local time, it is worth remembering that local time is UTC +2 in summer and UTC +1 in winter.

Careful observation will give you a good idea of the tide, several strand lines indicate a period of neap tides, whilst a single one indicates a large spring tide. Floating sand or small sea shells indicate the begginning of flood tide on a calm beach. The zonation of seaweed and barnacles gives an idea of how high or low the tide is. The black lichen *Verrucaria maura* makes a black line indicating the height of the higest tides, above this the yellow lichen *Xanthoria parientina*, the same one that you see on roofs, grows in bright patches. Below the high water mark various seaweeds, barnacles and shellfish live at distinct heights, ending with the nodding brown heads of kelp at the low water mark. ∎

Tidal flows and currents

IN ENGLISH WE GENERALLY use the term tide to refer to both the up and down movement and the sideways flow of the sea. In French the term *courant* (current) is used for horizontal flow in both rivers and the sea, thus the tidal atlases published by SHOM are called "*Courants de Marée*". Three volumes cover all of the Brittany coast. Admiralty tidal atlases of the area are also available and are often reproduced in miniature in almanacs. The SHOM atlases are covered in little arrows, these give a good overview of the complexity of the tidal flows and potential back eddies, but can be confusing at first if you are used to the more restrained Admiralty system. The SHOM tidal atlases are a very worthwhile investment.

Provided it is in the right direction, the tide can sweep the kayaker along on a magic carpet so, with the big tides found in Brittany, it is well worth doing some careful planning. If there are tidal flows, there are also back eddies. Each point and headland, big or small will create a back eddy behind it. If you have to go against the tide, it is worth thinking about how to make best use of them. Rocks, buoys, towers, islands and islets all have an eddy behind them, a good place for a rest, to allow people to catch up, or to assess a ferry glide.

Where the flow is constrained by a point, shallow water or any narrow passage, the flow will be accelerated. An area of rough water is often to be found where this faster moving water runs into slower moving water, so just after obstacles to the flow.

Although being "pinned", forced against an obstacle by the tide, is much rarer sea kayaking than in white water, it can happen and is very dangerous. Keep an eye on potential obstacles; moored boats, posts, buoys, rocks, mud, and make sure the tide is not carrying you onto them. If you are in danger of being pinned, lean towards the obstacle. If the current is too strong for you, exit the boat sooner rather than later…when it might be too late.

The flow is usually less strong along the edges than in mid channel. Flood tide in French is *le flot* and the ebb *le jusant*. ■

Rules and Regulations

THE CURRENT RULES and regulations for sea kayakers are as follows (law of 11 March 2008, section 240):

Any craft can navigate up to 300m offshore. To go more than 300m offshore a French kayaker has to register his boat, this regulation **does not apply to foreigners**. However, all kayakers must carry the appropriate safety equipment.

Up to 2nm offshore you must carry:
- buoyancy aid of at least 50 newtons buoyancy
- a means of attracting attention by light (preferably a strobe attached to the buoyancy aid, but a torch will do)
- a means of making an audible signal (whistle or foghorn)
- a means of bailing the kayak, a pump or bailer (this rule does not apply to self draining boats like sit-on-tops, interestingly a kayak with spray skirt is considered self draining, but you would be well advised to carry a pump anyway)
- a means of climbing back on board i.e. a self-rescue technique
- a towline (2-3 boat lengths) and an attachment point for being towed.

For between 2nm and 6nm you must carry all of the above plus:
- three red hand held flares, a signal mirror and a compass
- chart of the area (could be electronic), memory aid for international buoyage (available as vinyl stickers in chandlers).

The flares can pose a problem for English kayakers since the cross-channel ferry companies do not allow you to carry them and they do sometimes ask when they see the kayaks. They may accept carriage of flares in a proper flare box locked inside the car during the voyage. If you have not taken flares, in the very unlikely event of you being asked by a French coastal patrol boat it might be possible to argue that a PLB with GPS facility is both safer and surer.

For offshore paddles, a VHF, mobile phone in waterproof bag and a spare paddle, at least amongst the group, are also highly recommended. ∎

Driving with your Kayak in France

You are unlikely to run into any problems driving with sea kayaks in France. The load must be secure and marked with a red flag, but there is no need for any special board or signs. The toll booths on motorways sometimes sense the height and issue commercial vehicle tickets, just go to a manned booth when you come to pay and you will only pay the car rate. In any case you will have to choose a booth without a height restriction, usually on the right. There are no tolls to pay in Brittany!

Introduction

Rivière de Pont-l'Abbé in the rain.

Weather Forecasts

MODERN TECHNOLOGY has vastly improved both the forecasts and the ease of obtaining them. Many paddlers now have access to the internet:
The inshore forecast (*bulletins côte*) of Météo-France is the most useful for the kayaker. The coastal forecast (*météo rivage*) concentrates on how much sunshine a holiday maker can expect.
http://marine.meteofrance.com/marine/accueil?93025.path=marinecote
Previmer is an experimental site which has a huge amount of information in English on weather, sea state and tidal flows. You need to register to access more data and some of it is limited to prevent commercial use. http://www.previmer.org/en
Your favourite international weather site, for instance Windguru, Windfinder or Magic Seaweed will also cover Brittany.

Radio broadcasts:
France Inter on 162 kHz, Long Wave, at 20.30hrs and France Info, Brest 1404 kHz, Rennes 711 kHz, Medium Wave, at 06.40.
The Shipping forecast on BBC Radio 4, 198 kHz, Long wave, at 00.48, 05.20, 12.01 and 17.54, sea area "Plymouth" covers the Channel coast of Brittany and "Biscay" the Atlantic coast.

Harbour Master's Offices, Campsites and Sailing Schools often have a forecast on a notice board outside. Sailors on board yachts at anchor or fishing boats can be a good source of information during a long expedition. Regional newspapers have a weather page, a camp-site attendant will often let you have a glimpse at the forecast if you ask nicely. ■

Coastguard Bulletins

THE FRENCH COASTGUARD regional headquarters (CROSS) give regular weather bulletins on VHF. The time and channel used for the regular bulletins varies around the coast and can be found via a link from the Météo-France website, click on "Guide Marine" "télécharger" (download). An announcement is made on Channel 16 shortly before the broadcasts. Special announcements are made when winds may reach force 7 or above, again a warning call on Channel 16 is made beforehand.

The following details are taken from the *Guide Marine* of Météo-France.

CROSS Étel, channel 80 (emergency 24h/24: tel. 02 97 55 35 35), transmitters:
- Saint-Nazaire 7h45, 16h15 and 19h45.
- Belle-Île 7h33, 16h03 and 19h33.
- Île de Groix 7h15, 15h45 and 19h15.
- Penmarc'h 7h03, 15h33 and 19h03.

CROSS Étel, channel 63: experimental regular transmissions.

CROSS Corsen, channel 79 (emergency 24h/24: tel. 02 98 89 31 31), transmitters:
- Pointe du Raz 4h45, 7h03, 11h03*, 15h33 and 19h03.
- Le Stiff/Ouessant 5h03, 7h15, 11h15*, 15h45 and 19h15.
- Île de Batz 5h15, 7h33, 11h33*, 16h03 and 19h33.
- Bodic/Le Trieux 5h33, 7h45, 11h45*, 16h15 and 19h45.
- Cap Fréhel 5h45, 8h03, 12h03*, 16h33 and 20h03.

(*) From the 1st of May to 30th Sept., after an announcement on channel 16.

Coastguard lookouts will give weather information if they are called up on Channel 16, they usually ask enquirers to use working channel 10, they do not accept telephone requests for weather forecasts. However, they will give current observations over the telephone, the numbers are given below.

Atlantic Coast and South Brittany

Chémoulin (24h/24), tel. 02 40 91 99 00 [44380 Pornichet]
Piriac-sur-mer, tel. 02 40 23 59 87 [44420 Piriac-sur-mer]
Saint-Julien, tel. 02 97 50 09 35 [56170 Quiberon]
Le Talut (24h/24), tel. 02 97 31 85 07 [56360 Belle-Île-en-mer]
Beg Melen (24h/24), tel. 02 97 86 80 13 [56590 Groix]
Étel, tel. 02 97 55 35 59 [56410 Étel]
Beg Meil, tel. 02 98 94 98 92 [29170 Fouesnant]
Penmarc'h (24h/24), tel. 02 98 58 61 00 [29760 Penmarc'h]

*Passing in front of the Corsen Coastguard (CROSS Corsen).
Photo L. Malthieux*

VHF and Mobile Phone

A handheld VHF radio is an important piece of equipment for safety at sea. Unlike in the UK, no licence is required to use a handheld VHF with a power output of 6W or less in French territorial waters. If you hold a Short Range Certificate, this is valid for using a fixed marine VHF in France. Maintaining a listening watch on channel 16 is good for your own safety and the safety of others, and encourages sense of solidarity amongst mariners.

A call for help, Mayday or Pan-Pan, is likely to be picked up either by the coastguard or nearby ships. Weather forecasts can be obtained at regular times. Big ship movements can be monitored in busy areas like the approaches to Brest.

Channel 16 is the international calling and distress channel. It must not be used for routine communications. After a brief call on channel 16 move to a clear working channel. Channels, 6, 8, 72 and 77 are useful working channels, but listen for a minute to check that no-one else is using them.

Mobile phones can be very useful and the signal propagates well over the sea, but is often blocked close inshore by high ground. In emergency, dial 112 and ask for the CROSS. Phones can be operated inside a waterproof pouch. On a long expedition take every possible chance to dry out the phone and case, or condensation may render it inoperable. ■

Pointe du Raz (24h/24), tel. 02 98 70 66 57 [29770 Plogoff]
Cap de la Chèvre, tel. 02 98 27 09 55 [29160 Crozon]
Le Toulinguet, tel. 02 98 27 90 02 [29570 Camaret-sur-mer]
Le Portzic/Brest port (watch) (Ch. 8), tel. 02 98 49 11 96 [29200 Brest]
St-Mathieu (watch), tel. 02 98 89 01 59 [29217 Plougonvelin]

Channel and North Brittany
Ouessant Le Stiff (watch), tel. 02 98 48 81 50 [29242 Ouessant]
Brignogan (24h/24), tel. 02 98 83 50 84 [29890 Brignogan]
Île-de-Batz, tel. 02 98 61 76 06 [29253 Île-de-Batz]
Saint-Quay (24h/24), tel. 02 96 70 42 18 [22410 Saint-Quay]
La Clarté - Ploumanac'h (24h/24), tel. 02 96 91 46 51 [Ploumanac'h]
Bréhat, tél. 02 96 20 00 12 [22870 Bréhat]
Saint-Cast (24h/24), tel. 02 96 41 85 30 [22380 Saint-Cast]
Le Grouin (from 01.06 to 15.09), tel. 02 99 89 72 29 [35260 Cancale]. ■

Wind, Swell and Sea State

Trips can be planned well in advance to take account of tide, tidal flows and the nature of the seabed and coast. Wind, swell and sea state can be assessed just before starting out. However, the forecasts for these latter three are by their nature a broad sweep only giving an overview. On a small scale, wind against tide and clapotis, especially around headlands, can give harsher conditions. It is only years of experience that enable the forecasts to be put to full use in assessing what conditions will be like once you leave the shelter of the bay. ■

Photos C. Magré

Safe Paddling

THE MOST IMPORTANT safety decision is a good choice of where and when to paddle. The second is having appropriate paddling skills and the mental attitude necessary to make full use them. After that it is having the right equipment and keeping it in good condition.

After looking at the tide tables and weather forecast, study the maps and charts, appreciate the shape and nature of the coast and seabed; the areas likely to be sheltered and those exposed to the full force of the elements. Identify areas with their own special features, challenges and rewards.

Plan the trip; distance, timing, escape options, equipment necessary, appropriate clothing, what to do if the weather changes. Think about special hazards which might be encountered; tide races, large shipping, nature conservation areas.

Think about how you are going to feel on that choppy headland or in that tide race and rehearse staying calm and confident. It is not all about objective hazards. The same spot in the same conditions of tide, sea and wind, will feel very different in bright sunshine compared to gloomy weather. On a bright sunny day you may feel invincible, don't let the sunshine tempt you into a swell filled gulley a step beyond your skill level, on the other hand, don't let bad weather intimidate you.

Literally, "keep a weather eye open", for changes in the weather during the paddle.

Introduction

Carry food and drink to maintain your physical shape. Beware of sunburn or sunstroke. Hypothermia is an ever present danger, dress sensibly and carry spare clothes. Carrying at least one oversize cagoule or selkie in the group is a good idea. Put on over the top of everything else it can keep a cold paddler going. Paddle in a group within line of sight and voice contact. In even a 1m swell, paddlers disappear from time to time in the troughs. Plan ahead how you are going to communicate and what will happen if an emergency arises.

Do not be tempted to swim to safety except in exceptional circumstances like being swept onto rocks: stay with the kayak. Before going rock-hopping consider if anyone in the group has the skills necessary to come in and help you if it all goes wrong.

The coastguard (CROSS) is responsible for safety and rescue coordination on the sea. Call for advice or help sooner rather than later: North Brittany, CROSS Corsen, tel. 02 98 89 31 31 and South Brittany, CROSS Étel, tel. 02 97 55 35 35 or on VHF Channel 16. Once you have made a Mayday call the coastguard assumes all responsibility and only he can call off a search and rescue, you must follow instructions.

Make sure a home contact knows; who, where and when; so that the coastguard can be contacted in case of worries about an overdue group. Have back-up escape plans just in case and keep track of where you are and the nearest shelter and landing points.

It can be hard to assess tidal flow in open water. Transits on prominent objects or features on the coast can help. Take every opportunity presented by a buoy etc.,

If you are not very experienced

Start off in sheltered water. Choose neap tides and winds of force 3 or less. Paddle into the wind and tide on the way out, so paddling back will be easier and quicker. Avoid off-shore winds that could carry you out to sea. Avoid swell of more than 1m. Start off with short paddles.

to assess the force and direction of the current. Moored boats can often be observed from a distance, but be sure that the direction they lie in is due to current and not wind. Observing wind and water can give an idea of leeway, but always keep an eye on where you are on the water by orienting yourself relative to landmarks. Make corrections early enough if you are drifting off course. Soon after setting off, have a good look around to familiarise yourself for finding the way back.

Chart work based on 3kt over the water generally works well; however, get to know how fast you and your group travel by looking at the watch and map/chart from time to time on trips.

The compass is essential for navigating in many conditions; fog, sea fret, open crossings, travelling towards a flat coast without landmarks etc. The bearings to paddle on are best worked out in advance, but using the chart and a hand bearing compass with a rotating base plate at sea is possible. A boat mounted compass is easier for maintaining a course.

Develop and maintain your skill level. Towing is a fundamental skill. Another is the deep water rescue. The "one leg in over the outside and 360° turn" re-entry is commonly called *récupération à l'anglaise*, the "English rescue" in France. You might be asked to demonstrate it, make sure you can make a slick job of it! ■

Deep water rescue

Being able to effect a deep water rescue on anyone in any conditions is a fundamental skill. Practice it whenever a chance arises. Set the stopwatch to 1 minute!

"English" re-entry.

"T" rescue.

Some hazards

HERE ARE A FEW HAZARDS that you might be confronted with:

Whilst paddling

Being pinned (*en cravate*): this is uncommon in sea kayaking, but if it does happen is very dangerous. It is where the kayak becomes held by the current against an obstacle (rock, buoy etc.). Avoid getting into this position by keeping track of your position relative to any obstacles when paddling in tidal flows and currents. If it does happen, lean TOWARDS the obstacle and try to get on top of it to avoid capsizing. If a capsize does happen exit without panic and keep a clear head to avoid obstacles.

Shore-break, also *shore-break* in French: waves or swell dumping straight onto a beach, common on steep beaches and near high water. Landing can be hazardous and on steep shingle the undertow can wash you back into deep water. Study the bay carefully to find the least-bad place, wait for the tide to drop, or try exiting the boat and swimming in with the boat on a line. Decide how to make best use of the skills available within the group and make sure everyone knows the plan before committing to a landing.

Shallows (*hauts-fonds*): areas of shallow water which often raise large waves or even breakers, paddle around in the deeper water.

Bar (*barre*): a shallow bank often extending all the way across the entrance of rivers and estuaries and attendant rough water. Look out for deep water channels or wait for the tide to rise.

Sea caves (*grottes marines*): a major attraction for the sea kayaker, but also a potentially hazardous place. Assess the swell conditions and especially what happens when a large set arrives before venturing in. Breaking swell can carry a kayak onto rocks at the back of the cave or up to the roof. Backing in is often easier as the light seems to carry further and paddling out is quicker if something happens. Carry a waterproof torch. Don't crowd the narrow spaces. Someone should stay outside to warn of an approaching wave or to call for help.

Rips (*baïnes*): strong currents running out to sea through deeper channels on surf beaches. Their position alters as the tide rises and falls. Little danger for a kayaker in his boat, but could carry a capsized kayaker out to sea. Can be a useful way through the surf to land on the beach.

Bites and Stings

Jellyfish (*méduses* and *physalies*): can sting and detached tentacle fragments can run down the paddles to the hands even when the animals themselves have been avoided. Painful but seldom serious, be ready to call for help in case of a serious reaction. Try applying an anti-histamine cream.

Weaver fish (*vives*): small fish half-buried in the sand near the low water mark. The venom is very painful but heat labile, applying hot water makes the pain ease more quickly. Seek medical assistance in severe cases.

Sea urchins (*oursins*): wear shoes, the spines are sharp and easily detached. Only handle urchins with gloves. Broken off spines will be absorbed by the body over time. Keep the wounds clean to avoid infection.

Wounds and Injuries

Cuts (*coupures*): it is easy to get small cuts from sea shells, rocks, barnacles and small wounds from rubbing shoes or blisters. Long immersion in sea water tends to aggravate small wounds, so keep them clean and disinfected. Insulating tape is one of the few things that will stay on during prolonged immersion if wrapped around and back on itself.

Tendonitis (*tendinites*): this takes time to clear, so avoidance is the best policy. Keep rehydrated by drinking enough, hold the paddle in a light open grip, develop a relaxed paddling technique. Using a shorter paddle, less feather, some flexibility (not too much carbon) and smaller blades can help.

Back trouble (*mal au dos*): mainly due to poor handling of boats off the water; pair up, don't handle boats on your own. Pay attention to keeping an upright or slightly forward posture when paddling and not slouching. ■

The Bivouac or Over-night stop

WILD CAMPING is not allowed in France. Not to be confused with camping, the bivouac is a simple overnight halt. Any shelter is put up at dusk and packed away again at dawn. The best place is often at the top of the beach above the tide line. Publicly owned land may be easier to access than privately owned land.

There are many places along the Brittany coast where a discrete overnight stop will not pose a problem; indeed, there are some fantastic spots. Conservation areas and those owned by the Coastal Conservancy are exceptions, overnight stops are strictly prohibited. Too many people using the same site, will lead to problems, so this guide does not give any precise locations. Careful study of the 1:25,000 IGN maps will suggest possible spots. Local kayakers may be able to help pinpoint sites, but the best bivouac spots, like the best places for mushrooms in the forest, are something people tend to keep to themselves. If you are planning an overnight halt and do not know the area, start looking for a suitable place earlier rather than later. Leave no trace of your stay when you paddle off in the morning. ■

Respect the environment

BIVOUAC IN SUCH A WAY as to minimise impact and leave the minimum trace. Using a free standing shelter on the beach is better than trying to pitch a tent in fragile vegetation which may take months to recover.

*Bivouac at Belle-Île, Ster Vraz.
Photo Y. Dodard*

Do you really need to light a fire? If you do, use a site which has already been used before, for preference below the high water mark. Make sure the fire is out and the ashes dispersed before you leave.

Sea water is good for washing and the washing up, sand makes a good scouring pad. For a toilet, digging a scrape or using the foreshore near the low water mark is possible. However, why not wait until the public toilet at the next settlement along the coast.

Don't sneak up on animals or make sudden changes in course and alarm them. If paddling in a group don't encircle animals or drive them in a certain direction. Keep clear of bird nesting areas; terns; 15 April to 31 August, other birds; 15 March to 15 August. Ask wardens for advice, they may help you see things you would otherwise have missed.

Grey Seals are much less common in France than in the UK, only a few hundred individuals. This has increased from only tens of individuals in the 1970s. They are part of the grey seal population of South-West England and Wales and move freely across the Channel. Respect their space and allow them to approach you if they want to. Common seals are also at the limit of their range and found in small numbers in sheltered bays (i.e. Bay of Mont Saint-Michel). ■

Reporting Observations

Sea kayakers are well placed to make scientifically useful reports of sightings of sea creatures like dolphins and whales, basking sharks, turtles and sun-fish.

Useful addresses:

• Sea mammal research centre (CRMM), tel. 05 46 44 99 10 or http://crmm.univ-lr.fr/index.php/fr/accueil

• Basking Shark Study Centre (APECS), tel. 02 98 05 40 38 or http://asso-apecs.org/

• Sightings can also be reported to your national centre i.e. http://seawatchfoundation.org.uk/ which will pass them on.

01 The Wild Coast of Le Croisic

Difficulty: ✗ ✗ ✗ / ✗ ✗ ✗

Distance: 23 nautical miles (1 or 2 days)

Leaving and Arriving: Batz-sur-mer

Maps:
SHOM 7395
Navicarte 547
IGN 10230T

The wild coast near the Pointe de Penchateau.

From the Loire to the Vilaine

Salt making at Guérande.

Le Croisic ●

Beach huts at Batz-sur-mer.

FROM THE MOUTH of the Loire to Le Croisic the sea still reflects the colours and quietness of that great river. However, the "wild" coast has another character. Even in calm weather, the rugged coast, fringed with a rock garden of fallen blocks and tidal ledges creates an enchanting paradise for rock-hopping, the coast road and development could be miles away. In bad weather it really is wild.

The port of Le Croisic.

Launching, Landing and Parking:

Batz-sur-mer: launching from the Valentin beach, street parking in "Rue Appert".
Le Croisic: many small slipways but with limited parking in summer and traffic congestion: 1) Slipway at the side of the large jetty at Trehic near the local SNSM (RNLI); 2) Slipway inside the port near the harbour master's office, parking nearby; 3) Slipway on the east side of the Pen Bron peninsula, parking nearby.

The port of Le Croisic has 3 yacht basins and a wholesale fish market.

This paddle needs good weather conditions. Launch from Valentin beach, Batz-sur-mer at HW -3 (Port-Navalo) and turn west following the coast. Go in as close as you dare; the small cliffs, rocks and ledges create interesting sea conditions. This coast merits the name "wild" despite the built-up interior. Don't overdo it, it can be a dangerous spot for the inexperienced. Take care and keep an eye on the tide, it is easy to loose track of time in the excitement of rock-hopping

From the Pointe du Tréhic expect strong currents as all the water from the Guérande marshes passes in and out through the narrow gap between Le Croisic and Pointe de Pen Bron. Having left at HW -3 it should be with you. The main channel is on the south side.

The port of Le Croisic is an interesting spot in a kayak. Three separate basins, fishing boats alongside the fish market and pleasure yachts on pontoons; all against a backdrop of a beautiful old seafront. The summer crowds might discourage some paddlers from landing, a quieter alternative is opposite on the Pointe de Pen Bron.

Take the same route back once the tide has eased and continue past the launch spot, the small port of Batz-sur-mer with its yellow beach huts and all the small inlets you pass look inviting, but in bad weather they offer no landing or shelter. If the sea is calm, look out for Korrigans cave

Pen Bron seen from Le Croisic.

From the Loire to the Vilaine

(*korrigan* is a sort of Breton leprechaun) with its 3 entrances. The land rises and small inlets or gulleys provide shelter for fishing huts with their square drop nets and derricks. At Pointe de Penchateau, the vast beach of La Baule-Pornichet comes into view with its blocks of holiday flats and crowds of bathers. Faced with this, the undeveloped rocky islets of Les Evens start to look very attractive. Half an hour on a bearing of 110° will take you there. Enjoy the panoramic view of the Loire estuary and Vendée region, and then take the same route back.

Alternatives: This paddle could be divided into two trips, one to Le Croisic and one to Les Evens, or it would be possible to do it all from Le Croisic. The islet of Pierre Percée, 2.5nm south-east of Les Evens is another place to visit and good for sea boat surfing in the right conditions (tide coefficient of at least 90, a rising tide and easterly wind). From Le Croisic the creeks running up into the marshes of Guérande are very tempting to kayakers, but the marsh is a fragile, protected environment and kayaking is not encouraged. ∎

WEATHER, TIDE AND SAFETY

Paddling conditions vary completely with weather and sea conditions. Reflected swell makes the rock-hopping very unpredictable.
The escape options are very limited.
Although a low swell coupled with an offshore (north) wind make for a safe and easy paddle, experts will wait for the wind and swell to provide world class challenging and exciting paddling.
Tidal flows are not strong except where already indicated. The outbound flow, west and south, starts at HW (Port-Navalo) and the inbound, east and north, from -5.

Sea Kayaking Guide **Brittany**

02

The Island of Dumet

Difficulty: ✗ ✗ ✗

Distance: 13 nautical miles (1 or 2 days)

Leaving and Arriving: Anse de Lérat

Maps:
SHOM 7033
Navicarte 546
IGN 10220T

Ile Dumet. Photo D. Hottois

From the Loire to the Vilaine

Lérat Harbour.

Dumet

THE BOW OF THE KAYAK forging a way towards this island; the stuff of which legends are made. Long used by pirates, then a military base; now only the gulls haunt the Fort of Sébastien Vauban, ruined houses and the beaches and black cliffs of Dumet.

Launching, Landing and Parking:

Lérat harbour: on the road from Piriac to La Turballe, parking is limited in summer. There is the choice of launching from the beach or in the bay.

Piriac: 1) Piriac beach, if you can find a parking spot (parking charge in summer) or one of the few free spaces near the small beach in the port; 2) West of the Port, the square du Lehn offers parking and easy launching near the SNSM (RNLI) boat.

Quimiac: Lanseria beach, 5km north-east of Piriac, is further away but easier access and parking.

Gathering shellfish at Piriac. Photo C. Magré

The "tomb of Almenzor".

Leave the attractive bay at Lérat around HW -3 (Port-Navalo), the rising tide will give you deeper water, and follow the coast north-west, passing the grave of Almenzor, a huge eroded rock named after a legendary knight. The majestic beach and headland of Castelli, dominated by the coastguard lookout, are a potentially tricky spot as the rocks extend far out to sea. Regarding the weather, it might be well to heed the local saying: *"Côtes de Dumet bien découpées, pluie à redouter, brume sur l'île aux oiseaux, il va faire beau"* (The coast of Dumet in sharp relief, rain is on its way; the bird island hidden in the haze, the sun will shine).

Pointe du Castelli is the jumping off point for the 4 mile crossing which should take a little over an hour on 315°. Take time to look behind you as the coast unfurls from the lighthouse of Le Four, sweeping along the coast of Piriac to the cliffs of the Rhuys peninsula. On arrival, explore the surf around the rocks then circumnavigate the island. The dark rocks in various formations create an atmosphere typically Breton, contrasting with the light colours of the mainland. Dumet is part of the same ridge as the islands of Houat and Hoëdic and has the same geology. On the north-east side a lovely beach offers an easy landing and a temptation to relax. However, make the effort to

Heading off to Dumet. Photo C. Magré

From the Loire to the Vilaine

explore on foot and appreciate the fort, the ruins and the contorted pine trees, a witness to the wind. The island has a long and turbulent history as a staging post for pirates and invaders, Romans, Vikings, Spanish, Dutch, and of course English. The fort, together with a permanent garrison, was established to protect the coast.

Nowadays the gulls are kings of the island (one nest for every 10 m²): 6000 pairs of herring gulls and 200 pairs of lesser black backed gulls. One would never think that in the 1950s these birds were almost wiped out by the famous singer Colette Renard – English speakers who may not be familiar with her songs will find them on the Internet. A friend of the owner, she spent numerous summers on the island with her 2 dogs…and her tame mongoose! The latter, not finding any snakes, set about the eggs and chicks. Its appetite for these delicacies decimated the gull population.

For the return crossing, a heading of 120° will take you to Piriac and allow you to enjoy this beautiful village with its small port. Remember to go far enough offshore to skirt the rocks on the way back to Lérat. ∎

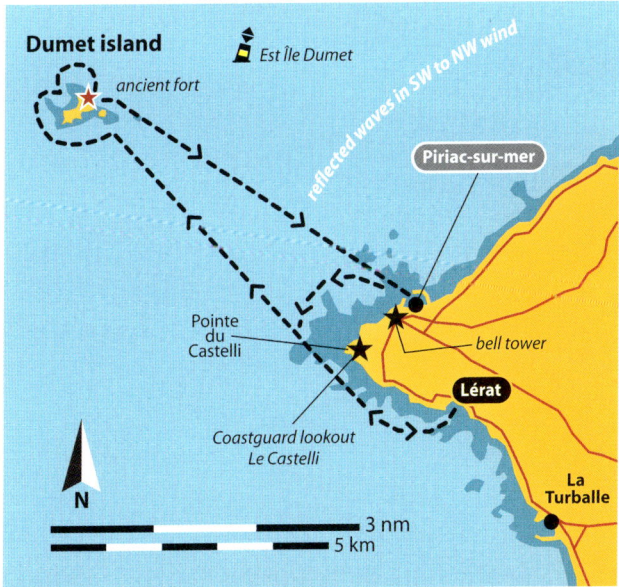

WEATHER, TIDE AND SAFETY

Take care during the crossing as shallow sandbanks may set off breaking waves if there is any swell. This is more of a hazard at LW. Choppy seas are also to be found around the east cardinal "Basse Est Île Dumet". The local name for the coast between La Turballe and Castelli is the "Wild coast of La Turballe", an apt description in wind and swell. Tidal flows are weak, but the general drift runs south from HW then offshore towards the island from HW +3 to +6, then north until -4 and finally towards the mainland until HW.

03 The Gold Mine

Sea Kayaking Guide — **Brittany**

Difficulty: ✘ ✘ ✘

Distance: 15 nautical miles

Leaving and Arriving: Loscolo Beach

Maps:
SHOM 7033
Navicarte 546
IGN 1022OT

The beach at Pointe du Bile.

From the Loire to the Vilaine

Penlan lighthouse.

Pénestin

Launching, Landing and Parking:

Loscolo: a lovely beach with plenty of parking.

Pointe du Bile: similar to Loscolo, but with more islets. At LW a portage with *bouchots* everywhere. Take care not to impede farmers with their tractors on the beach, they have to make the most of limited working time at LW. There is also slightly less parking than at Loscolo.

Poudrantais: beside the sailing school: at the southern end of the Gold Mine beach, limited parking.

If you want to do the paddle in the opposite direction:
1) Slipway at Tréhiguier on the left bank of the Vilaine; 2) At the mouth of the Vilaine in the port of Billiers, limited parking.

THIS SECTION of coast is less inhabited, and characterised by mussel farming. The Pointe de Bile a hedgehog with its spiny islets and *bouchots*: then the beach called "Mine d'Or" —The Gold Mine, made even brighter by its ochre cliffs. The estuary of the Vilaine with its banks of mud makes a broad triangle in these peaceful waters. Finally, a secret is hidden behind the headland of Penn Lann.

Bouchots are poles used for mussel farming, strings of mussels are wound around the poles to mature. A farmer measures his farm in kilometres of poles. Stretching from near chart datum to LW neaps, their positioning is a compromise between ease of access and maximum underwater feeding time for the mussels.

Surfing at low water off the Pointe de Penlan.

Low water at Loscolo, launching near the bouchots.

Launch from Loscolo at HW -3 (Port-Navalo) and paddle south to meander your way around the two larger islands off the Pointe de Bile, enjoying the ochre cliffs and jumbled black rocks. Then head north again past the Pointe of Loscolo and between the island of Belair and the Pointe de Cloedeneu. This is locally popular for "fishing" for shellfish at low tide. If the sun is shining, your attention will now be seized by the varied ochre shades of the long cliffs of the "Gold Mine" which frame and reflect the superb beach. Further along, secluded little beaches, very attractive at half tide, mark the entry of the estuary of the Vilaine.

Head straight north across the estuary towards the prominent headland opposite, the Pointe de Penn Lann, with its fortified buildings dominating the scenery. To the summit of the point, the white and red striped lighthouse of Penlan (or Penn Lann) peeps out between the trees. Once around the point you enter a hidden world, the narrow opening leading to a beach and behind that it widens into a broad estuary with a river snaking between wild mudflats and saltings, alive with lark song. It is possible to paddle upstream several kilometres, as far as the village of Billiers, or even beyond if the tide is high enough.

On the way back head up into the estuary of the Vilaine. This river has done nothing to deserve its name (*vilaine* in French=ugly), it has an attractive air, with its water, long cliffs, and its glistening mud banks. The flat bottomed boats of the mussel farmers, (*plates* in French) Indian file on their moorings. In fact the construction of the dam at Arzal in the 1970s has reduced the flood flow of the river, mud is no longer washed out to sea in annual floods, leading to a build up of sediment. The poles and pillows of the shellfish farmers are still arranged in neat lines, but the farmers complain that they are being swallowed slowly by the mud.

From the Loire to the Vilaine

Once you think you've gone far enough, the tide, which should now be ebbing, will carry you seaward again. Just take care to stay in the channel to avoid the mud banks as they emerge. On the return, you will pass the Gold Mine beach again. Not just a name, this is a singular geological phenomenon, formed by an ancient river, traces of whose banks can still be found on the northern side. In the 19th century gold was actually extracted from the sediments, but the returns were poor and mining was abandoned during World War 1. The evening sun makes the cliffs even brighter. Paddle around a final headland, and you arrive back at Loscolo. ■

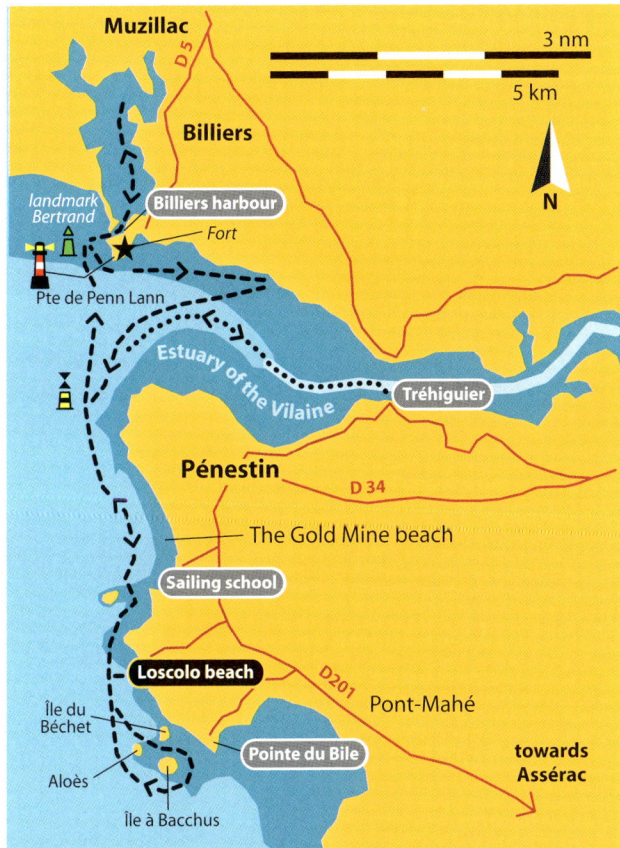

WEATHER, TIDE AND SAFETY

Take care of the current in the estuaries, this follows the ebb and flow of the tide, outside of the main channels the current is much less. At Loscolo watch out for rocks, awash at mid-tide, these are a trap for the unwary and landing at HW in swell may be difficult. If there is some swell from the south-west, the mouth of the Vilaine may produce superb long shouldered, slow breaking waves towards the end of the ebb. If you are lucky enough, make the most of them for a spot of surfing.

The Berno tide mill on Île d'Arz. Photo C. Magré

Learn more

The Gulf of Morbihan

Mor bihan means "little sea" in Breton, it is a vast area of almost enclosed sea. When the weather is bad there is always a paddle to be had in the sheltered upper reaches. On the other hand, swift currents formed by the ebb and flow around and between the islands near the entrance create rivers in the sea, complete with white water features. These are fiercest during spring tides and with wind against tide. An area of 110 km² drains through an entrance barely 900m wide.

The Gulf can be divided into 4 areas for navigational purposes. (SHOM) These are shown on the map.

❶ **The entrance**, defined by a line joining Pointe de Kerpenhir, Pointe de Locmiquel, Pointe de Berchis, Île Berder, Île de la Jument, Hent Tenn, Pointe de Kerners, Pointe de Motenno, Pointe de Port-Navalo.

This area is characterised by strong currents, no real period of slack water, and numerous back eddies along the sides. The main dangers: the rocks called the Petit Mouton (Little sheep) create a dangerous stopper during the ebb, the channel marker the Grand Mouton (Big

Proposed Conservation Areas

Two proposals are currently under consideration, enhanced status for the Gulf of Morbihan and a marine conservation area from Gurande to Quiberon. If these are confirmed, additional regulations might affect kayaking in the area.

The Gulf of Morbihan and surrounding area

sheep) forms an equally violent back eddy, then there is the Perche des Tisserands (the Weavers' pole) (during the flood tide) and the port buoy La Jument (the Mare), respectively south-west and north-east of the island Er Lannig. Becoming pinned against any of these obstacles could prove fatal.

The worst conditions are found with wind against tide. The larger the tidal range, the stronger the peak flows at mid-tide and the more challenging the boils and whirlpools will be wherever the counter-currents meet. Even when all looks quiet, it is an area for experienced paddlers only. The flood tide starts at HW -6 (Port-Navalo) but there is a progressive delay between the entrance and the north of this zone where the flood starts up to 1 hour 30 later about HW -4.30. The ebb starts about HW +1.30. The Pointe de Port-Navalo is a particularly tricky place with the ebb tide against a south or south-east wind, the Pointe de Kerpenhir will prove equally challenging in a flood tide against a north-east wind.

❷ **The west of the gulf**: between a line joining La Jument and Hent Tenn up to a line from the north of the Île aux Moines to Pointe d'Arradon and the southern point of Île aux Moines and the Pointe de l'Ours (2 miles east of Kerners). This has wide expanses of water with strong "rivers" of moving water especially around mid-tide. Good knowledge of the ferry glide and transits to cross these is essential. The flood tide starts around HW -4 and the ebb HW +1.45.

Learn more

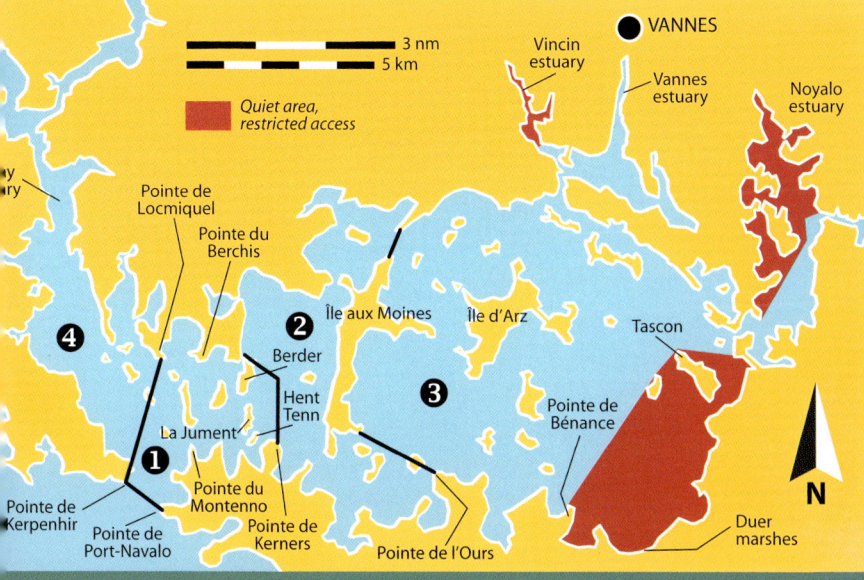

Congested waters– in the tide at La Jument.

Learn more

❸ **The east of the gulf**: this is a calmer zone with less current and a complicated pattern of islands. Two main flows correspond to the two principle estuaries; Vannes (running north of Île aux Moines to Vannes) and Noyalo (running from South of Île aux Moines to the south of Île d'Arz up to Saint-Armel). Large areas of mud and sand are uncovered at low water. An area of mud and sand banks south of a line joining Pointe de Benance-Île Bailleron-Île Tascon and Corn Bihan is a bird reserve where navigation is prohibited. The flood tide here starts about HW -3.30 and the ebb HW +2.

❹ **The Auray estuary** : on the west of the gulf, this is more of a linear feature without obstacles to the ebb and flow of the tide and has the characteristics of a normal estuary, provided you avoid the strong currents at the mouth of the gulf. The flood tide starts at HW +5.15 (Port Navalo) and the ebb starts at HW +0.45mins. This is because water is still running up into the Auray at the same time as it has started running out through the entrance to the gulf. The tide does not turn at Saint-Goustan at the top of the estuary until HW +1.

In brief:

The strong tides in the entrance, contrasting with the more sheltered areas and the 30-40 islands (almost all privately owned except for Île aux Moines, Île d'Arz and Île d'Ilur) provide inspiration for a wide range of trips depending upon what interests you.

It is advisable to paddle the entrance with the tide; unless you really enjoy fighting the tide in the back eddies.

The ebb tide runs stronger than the flood and much stronger during

The Gulf of Morbihan and surrounding area

springs than at neap tides.

Branches stuck in the sand indicate oyster beds with their lines of pillows on metal stakes. Keep clear of these areas if you don't want to scratch or hole your kayak, damage your paddle or become stuck as the tide drops. Exploring shallow areas on a flood tide will reduce the risk of being caught on sand or mud banks.

The SHOM tidal atlas *Côte sud de la Bretagne* (South Coast of Brittany) has hourly detail on tidal flows. It is very strongly recommended that you invest in a copy before exploring the Gulf.

The pleasures of the Gulf:

- paddling in strong tidal flows, these can be very helpful in covering ground in less demanding areas as well as providing world class play spots.

- exploring and keeping track of where you are in the pattern of islands can be tricky but also very rewarding.

- tidal mills, bird life, megalithic monuments, traditional fishing boats like the two masted *Sinagots*, *Forbans du Bono* (Buccaneers) and *Guépards du Golfe* (Cheetahs).

- on spring tides for the most adventurous: 1) flood tide; the north of Île de la Jument, north of Île Berder, south of Île Longue, the Grand Mouton, Kerpenhir Point, Toulingat Point on Île aux Moines. 2) ebb tide; the north of Île de la Jument, south of Île Berder, between Île de la Jument and Île Hent Tenn, the Grand Mouton. ■

Enjoying winter sunshine on Iluric.

Learn more

Watch out for other boaters

The Gulf of Morbihan has become a victim of its own beauty. From May to the end of September there is heavy pleasure-boat traffic especially on the main channels between Vannes and Port-Navalo. Not all of the water users respect navigation rules and some may be less than expert in their boat handling. Take care in these channels. If you are in a group, try to keep together, this is less easy than it sounds.

When the tide is running it is easy to lose sight of each other when waiting for other boats, especially if some are better at estimating the ferry angle than others, or whilst concentrating on navigating boils and eddies. Look ahead and be prudent. Try out the weaker currents higher up the Gulf before tackling the fast flows.

50 | Sea Kayaking Guide **Brittany**

04

The Islands of Boëd and Boëdig

Difficulty: ✘ ✘ ✘

Maps:
SHOM 7034
Navicarte 246
IGN 09210T

Distance: 6 nautical miles

Leaving and Arriving: Bararac'h harbour

The Monk.

The Gulf of Morbihan and surrounding area   51

A channel in the saltings.

Séné

FOUR POSTCARDS illustrate this trip. The first would be of the small "island", Île de Conleau; the second the famous pink house which marks the entrance of the channel to Vannes. The small chapel in the sea on the peninsula at Boëdig would be the third and the fourth, close by, the well known "Rocher du moine" (the Monk's rock). Don't forget to take along a bottle of white wine.

Launching, Landing and Parking:

Near Port Anna, Bararac'h has a slipway on the end of the headland Pointe de Bellevue, in the parish of Séné. This is one of the landing places for boats to Île d'Arz. There is a large parking area, but even this might be full during the season.

Port Anna itself is also a good starting point.

The beach at La Pointe du Bil: east of the Île de Boëd, near Moustérian. Launching here makes use of the rising tide; a large parking area but busy in the season. Arrive early and leave late to avoid the crush.

Sea lavender at high water.

The pink house shows the way to Vannes.

Leave from Bararac'h at HW -1 (Port-Navalo) and paddle out through the entrance, passing Port Anna and the pink house, a famous landmark for sailors approaching Vannes, there may be some current against you in places.

To your left you will see the end of Île Boëdig with its chapel in silhouette. Take the inside channel, with its lines of moorings, between the islands and the mainland. Some rotting hulks lie on the saltings amongst the reeds and mudflats. The water is very shallow in places, at low water a line of sand banks link Boëd with Cadouarn on the mainland, allowing crossing on foot. In winter keep well out to sea to avoid disturbing the flocks of wintering Brent geese, but in summer you can thread your way along a small channel amongst the Salicornia and sea lavender.

The return trip is along the south side of the islands. At the south east tip of Boëd a square rock tower perched on a rock stands guard. This is the Tour des douaniers (customs tower) which was used by customs officers to levy tolls on boats entering Vannes. The Île d'Arz is to the south-west, continue past the lovely beach and on past Boëdig,

Boëd tower at high water.

The Gulf of Morbihan and surrounding area

a beach, pine trees, a recently restored manor and the farm will let you know that you are on the right course.

Did you remember to bring along the bottle? Now is the moment to take it out. On the west tip of the island is the Monk, a rock, sculptured in 1901 and painted white. The tradition is for sailors to salute the monk as they pass by downing a drink and saying *"Doublant le moine, il faut saluer d'un coup de blanc sans respirer. Bon vent, belle mer et bon courant, te porteront assurément"*. He is then sure to bring you a favourable wind and tide, and a calm sea.

Between the two westerly points of Boëdig lies a scene in miniature encompassing the delights of the Gulf, rocks, beach and a chapel. The pink house will be your guide back into the channel to Vannes. If the tide is still high enough you can prolong the trip by exploring further upstream along both arms, the channel towards Vincin and the main channel to Vannes.

Alternatives: If you have time, stop at the bar "Le Corlazo" at Conleau, 200m west of where the ferries come in. This bistro is the start and finish of the famous "Bar to Bar" regatta. This race is between "Le Corlazo" and another bar "La Trinquette" on the island of Hoëdic and back. ■

WEATHER, TIDE AND SAFETY

There is a risk of going aground in the shallow water between Boëd and the mainland. The paddle can be done in the opposite direction, but bear in mind that the shallow areas dry quickly after HW.

05 A Tour of the Gulf of Morbihan

Difficulty: ✗ ✗ ✗

Maps:
SHOM 7034
Navicarte 246
IGN 0921OT

Distance: 13 nautical miles

Leaving and Arriving: Arzon, Kerners slipway

Île d'Arz, Pointe de Brouel.

The Gulf of Morbihan and surrounding area

Arzon

A twin-masted Sinagot.

THIS PADDLE THREADS its way along the necklace of islands around the Île aux Moines and the Île d'Arz: a rocky island, a wooded island, a strictly private island… Here and there a house peeps out of the vegetation, an apple tree, a ghostly white group of cattle egrets in a bush, a speck of beach, an ochre cliff. Paddle gently and enjoy being taken by the current.

The island of Mouchiouse is surrounded by oyster beds.

Launching, Landing and Parking:

Slipway at Kerners: near Arzon, adjacent to Bilouri beach. Parking is prohibited in the turning area. Congested in summer and at the end of a cul-de-sac, the nearest parking is 150m away. A trolley would come in handy.

Slipway at Logeo: further east, very busy in the season with pay parking.

Slipway at Lindin: inside the bay of Lindin, launching possible from the beach at the village (HW +/-3).

Slipway at Pointe du Ruaud, near Sarzeau, this is only usable from mid-tide onwards (HW +/-3).

Slipway at Arradon, at the other end of the Gulf, during the season you have to park in the upper car park, you may be able to drop off the boats nearer the water. (trolley useful) The nearest slipway is that used by the sailing school. In summer, the marina slipway is only accessible by car to pass holders.

Channel between Île d'Arz and Île de Lerne.

Leave from Kerners around HW -1 (Port-Navalo) and head east past the headland of Saint-Nicolas and then out amongst the islands. If you take a northerly route you will pass close to a traditional naval dockyard, hidden in a small bay on the east side of the Île aux Moines.

A southerly route takes you island hopping to Govihan; then Stibiden, round and densely wooded; Godec with its ancient stone breakwater; and Iluric defended by banks of mud and rocks on the west, nice beach on the east. The next island, Ilur, is well worth a special visit (see paddle 06).

The Pointe de Brouel on the south-east coast of Île d'Arz (Captains Island) is a favourite lunch spot for kayakers. On the east of the island there is a branch of the well known Glénan sailing school. This time, pass between Arz and Île Ilur to near Île Lerne, then paddle towards the slipway at Béluré on the north coast of Arz. This is where the ferries shuttle across to Conleau.

From here, following the coast of Île Arz, will take you past the tide mill at Berno which has recently been restored. Alternatively continue westward to the the island of Drenec and the two Logoden isles (mouse in Breton). There is a fine panoramic view from Petite Logoden (little mouse), a good stopping place. Skirt the rocks around the next island Île Holavre and then head for Île d'Irus. The tide can run strongly here, especially on spring tides, watch out for the ferry from Port Blanc across to Île aux Moines near the Pointe de Toulindag.

Landing on the Île aux Moines on the beach may be easier than at the slipway;

The Gulf of Morbihan and surrounding area

however, during the summer, the beach is buoyed off as a swimming area only. Blue and white bathing huts give a gentle old fashioned feel to the place.

Continue down the coast, and over the wide expanse of water it is possible to discern the Île Berder with its square tower, Île de la Jument with its heronry and salmon coloured house, the bell tower at Arzon and the port at Kerners. Along the coast of Île aux Moines a few houses peep out, little cliffs, plum trees, tiny rocks, a colony of egrets perching in a tree, a small beach opposite Île Creizic, a sunken boat...time glides past.

Further south the coast seems more remote, with higher cliffs and pine trees. In May the asphodels defend the cliffs with their lances of flowers along the rampart. Kerners is in front of you across the channel, a ferry glide from near the Pointe de Penhap will make best use of the ebb tide. ∎

WEATHER, TIDE AND SAFETY

This is a paddle which makes good use of the tidal flows in the Gulf. You should aim to take the rising tide to the top of Île d'Arz and then the ebb along the shore of Île aux Moines. If you find the tide against you, keep close along the shore and use the back eddies. Starting from Arradon will require the opposite timing, out with the ebb and back with the flood. The complicated pattern of islands can be surprisingly difficult to untangle, it is very easy to get confused and end up in a different place altogether. Keep a careful watch on your position and where you are going.

Sea Kayaking Guide — **Brittany**

06 Towards the Island of Ilur

Difficulty: ✘ ✘ ✘

Distance: 9 nautical miles

Leaving and Arriving: Séné, slipway at "Le Passage"

Maps:
SHOM 7034
Navicarte 246
IGN 0921OT

The north beach on Ilur, the island of Arz is on the horizon

The Gulf of Morbihan and surrounding area

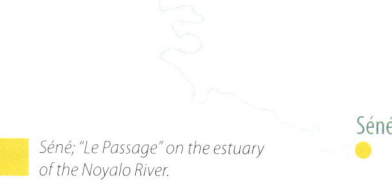

Séné; "Le Passage" on the estuary of the Noyalo River.

Séné

The chapel in Ilur.
Photo C. Magré

ENJOYING THE PEACE of the islands deep inside the Gulf, you will discover the pearl of this inland sea: Ilur. Abandoned in the 1950s it has remained unspoilt and retains its old-fashioned charm.

Acquired by the Conservatoire du Littoral (Coastal Conservancy), it is a birdwatcher's paradise with numerous waders, geese, shelducks, herons...

For the botanist, according to the season, "lords and ladies", wild hyacinths and fungi are common inland.

An island lost in time.

Launching, Landing and Parking:

Montsarrac, the Séné side of the river Noyalo facing Saint-Armel:
1) Visitors slipway and parking;
2) Slightly higher up on the same side, the slipway at Garenne (muddy at LW). This area is called "Le Passage" (the crossing) because a small ferry joins Saint-Armel and Séné across the Noyalo.

Saint-Armel bank: launching possible, but it can be impossible to find a parking spot.

Beach at Pointe du Bil at Séné: opposite Mousterian, permits a direct line to Île de Bailleron.

Slipway at la Pointe du Ruaud, to the south near Sarzeau, only useable above half-tide. Easy access to Iluric and Île des Œufs.

The island of Iluric from Ilur.

Leave Montsarrac at HW -1 (Port-Navalo), set off towards the marvellously geometrically square island of Quistinic and then head towards the north end of Tascon. The next island, Bailleron, is managed by the University of Rennes for marine and biological studies. Navigation is forbidden in the nature reserve which extends towards the mainland across the marshes of the Marais du Duer up to the Rhuys peninsula.

Island hopping from Pladic to Penn Blei then Île des Œufs takes you in the right direction, watch out for the branches stuck in the mud indicating oyster

beds; keep clear. Depending on the tide, it might be possible to pass amongst the islands, if not, it will be necessary to go around both Iluric and Godec and turn back to Ilur. Ilur is owned by the Coastal Conservancy, and is noted for its protected landscape, its old village and the diversity of habitats.

Land on the beach on the west coast. A cleared path between the sea and lagoons leads inland towards the old village. The landscape and wildlife can vary greatly according to the season.

The village on Ilur.

The Gulf of Morbihan and surrounding area

The village has been restored, together with its small chapel. The path continues to the muddy east shore and then up onto higher ground which provides a panoramic view of the Gulf. Turn back northwards to return to the landing beach. There are several other walks, go and explore; but respect the natural environment.

Back at the boats, take a more northerly course back, passing south of Pointe de Bilhervé on Île d'Arz and north of the headland at Tascon. The grove of trees at Péchit and the small white hut at Le Passage, Saint-Armel can be seen from far off, giving something to aim at.

Before arriving back at the slipway, if you want to experience more tranquillity and the tide is high enough, take a look at the maze of channels in the ancient salt workings of Hézo by turning right at Montsarrac and heading south. A calm and beautiful spot. ∎

WEATHER, TIDE AND SAFETY

This paddle is described at HW, it is feasible at all states of the tide, but watch out for oyster beds, especially between Île des Œufs and Godec.
If starting at HW, take a look at Hézo before starting off for Ilur. Leaving from Ruaud makes for a short paddle to Ilur, giving more time for exploration on foot.

07 The Mouth of the Gulf of Morbihan

Difficulty: ✘ ✘ ✘

Maps:
SHOM 7034
Navicarte 246
IGN 09210T

Distance: 9 nautical miles

Leaving and Arriving: Arzon, slipway at Kerners

In the tide at Kerpenhir. Photo P. Mallard

The Gulf of Morbihan and surrounding area

The twin stone circles of Er Lannic.
Photo C. Magré

Arzon

BOILS AND WHIRLPOOLS, stone circles and an ever-moving carousel, where the placid twin stone circles on the island of Er Lannic are often completely surrounded by swirling white water. The entrance of the Gulf is a zone of turbulent water, strong currents, standing waves, boils and whirlpools.

It is easy to be carried along by the current, but disconcerting as the land flies past. Keep paddling, look ahead, practice your support strokes and wear a helmet.

Thrills are guaranteed!

Launching, Landing and Parking:

Slipway at Kerners: near Arzon, adjacent to Bilouri beach. Parking is prohibited in the turning area. Congested in summer and at the end of a cul-de-sac, the nearest parking is 150m away. A trolley would come in handy.

Larmor-Baden Port: congested parking in summer, a wide slipway to the west and a tiny beach to the east.

Pointe du Berchis: a lovely beach, but difficult parking.

Port-Navalo harbour, if you want to do the paddle in the opposite direction: slipway to the east of the harbour master's office, pay parking in summer.

Port-Navalo headland, outside coast: Port Blanc beach, access by some steps, parking difficult in summer.

Locmariaquer: 1) From the first beach north east of the Pointe de Kerpenhir beside the panoramic table; 2) Beside the sea below the Pierres Plates Dolmen (chambered cairn).

Breaking-in to the ebb tide near Île de la Jument. Photo P. Mallard

Leave Kerners on the ebb tide about mid-tide. Head north and west towards the cross on the island Hent Tenn. Between this island and Île de la Jument there is a good play spot with a strong tidal flow and an equally strong back eddy. The first challenge is to manage the ferry glide across, and the second is to try to paddle back up along the edge; the sea seems to be sloping up-hill.

Pass north of the Île de la Jument and enter the famous race of the same name. This reaches 8kts on spring tides. Practice your white water skills of breaking in and breaking out, use the back eddy to paddle up and break in again, welcome to the magic roundabout. A ferry glide will take you across to Er Lannic with its striking megalithic monument. This island is a bird reserve and landing is prohibited during the nesting season from 15 March to 31 August; but you can look from the water. There are two circles of stones, but the southern one is now underwater, this island was attached to the mainland when the circles were built about 7,500 years ago.

Rejoin the tide and once past the Pointe de Motenno, the courageous can take their chances in the violent triangular back eddy of the Grand Mouton, a green channel marker in the middle of the flow. Don't get pinned against it. Breaking in might well give you some rolling practice. Calmer water is found in the eddy near Le Faucheur (the sickle or scythe), a white rock on the side of the Rhuys peninsula. Port-Navalo has an attractive bay in which to rest but it is worth going to the beaches on the Locmariaquer side to picnic. The ferry glide is easier than it looks due to back eddies, but the entrance itself with ocean waves meeting the ebb tide

The Gulf of Morbihan and surrounding area

can be very rough; it dies down as the tide eases. Paddle along to Les Pierres Plates dolmen (chambered cairn), a fine example of this type of megalithic monument, go inside and feel the engraved cup and ring patterns on the stones in the dark. The beach in front of it is a good place to watch families collecting shellfish, or have a go yourself, they will probably lend you a rake.

The return paddle is with the flood tide, remember that it doesn't turn until about 1hr 30 after low water. The Pointe de Kerpenhir, right in the entrance makes a play spot on the flood tide, but the rocks are close underwater. After this keep out into the current to avoid getting swept up the Auray river.

Head towards the south of Île Longue with its white water playspots and then on to Île Gavrinis with its famous restored and illuminated chambered cairn. Access to this is restricted to visitors using the boat from Larmor-Baden, so you cannot land. What a pity! From Gavrinis ferry glide across to the western side of Île de la Jument and the southern branch of the tide will carry you rapidly back to Kerners.

Alternatives: The tidal causeway between Île Berder and Larmor-Baden creates a good standing wave once it is covered by the flood tide, to get back against the tide from here you need to hug the shore.■

WEATHER, TIDE AND SAFETY

This paddle requires good white water skills and an ability to read the water. Not recommended for beginners. Watch out for boat traffic. Once in an eddy, get your bearings, it is easy to become disoriented in the rapidly moving water. If you are not sure, start off on a moderate tide with little swell at the entrance and practice using the eddies to make ground up-tide. The playspot at the Île de Berder can be busy with short-boaters, look ahead before dropping into it from the south side and wait your turn.

Sea Kayaking Guide | **Brittany**

08 Up and down the Auray estuary

Difficulty: ✗ ✗ ✗

Distance: 15 nautical miles

Leaving and Arriving: Locmariaquer

Maps:
SHOM 7034
Navicarte 246
IGN 0921OT / 0821OT

Locmariaquer.

The Gulf of Morbihan and surrounding area

Auray

Le Bono and Le Forban, its traditional boat.
Photo C. Magré

THE AURAY TIDAL RIVER is steeped in history. The living tradition of working people, oyster farmers, fishermen and millers seen cheek by jowl with the rich merchants of Saint-Goustan and owners of grand mansions. Megalithic and bronze age monuments are hidden in the vegetation on the headlands. On the water you may see the *Forbans du Bono* (Bono Buccaneers), superb traditional sailing ships still in use for fishing and pleasure.

Launching, Landing and Parking:

Locmariaquer, 1) From the first beach north east of the Pointe de Kerpenhir beside the panoramic table; 2) Beside the sea below the Pierres Plates Dolmen (cromlech or chambered cairn), a large car park, but a long walk down the beach to the sea at low water; 3) The port of Guilvin, difficult access and congested parking.
Left bank of the river:
1) Larmor-Baden, leave from here at HW -4 (Port-Navalo); 2) Pointe of Berchis, a lovely beach, but tricky parking; 3) Slipway at the port of Parun, parking beside the naval base.
Port de Port-Navalo, slipway east of the harbour master's office, pay parking in summer, start off towards Kerpenhir and return via Le Petit Veizit (less easy to find the way).
Note: Le Bono and Saint-Goustan are possibilities at quiet times of the year, but very congested in summer.

Port of St Goustan (Auray). Photo C. Magré

Leave from the beach at Kerpenhir, north-east of the point, beneath the pine trees HW -3 (Port-Navalo). Paddle up the Auray keeping to the Locmariaquer side and pass the lovely curved houses of that town. Now head towards the point of Fort Espagnol with Port Parun on the opposite bank. From here the channel narrows after Kerdréan Bay and houses peeping out on the point of Berl indicate where the land starts to rise on either side. Rocher tumulus is on the right, well hidden.

Take the right fork towards Le Bono, the waters' edge is lined with small quays and piles of red clay tiles. Le Bono was one of the first centres of oyster production and famous in the 19th century for its oyster spat, collected on stacks of curved clay tiles laid on the river bed. Fishing has always been important for the inhabitants of Le Bono. Their boats carry the surname of Le Bono families who were once considered dubious by neighbouring villages. Forbans were equipped with trawl nets and passed the summer offshore amongst the islands.

At the old suspension bridge, take a detour to visit the port, then turn back downstream to the main Auray. (translator's note: a very attractive lone girl was

sitting on a rock beside the water playing the flute when I paddled under this bridge; could I have been dreaming? Everyone else stopped paddling and drifted along to the music; we were all in the same dream). Almost opposite the point of Kerisper, the charming Plessis lake can be visited at near high-water. After another bend, the mud banks lead towards the motorway bridge at Kerplouz. This is not the most inspiring arrival at Saint-Goustan, but the old quays and bridge further on are splendid.

Kerouach tide mill.

The Gulf of Morbihan and surrounding area

Benjamin Franklin landed here on 4 December 1776 as US ambassador to negotiate the first alliance between France and the USA at the dawn of its independence from the UK. For the kayaker it is probably easier to land on the small slipway near the historic stone steps leading up to Auray.

Make use of the ebb tide to carry you back down the river and look out for things you missed on the way up. Back at Kerpenhir, take the time to walk to the fine chambered cairn of Les Pierres Plates before driving off.

Alternatives: High water allows you to choose between some themed paddles: 1) Tide mills; Kerouac'h, Moustoir and Roch Du. 2) Islands: Grand Huernic, Sept Îles, Runio, Grand Veizit and Petit Veizit. If you have time it is possible to penetrate far up Le Bono estuary to the Plougoumelen tide mill or even further on a big tide up beyond the N165 (coefficient more than 80). ∎

WEATHER, TIDE AND SAFETY

Watch out for oyster beds, there are very many downstream of Fort-Espagnol. Parun is a good place to leave from if the tide times are difficult since you can head either up or down the estuary. Near the Pointe of Kerpenhir the water can be rough with wind against tide. Tuck in close to the bank, especially on the way back, to make sure that you are not carried out of the Gulf with the tide.

09 The Crac'h Tidal River

Difficulty: ✖ ✖ ✖

Distance: 8.5 nautical miles

Leaving and Arriving: La Trinité-sur-mer

Maps:
SHOM 7034
IGN 0821OT

The Crac'h with its oyster boats.

The Gulf of Morbihan and surrounding area

La Trinité-sur-mer

The Crac'h.

THE NAME OF La Trinité-sur-mer is synonymous with blue-water racing and sailing regattas. Our trip turns its back on these challenges to follow the kayakers' path between sea and land. We tread three worlds, firstly the sea with its yachts and beaches backed by holiday homes; secondly, the domain of the oyster farmers; and finally, the brackish upper reaches, merging into field and forest.

Île Cuhan.

Launching, Landing and Parking:

Finding a good launch and parking spot is not easy.
Slipways in La Trinité-sur-mer harbour: 1) Slipway at the sailing school (Éric Tabarly breakwater) reserved for the use of the school (ask permission), handy out of season; 2) Slipway beside the tourist office; 3) Small slipway on the Loïc Caradec breakwater in the town centre; 4) Slipway inside the dockyard.
The beach at Kervilhen: the open sea, crowded in summer and a difficult launch in rough seas.
Below the Kerisper road bridge: slipway for commercial fishermen only, but launching and landing tolerated as long as you park the car further up.
Passage du Lac, right bank: a third of the way along the paddle, upstream of the tide mill, slipway near the campsite.

The "Moulin du Lac", tidal mill.

Trinité-sur-mer developed as a port for the export of pit props to Cardiff for the coal mines of South Wales, payment being made in coal on the return voyage. The trade declined in the 1930s and it has now become a famous centre for leisure boating. Leave at HW -2 (Port-Navalo) from the sailing school slipway at the south of the quayside. You are among the blue-water yachts and second home owners. The forest of masts inside the marinas is extremely dense. The elegant arc of the Kerisper bridge, opened in 1958, spans a narrow section of the estuary. It replaced a metal "Eiffel" bridge destroyed during the war, and offers a fine

The Gulf of Morbihan and surrounding area

In front of the "Moulin du Lac".

view over the large expanses of water upstream and the brightly-coloured flat-bottomed oyster boats (*plates*) on their moorings. The island of Cuhan is to the side in a corner out of the main stream, which heads north. However, there is a secondary channel around to the east of it.

At low tide this area is a wide expanse of mud, but the main channel permits navigation as far as the bay of Saint-Jean. A succession of charming meanders follow this open area. From time to time the outline of a chateau in the distance, or the silhouettes of some trees close by, diverts attention from the oyster farming. The oyster beds covering half of the tidal zone in the vast bays disappear here, but oyster sheds, derelict oyster huts and smartly renovated cottages jostle for position on the shore in a ramshackle line. Each oyster farmer moors his boat in front of his house. Higher up on the banks there are a few holiday homes.

Little inlets hide one or two cottages, an ancient barge rots on the mudflats, the branches of the ancient oaks lining the banks lean down and out over the water surface, enlacing these limpid pools. Landing places are plentiful, but are often on private property; a good place to stop is in the tiny harbour near the tide mill downstream of the Passage du Lac.

The forested shores of the bay of Saint-Jean indicate that the nature of the river has changed. A large country house faces the last oyster quay, the latter littered with abandoned boats, oyster tiles (for collecting spat), the invading forest never far off. At high water this is often mirror calm. A cross and crucifix on a point: the two side branches each lead to a tide mill, to the left Kergoch, beautifully restored, except for the waterwheel; to the right Béquerel, now sadly demolished.

The return journey offering a different perspective will be equally interesting. ∎

WEATHER, TIDE AND SAFETY

To avoid problems with the mudflats, a rising tide is recommended for this paddle. It can be done in two parts starting from the slipway near the campsite "du Lac". If heading either upstream or downstream, a rising tide is preferable as the large expanses above Kerisper are not very interesting when paddling hidden in a tortuous channel with only muddy slopes on either side.

10 Belle-Île

Maps:
SHOM 7032
Navicarte 545
IGN 0822OT

Difficulty: ✘ ✘ ✘

Distance: 42 nautical miles (3 or 4 days)

Leaving and Arriving: Quiberon

Arches and caves at Domois.

The Gulf of Morbihan and surrounding area

The headland of Arzic, on the east of Belle-Île.

Belle-Île

THE PADDLER, could be in a painting by Monet as he glides between the needles of Port Coton, but hopefully will never be in a Dantesque photograph by Plisson as he rounds the Pointe des Poulains. Contrast the soft sheltered inner coast with the fantastically eroded and foam flecked wild coast, kneaded by the ocean swell. The magic of feeling so far from civilisation; whilst seeing the outlines of hikers sixty metres above you on the coastal path.

Launching, Landing and Parking:

Car park at the Pointe du Conguel, on the east side of Quiberon. Traffic jams are frequent on the single road across the isthmus of Quiberon, so you might have to arrive the night before for an early start! The car park has a height barrier, but a removable post on the left side of the west entrance allows access with kayaks on the roof rack (this is for access by Council workers), just put it straight back.

Port Haliguen : 2km further north.

Crossing with the Ferry: *La Compagnie Océane* operates a vehicle ferry to the island from Quiberon and can take cars with kayaks or just kayaks. Contact them on 0820 056 156 to make a reservation. In the event of bad weather it is usually possible to find a place on the ferry to take you back to Quiberon; except on Bank Holiday weekends.

Pause amongst the rocks at Bornor. Photo Y. Dodard

Leave at HW -1 (Port-Navalo) from the Pointe du Conguel. Launching is possible either side of the headland depending on sea conditions. The crossing should take about 3 hours in good conditions. Landfall should be made at the Pointe de Taillefer, head north-west, passing Port Fouquet and then Port Jean, where a stop is possible. The dissected, protected and attractive coast leads on to Port Sauzon, a charming inlet with its pastel coloured cottages. You've probably already seen the postcards of the two lighthouses and the "Hôtel de la Plage"; now you are paddling in it!

Start off again along the coast, past numerous huge rocks, before the two beaches of the Port de Deuborh (also a good place to stop), then the almost mythical Pointe des Poulains. Here you will have to make the decision whether to go on or not. This can be a rough stretch of water and a passage at low water slack is recommended. Monet tried to capture the wildness of the sea as well as calmer waters during his stays on Belle Isle. However, it is the photographer Philip Plisson who famously captured the Pointe de Poulains on a very rough day; scary stuff! It is worth making an internet search and taking a look at these pictures, you will not be on the water if it is anything like that.

Foam.

The Gulf of Morbihan and surrounding area

The swell on the west coast of Belle-Île can have particularly unpredictable patterns, so keep a weather eye out for freak waves and watch out for the reflected waves. You should be sure of your weather window and predicted swell height. Once committed to the Pointe des Poulains on an ebb tide, there may be no way back.

You are now on what the inhabitants of Belle-Île call the "outside coast". Look ahead to the fort of Sarah Bernhardt. If you can stop and look at it without being in too much of a cold sweat, the rest of the paddle should be alright! Landing on the large beach of Ster Vraz is easy, from here you can look and assess the coast and conditions. Ster Ouen is a lovely small inlet, a refuge for the yachtsman.

Depending upon the weather and swell, the wild coast of Belle-Île can be: 1) paradise; caves, narrow defiles, cliffs. 2) challenging; paddling 1–2 miles offshore to avoid the clapotis. 3) a nightmare to be absolutely avoided. In the third case, stay on the sheltered north coast of the island, land from time to time to walk out to the headlands and admire the coastal scenery and catch the ferry back.

Set off again from Ster Vraz if the conditions are good. The peninsula of Vieux Château, shaped like a hand on the map, is the domain of herring gulls. From the sea it is an impressive series of deep bites out of the black rock; at mid-tide groups of goose barnacles (*pouces-pieds*) can be seen stuck to the rocks: these animals are a good indicator of an exposed shore.

The small, high island of Roc'h Toul is typical of the islands along this coast, in that although wild and inaccessible to humans it provides a sheltered passage on its inside giving a welcome break from the rough seas on the outside.

The famous cave of l'Apothicairerie (the Apothecaries) is situated below a flat building on a point. The entrance is to the west, this is often rough; only attempt an entry in good conditions. Inside, a huge window created by a rockfall gives it particular charm. The powerful waves are rapidly eroding the coast here. In mediaeval times an inhabited islet, Lonèques lay off the point.

BEFORE LEAVING

Do your chart-work and plot your course in advance, with headings calculated for each hour of the crossing. Using a GPS can help you correct your course for leeway on a regular basis. The Pointe de Taillefer is a good place to make landfall.

Make use of the ebb tide for the outbound crossing. The tide flows south and around both ends of the island from HW to HW +4, east to west HW +5 to HW -6, north-east HW -5 to HW -2 and east HW -1 to HW. Tides are not strong along the outside coast, but can be fast on the east coast, the north-west point and between Quiberon and the island. Careful study of a detailed tidal atlas is strongly recommended before you set off. Neap tides will make the planning easier.

Since you will be away for at least 3 days, look at the long range weather forecast.

Locmaria.

Cliff to cliff, cave upon cave, gulley after gulley, the paddle continues; punctuated now and then where rock fortresses protect the coast and sometimes allow a landing (Port de Kerlédan, Port Skeul). Do not be tempted into the bay of Port Donnant to have a closer look at the magnificent beaches. The gently sloping beach and rock outcrops can generate large breakers. Cut across towards the Pointe du Grand Guet.

Had enough yet? No…well here is the second course; Baguenèrez islands to Port Kerel. First is Port Coton, laced with needle rocks (a favourite inspiration for Monet) then Port Goulphar, easily recognisable by the "Hôtel du Grand Large" painted pink. If it is calm, the succession of arches and tunnels ahead will make any kayaker smile. High, majestic, narrow, or twisting; just enjoy yourself. The area around Bornor is another nice stretch taking you to Port Kérel. A fault in the rocks makes a deep gash into the plateau of Belle-Île. A good landing place on the sand, but a long portage at low water.

Now you have finished the second course, and completed the most committing section of coast. However, Belle-Île has still much to offer. The fine pale sand of the beach at Herlin and, next door, the

Sauzon. Photo D. Hottois

welcoming pebble strand of Port Gwenn. The coast is still as high, but less dissected, no islands and no more caves, but lots on indentations to be explored between the headlands of Saint-Marc, Pouldon and Skeul (ladder). If you are making the trip over three days, this might be an area to cover rapidly to gain ground. If you have four days, take time to enjoy the lichen-spotted folds of rock. Anywhere else this would be considered a first class section of coast, but you have been spoilt by the last couple of days.

After the point of Skeul, you are back in a zone with strong currents, it would be best to time the trip to go with the tide. There can also be clapotis in an easterly wind. In springtime the cliffs are covered in places with pink mesembryanthemums. This invasive species from South Africa, with its leaves like green claws, is displacing the native sea pinks (*Armeria maritima*). The popular beach at Port Blanc is a good place to stop, as is the well hidden inlet of Port Maria. Both give access to the picturesque narrow lanes of Locmaria.

Once past the headland of Kerdonis, with its little lighthouse, you are on the "inside coast", the headland of Taillefer is on the horizon. The coast is less rugged with many beaches, including the fortified beach of Grand Sables. The points between the sandy bays are truly delightful, especially those of Bugul and Gros Rocher. It is easy to find a secluded spot. Beyond the point of Ramonette lies the harbour of Le Palais deep in an inlet, dominated by a fortress. This, the capital of the island, has its charm, but is busier than Sauzon. The shop fronts are very close to the shore and flooding by the sea is not uncommon.

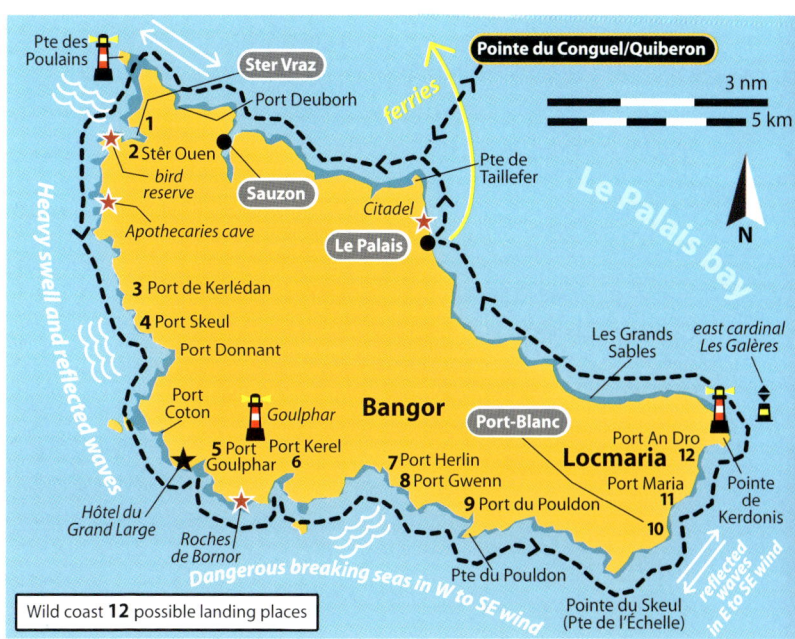

Learn more # Cliff Birds

The Raven (*Grand Corbeau*): a widespread and adaptable bird, but very rare in France, where it is accused of killing lambs. It only nests on cliffs or in old quarries. Pure black with a large wingspan (1.2m), it is a champion of aerial acrobatics. In addition to the well known deep croak, it can make other calls and imitate other sounds. A pair live in the same area throughout the year, surviving on an eclectic diet of carrion, insects, worms, seeds… and the eggs of seabirds.

Photo A. Audevard

The Chough (*Crave à bec rouge*): easy to recognise, this small member of the crow family is black with red feet and bill, and has a characteristic whistle which slowly drops in tone. It has a buoyant flight and does acrobatics around the cliffs. It likes a cliff topped with short grassland, if there are a few sheep around, so much the better. It feeds on insects, spiders, caterpillars etc. and lives in pairs in the same area throughout the year.

Photo © patou-Fotolia.com

The Rock Dove (*Pigeon biset*): despite looking very like the familiar feral pigeon, this is a very rare species. Interbreeding with feral domestic pigeons has reduced their numbers on the sea cliffs they used to inhabit. In France, pure Rock Doves are only found on Belle-Île and in Corsica.

The Kittiwake (*Mouette tridactyle*): a small delicate gull, this is a bird of the open ocean which only visits the coast to breed. The nesting colonies on sea cliffs are easy to recognise, it is the only gull which uses some twigs or straw and mud to make a little nest. White and grey with black tips to the wings; "dipped in ink". Its flight is light and graceful, almost like a tern. Around the nesting colonies you will hear their call "kittiwake-kittiwake" (*Kiti! Ouek!* in French!). In winter they roam as far as the east coast of America. ■

The Gulf of Morbihan and surrounding area

Approaching the Pointe des Poulains.

Belle-Île was briefly occupied by British forces from 1761-63. Once British troops had landed on the beach of Port Andro the French defenders retreated to the fortress, expecting to hold out until help arrived, but the British naval presence made relief impossible. The island was later returned to the French in exchange for Minorca. It had been captured as a bargaining chip in the war over Canada, but was not needed once the tide of battle turned in North America. In a final twist, the current population of Belle-Ile is largely descended from French refugees deported from Acadia (Nova Scotia) during this time.

After Le Palais, it is time for the crossing back to the mainland. The last stopping place is the little beach just before Taillefer. The crossing will take 2-4 hours; leaving at HW -4 to HW -5 will make best use of the flood tide. The tide will be flowing from west to east, so a long ferry glide is necessary to avoid being pushed too far east. ∎

WEATHER, TIDE AND SAFETY

This expedition is for experienced groups only and needs a period of settled weather. Winds above force 3-4 and a swell of more than 1m will make things difficult and the caves largely inaccessible.

Watch out for the ferries going to and from the island, plan your course to keep out of their way. They won't necessarily see you in the swell or take evasive action.

It is possible to explore the outside coast by crossing directly to Pointe des Poulains and then crossing back from the Pointe de Kerdonis. Kayakers making a long expedition taking in Belle-Île, Hoëdic and Houat often choose this alternative.

11 Houat and Hoëdic

Maps:
SHOM 7033
Navicarte 546
IGN 0822OT

Difficulty: ✗ ✗ ✗

Distance: 28 nautical miles (2 days)

Leaving and Arriving: Quiberon

The curving beach at the north tip of Houat.

The Gulf of Morbihan and surrounding area

Lighthouse La Teignouse. Photo C. Magré

Houat

Fishing is still important on Houat.

SIMILAR BUT DISSIMILAR, two siblings, Houat and Hoëdic! The duck and the duckling in Breton. Both isolated and steeped in marine culture, both parts of the same rock formation, but very distinct. Houat has some of the character of Belle-Île; Hoëdic is more like the Glénan islands.

Both had an unusual administration well into the 20th century: the priest was also mayor, judge, customs officer, postmaster, teacher, doctor and midwife!

Houat is verdant and Hoëdic sandy.

Launching, Landing and Parking:

Car park at the Pointe du Conguel, on the east side of Quiberon. Traffic jams are frequent on the single road across the isthmus of Quiberon, so you might have to arrive the night before for an early start. The car park has a height barrier, but a removable post on the left side of the west entrance allows access with kayaks on the roof rack (this is for access by Council workers), just put it straight back.

Port Haliguen: 2km further north.

Harbour at Saint-Gildas-de-Rhuys: a possible launching spot, 7.5nm crossing to Houat. (or 9nm from Port-Navalo).

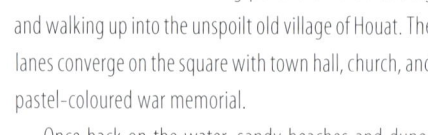

Houat, north coast. Photo R. Bate

Leave from either side of the headland at Conguel at HW -1 (Port-Navalo). Follow the rocks and islets out to the lighthouse, La Teignouse (bulldog), in the midst of chaotic seas and current, the name fits well. This is not the most direct route, but the light is an interesting one, making you think of a birthday cake with a single candle on the top.

Cross the deeper channels and follow along the line of rocks and islets that make up the Chaussée (causeway) de Béniguet leading south-east towards Houat. These are all a bird reserve, but in any case there is little opportunity for landing. Make landfall on Houat (pronounced "ouwat") at the north-west tip and skirt the northern coast. At low water there are several small beaches amongst the cliffs you could land on. Port Saint-Gildas is still an active fishing port. It is worth landing and walking up into the unspoilt old village of Houat. The lanes converge on the square with town hall, church, and pastel-coloured war memorial.

Once back on the water, sandy beaches and dunes dominate the coast. Beyond the point, the bay is a well known sheltered anchorage. The old port (*vieux port*) has a welcoming flat terrace. Then once again we are back on a rocky coast.

A house on Hoëdic with its handcart.

The Gulf of Morbihan and surrounding area   85

Three islands lead the way into the channel across to Hoëdic. The current runs strongly through here, use the various rocks and navigation marks as transits to avoid being swept off course. The crossing should take about one hour, the Pointe de Vieux-Château (Old Castle Point) is a good place to aim for. Follow the coast north, Hoëdic (pronounced "oedique") is much lower lying than its sister Houat.

The harbour at Argol can be very busy in the summer, luckily the north and east of Hoëdic have many fine beaches very suitable for landing. The southern end, which has rocky ledges exposed at low water presents more problems. A circumnavigation using the kayaks looks like the best option, but it is well worth exploring inland on foot. Areas of the island are covered with a bleached lichen, looking a bit like snow, otherwise it is marram grass, gorse, marshy patches of reeds and the machair (this Gaelic word seems to be the only one which fits for this grassy, herb rich, fragile coastal vegetation). Hoëdic has 46 plant species of conservation interest, keep your eyes open and close to the ground, but keep to the paths as well. The "sunken" fort is well hidden and is now a hostel. Although Hoëdic was the site of numerous naval confrontations with the English throughout the 17th and 18th centuries, this new fort, built in the 1850s was redundant before it was completed. The village with its single long lane, emerging out of and returning into the dunes is very attractive. Hoëdic was ruined, and much of the population forced to emigrate when, following a shipwreck in 1931, the press started a panic against eating locally caught lobsters and crabs with its scare-stories about what they had

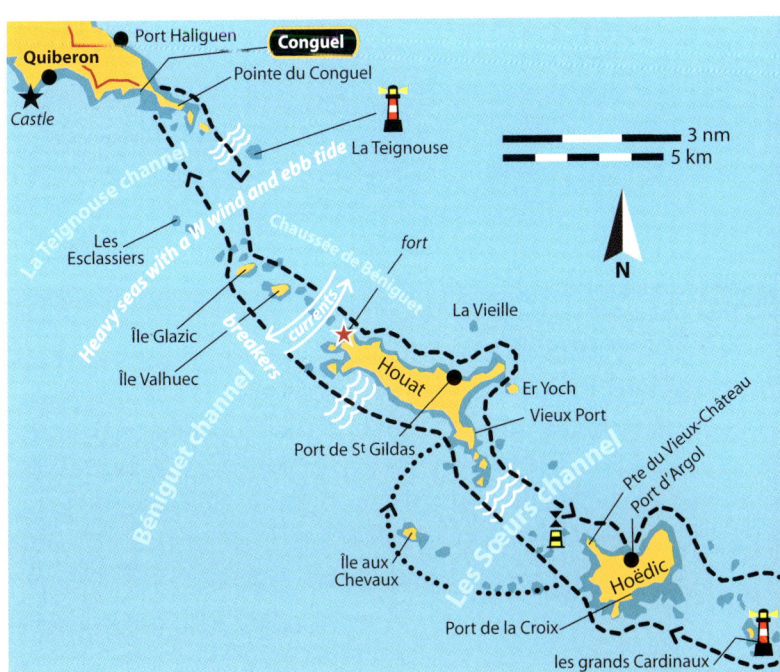

Hoëdic lily. Photo P. Bisset

been eating (corpses?). A slow recovery started in the 1960s as tourism developed. To sum up, Hoëdic is just as nice as its sister, but being further offshore has an air of remoteness, it really is that distant island of your dreams.

After paddling back across the Passage des Sœurs, follow the south coast of Houat, the beaches on this side of the island are wilder and the rocks more severely eroded. There are even goose barnacles (*pouces-pieds*) visible on the cliffs below mid-tide, biologists take these as an indicator of a very exposed shore. The ever present wind has blown the sand to create dunes on the very tops of the cliffs! The short west coast of Houat is lovely, but often very rough, Belle-Île, which can be seen to the west, in a microcosm. The paddle back to Quiberon can be made by the shortest possible course.

Alternatives: Follow the rocks east of Hoëdic to visit the lighthouse on the Cardinaux. Île Dumet can be seen from here, not so far away. It is also possible to make use of the tide to take in Île aux Chevaux on the way back from Hoëdic to Houat. This islet, formerly used by both islands, is now owned by the Coastal Conservancy. ■

WEATHER, TIDE AND SAFETY

A paddle only to be undertaken by a competent group in good weather conditions. The currents between the islets of the Chaussée de Béniguet, off the western end of Houat, in the Passage des Sœurs and around the Cardinaux islands can be very strong. Running north from HW -5 to HW -1 and south from HW +2 to HW +5. Detailed study of a tidal atlas and doing the chartwork before leaving is highly recommended. In these areas heavy seas can develop with wind against tide. The south coast of Houat is protected from the swell to some extent by Belle-Île, but watch out for a rogue set. This paddle can be combined with a trip to Belle-Île, Hoëdic to the Pointe de Kerdonis should take about 2.5 hours, or you could do Houat to the Pointe de Taillefer.

Food for Free

One way of getting some fresh food during your expedition is to keep your eyes open; above the strand-line, on the rocks and at the water's edge are various edible plants. You can collect a small quantity for your own consumption provided you are sure that:
- you have correctly identified the plant,
- that the plant is healthy and growing in large quantities,
- that the environment is a clean one (for seaweed the same advice as for shellfish, check advice from the local authorities),
- that the plant is still attached or rooted.

Seaweed

Thongweed, *Himantalia elongata*, (*Haricots de Mer* in French), cut into sections, cook in fresh water and fry with onions to accompany rice or fish.

Thongweed

Laver bread, *Porphyra umbicalis* (*Nori*) can be eaten raw or cooked, cut finely it is good to flavour omelettes. Similar species are used in Japanese cuisine.

Dulse, *Palmaria palmata*, (*Dulce*), sliced thinly it can be eaten raw in salad, cooked it can flavour a soup.

Pepper dulse

Pepper dulse, *Usmunda pinnifida*, (*Poivre de Mer*) used as a condiment to flavour salads, vegetables and starchy food.

Shoreline plants

Marsh samphire, glass-wort or Salicornia (*Salicorne*), small succulent stems, collect in spring or summer, eat raw or cooked, fried in oil: yum! yum!

Marsh samphire

Sea Purslane (*Obione*), can be eaten raw in a salad or cooked.

Sea beet (*Bette marine*), the wild ancestor of beetroot, sugar beet etc., the leaves can be eaten like spinach.

Sea beet

Wild rocket (*Roquette sauvage*), eat in salad.

Rock samphire (*Criste marine* or *Perce-pierre*), many seaside plants are called samphire, this is the fleshy one with shoots at all angles, growing on rock and cliffs often very close to the HW mark. All parts are edible and good. It was called "crest marine" during Shakespeare's time, which sounds very like the current French name. This name is still in use in Canada. ■

Wild rocket

Rock samphire

Sea Kayaking Guide | **Brittany**

12 The Quiberon Peninsula

Difficulty: ✘ ✘ ✘ / ✘ ✘ ✘

Distance: 13 nautical miles

Leaving and Arriving: Isthmus of Penthièvre

Maps:
SHOM 7032
Navicarte 545
IGN 0821OT

Fortblanc beach

The Gulf of Morbihan and surrounding area

Portaging across the railway line. Photo D. Hottois

Quiberon

Surf at Penthièvre. Photo R. Bate

A PENINSULA so close to being an island... connected to the mainland by a sand spit only twenty-two metres wide. The famous *côte sauvage* (wild coast), facing the wind and swell, cliffs fringed with rock fangs and white water; what a contrast to the lee side which is rocky, but lower and fringed with sandy beaches. Quiberon is a large town and between the headland of Conguel and the Château Turpault you pass a noisy urban landscape. It is well worth tolerating the disturbance, both coasts are so splendid. In this case, *the game is worth the candle*.

Launching, Landing and Parking:

Penthièvre isthmus: 1) Car park near the biscuit bakery, the handiest; 2) Parking on the east side, you will need to portage to the start.

If you are staying on the peninsula there are numerous possible start points from the beaches of Quiberon, Portivy or Port Haliguen.

Approaching the headland of Beg en Aud.

It may be a surf launch at Penthièvre. Think about how you would land again if you had to, near the fort may be easiest. Leave at HW -4 (Port-Navalo). Then head south-east along the coast, this section along to Beg en Aud will give you a chance to assess conditions. There are small beaches to land on and the harbour at Portivy, but after that, conditions may become rougher and escape difficult.

From the arrowhead of the rocks of Beg en Aud to the headland of Percho, with its ruined observatory, the scene is set; high cliffs, savage rocks, salt spray. From Percho to Porz Stang, the bottom of the cliffs is fringed with sandy beaches. These are well known surf spots, so keep far enough out to avoid breaking waves and getting in the way of the surfers.

Beyond Porz Stang, the impressive cliffs become lower and less steep. At Beg er Goalennec they are only 10 metres high; the restaurant is a good landmark and civilisation looks not far away. However, this is often a very wild section for the kayaker; swell, clapotis, breakers and rollers, rocks. Rounding the headland of Beg er Lan and the Château Turpaut you enter a zone where the tidal flow can have a substantial effect, flowing eastbound during the flood and westbound on the ebb. Take care of the ferries when crossing the harbour mouth at Port Maria. In places waves can break far out to sea, so look ahead and plan your course. The point of Conguel is a good place to stop, shelter can be found on either side.

The return journey is along the sheltered lee side of the peninsula which is less rocky and lower, with more houses, but with some rocky headlands and isolated

The Gulf of Morbihan and surrounding area

rocks out to sea. The harbour at Port Haligen is worth looking at, if only for the lovely and amusing sculptures opposite each other on the entrance breakwaters. You pass the National Sailing School, the little port of Orange, then, once past Kerhostin, the isthmus narrows beyond the fort. At its narrowest point there are two slipways, near the biscuit bakery. There is a small retaining wall to climb over and then the railway line to portage before arriving back at the car park. Small trains, locally called the "cork screw" run on this line, in and out of Quiberon, one way of beating the traffic jam caused by the single road access to the peninsula.

Alternatives: You can make a trip out to Île Téviec before starting off around the peninsula. From Conguel it is worth making the detour to go and see the Teignouse lighthouse; the candle on the cake. ∎

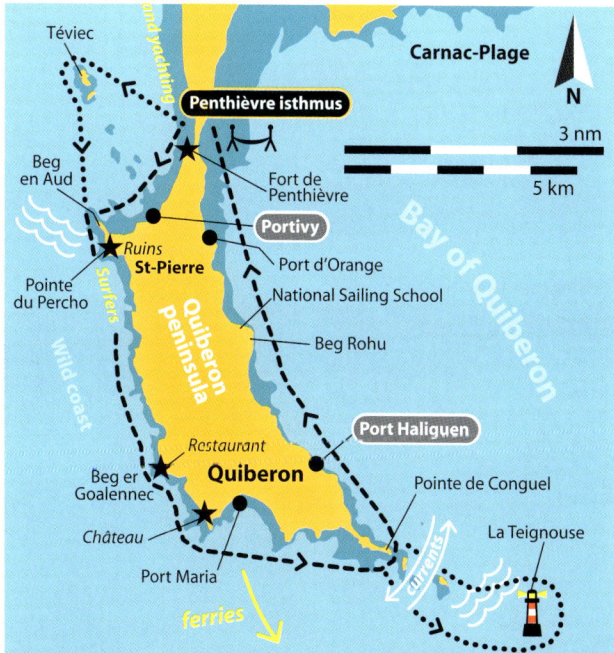

WEATHER, TIDE AND SAFETY

This can be an easy paddle, or a very challenging one depending upon the wind and swell. Keep a weather eye open to avoid unpleasant surprises. It is possible that no landing place can be found on the wild coast; the small beaches are very steep with dumping waves and can disappear completely on a very high tide. The inside sheltered coast has gently sloping beaches that can result in a long portage at low water; best to plan your landing at mid-tide or above.

The tide runs fast around the tip of the peninsula. Westbound from HW +1 to HW -6 and eastbound HW -5 to HW. If the conditions start to look too serious, do not hesitate to turn back. A sheltered paddle sticking to the east side is a good alternative.

92 — Sea Kayaking Guide — Brittany

13

The Ria d'Étel (North)

Difficulty: ✘ ✘ ✘

Distance: 11 nautical miles

Leaving and Arriving: Saint-Cado slipway

Maps:
SHOM 7032
Navicarte 545
IGN 0820OT

Oyster farming in the Ria.

Around Lorient

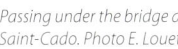

Passing under the bridge at Saint-Cado. Photo E. Louet

Étel

BRANCHES BENT by the wind? An octopus with mud rather than suckers on its arms? An aerial view of the north of the natural harbour of Étel makes you think of both.

Exploring this maze you find stretches of water and mud, reflecting the sky like a mirror, surrounded by a countryside punctuated with pines and great oaks. From time to time a flight of egrets or a flock of terns, with their strident cries, break your reverie.

A halt at an oyster farm will let you taste a condensed drop of this sea.

The north of the Île des Moines.

Launching, Landing and Parking:

Saint-Cado slipway: beside the harbour of Saint-Cado, large car park.
Saint-Cado beach: 200m from the slipway, by the campsite.
Pointe de Kerantréh, at the place called La Vieille Chapelle, a patch of sand allows landing or a launch site for several channels.
Étang de Kergoh at Nostang: beside the N158, access by a bridge to the Nostang branch of the harbour (avoid low water), limited parking.

The forest path.

Leave HW -2 (Étel=Port Tudy +20 minutes) from Saint-Cado. A 12th, possibly 9th, century chapel on the island is dedicated to Saint-Cado (The 6th century Welsh St. Cadoc who preached in this area). Nearby, the spindly bridge over to the island was reputedly built by the devil in return for the soul of a black cat, others say that Cado himself built it. In front, the picture postcard image of a tiny island, Nichtarguer, with its tiny house; a circumnavigation is a good warm-up before setting off. This harbour is a miniature version of the Gulf of Morbihan, but less visited.

Head north, the first island is Île de Fandouillec, then cross the channel to the peninsula of La Forest, there are some lovely walks here. The famous royalist rebel Georges Cadoudal hid himself here during the French revolution.

Paddle on to the point of Kerantréh, the only easy all-tide landing in the harbour. At La Forest and Kerantréh, viewpoint indicators will enable you to understand the layout of this maze a little better. Just beyond here at the point of Beg ar Vil, the channel to Nostang separates from the Landévant river. The channel markers are placed by the locals, so keep an eye on the water depth, their placement is sometimes only approximate.

Once past the last of the oyster farm buildings, the

In front of Saint-Cado.

Around Lorient

Sea campion.

channel turns north-west and the banks start to rise. At high water it is fun to find a route amongst the raised blocks of stabilised mud, *schorre*, which are everywhere along the banks. Here and there an old hulk rots in the mud, a heron takes flight, its wings apparently in slow-motion. Before arriving at Nostang the channel turns north again and becomes wider. A causeway marks the entrance to the Étang de Kergogh, an almost enclosed lagoon. If you turn east, under a small bridge, the estuary turns into a river. An ancient and lovingly restored homestead can be accessed by landing at a small beach below the bridge. It is now used as a hostel.

Follow the same route on the way back, the ebb tide will help, but keep in the channel to avoid going aground on the mud. Before landing, make a tour amongst the deserted islets of Niheu, des Moines and de Riech. If there is still enough water, paddle under the bridge of Saint-Cado. If this is not possible, you can land on a small beach east of the bridge on the mainland. The famous neolithic site of Kerdruelland is nearby. This was only discovered in 2006 and because it had not been

Looking across to Nichtarguer. Photo C. Magré

disturbed it is of more archaeological interest than the famous sites such as Carnac which had been "restored" over many centuries. They found that the site had been carefully dismantled again during the stone-age rather than being simply abandoned. This lead to a re-evaluation of all apparently ruined neolithic sites.

Alternatives: 1) A circuit of the islands of Saint-Cado, setting off under the bridge; 2) Explore the Landévant river as far as the tide mill at la Demie Ville.

Of course, there are many other possibilities, and it is good to be helped by the tidal flow. But even if at low water, the channels are navigable, the ever-present mud makes landing almost impossible, except at the spots already indicated. ∎

WEATHER, TIDE AND SAFETY

High water at the port of Étel, 1 mile from the entrance, is about 20 minutes after Port Tudy, the Pont-Lorois bridge is a further 20 minutes later, an extra hour at Saint-Cado, 1hr 30mins between the point of Verdon and the point of Kerantreh and 2hrs 15 minutes at Nostang. Slackwater is very short and the tide attains maximum speed at Pont-Lorois in under an hour.

This is an easy paddle, but does have three potential difficulties: 1) following the channels; 2) landing after mid-tide can be very difficult; 3) watch out for oyster beds. It is possible to paddle faster than the tide, but the water level drops much faster than you would imagine on the ebb; this is typical for these harbours with a bottle-neck at the entrance.

Salt Marsh and Mudflat

These are the two formations found in the estuaries. The salt marsh (*schorre*) develops on mud stabilised and stratified by persistent vegetation which is salt tolerant, sea purslane (see photo), sea lavender, sea pink, Salicornia and various grasses like Spartina. This forms discrete blocks, only flooded on spring tides. Amongst these, the mudflats (*slikke*), are areas of soft mud, gently shelving towards the channels. These don't look very attractive, but are home to a vast assemblage of life, animal and micro-algae which form a vital resource for fish, shellfish and birds.

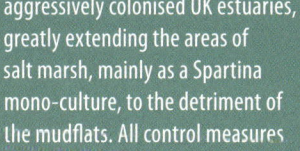

This is a dynamic ecosystem. Although the salt marshes take decades or centuries to develop, in places they are retreating and you see mud blocks, now bare of vegetation, making eroding micro-cliffs in the mudflat, in other places they are gaining ground and you see a sloping surface of vegetation extending over the mudflat. Often Salicornia and Spartina are the pioneering salt marsh builders. Spartina grass, with its spiky leaves and rice-like flowers is an interesting plant. We always had native European species, but in the 1830s a foreign Spartina from the east coast of North America made its way to Southampton Water in England and mated with the native species. The result was initially a sterile hybrid, but by 1860 this had developed into a fertile new species. This aggressively colonised UK estuaries, greatly extending the areas of salt marsh, mainly as a Spartina mono-culture, to the detriment of the mudflats.

All control measures were in vain and the ecology of the estuaries apparently changed forever. However, in the late 1960s it started to die back, the best guess being that the initial clones, now more than a century old, were dying of old age. The mudflats are slowly regaining ground to this day. The new Spartina was introduced into many places, including France, for erosion control and soon became a problem, aggressively extending the salt marsh. Control measures are being tried, for example in the Anse de Kernic (paddle 38), but it is likely that nature will have to take its course. ∎

14 The Ria d'Étel (South)

Maps:
SHOM 7032
Navicarte 545
IGN 0821OT

Difficulty: ✘ ✘ ✘ / ✘ ✘ ✘

Distance: 6 nautical miles

Leaving and Arriving: Saint-Cado slipway

Turbulence near the bridge at Pont-Lorois. Photo C. Magré

Around Lorient

Étel

White water near the island of Gravignez. Photo C. Magré

AN IMMENSE CURVE of sand and dunes links the Quiberon peninsula with that of Gavres near Lorient. The inland sea, *ria*, of Étel drains through this by a narrow channel. The narrowest point is where the Pont Lorois bridge crosses it one mile above the harbour of Étel. This channel is like a powerful river, with very strong tidal currents, which flow upstream as well as down.

The entrance of the channel. Photo C. Magré

Surfing on the bar of Étel. Photo C. Magré

Launching, Landing and Parking:

Saint-Cado slipway: beside the bridge of St. Cado, large car park.
Saint-Cado beach: 200m from the slipway, campsite.
Étel : it is possible to launch from the large slipway used by the lifeboat, large car park.
Vieux Passage: right bank of the ria, limited parking.
Opposite Étel: slipway in the harbour at Le Mogouër, limited parking.

Le Magouër.

Leave from the slipway at Saint-Cado at HW +4 (Étel=Port Tudy +20 minutes). This will give you time to visit the ship graveyard and have a picnic. It is a lovely departure spot, just beside the arched bridge over to this village-island: a fountain, a chapel, a crucifix and some cottages packed close together.

Opposite is the tiny island of Nichtarguer with its single cottage. Just a few paddle strokes towards the south-west and you start to feel the current. The narrowest place is downstream at the famous Pont-Lorois bridge. Getting there is just a matter of letting the tide take you, playing as the current takes you around rocks and islets.

Once past, there is a rural, rocky meander. Sand appears after the charming little harbour of Vieux Passage on the right bank. The harbour at Le Magouër is equally pretty, but is famous for its ship graveyard, mostly tuna boats, with their glistening sides like beached whales.

Land just before the mouth of the river on a scalloped beach on the right bank, not far from a pile of rocks, to admire the well known Étel entrance bar. A signal mast, the Fenoux, displays coded instructions for incoming vessels to cross the bar safely and avoid the shifting sand banks.

Paddle back up to Étel where the maritime heritage is still evident, with the coastguard headquarters and a school for maritime and oyster farming studies. The area lived by tuna fishing and canning. Oysters are now the main activity, but even this is threatened like everywhere in France, by disease.

Around Lorient

101

If you have time, and the tide is high enough, explore the side stream of the Anse de Poumeno. Then it is back up and under the bridge. If the flood tide is running strongly, keep the right-hand side, but once under the bridge quickly cut across to the left to avoid some rocks which are right in the middle of the tide flow on the next bend.

It is worth spending some time around the bridge, getting to know the currents and counter-currents, playing at breaking in and breaking out and ferry gliding; enjoy yourself! ■

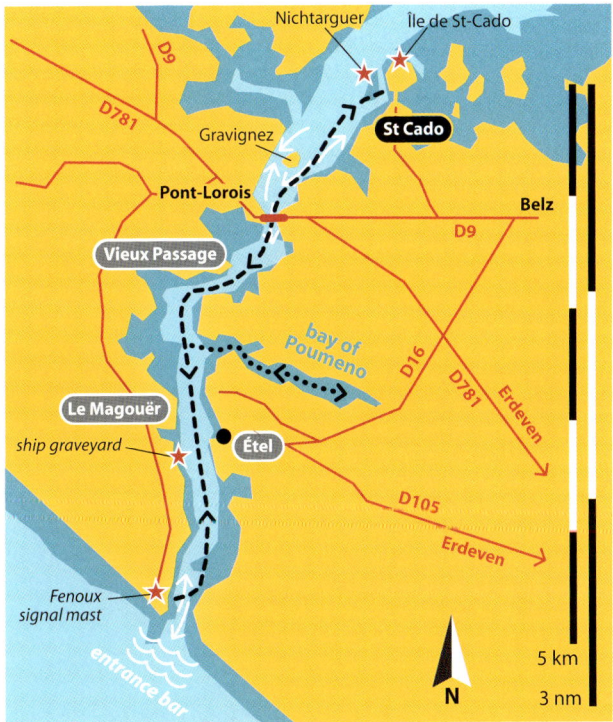

WEATHER, TIDE AND SAFETY

The reference port for Étel is Port Tudy, HW at the Pont-Lorois bridge is about 20 minutes later and about one hour later at Saint-Cado. The period of slackwater is very short, the current under the bridge attains maximum flow about one hour after the turn of the tide, maximum flow can be 5kt on the flood and 6kt on the ebb. Some knowledge of white-water paddling is necessary to get the most out of this paddle, local paddlers often come just to play around the bridge.

The entrance bar can be crossed around HW, wind against tide is to be avoided. Depending on the swell height, the sea can be monstrous or completely flat. However, waves can break without warning at any time, take care!

102 | Sea Kayaking Guide | **Brittany**

15

The Blavet

Difficulty: ✘ ✘ ✘ / ✘ ✘ ✘

Distance: 18 nautical miles (1 or 2 days)

Leaving and Arriving: Port-Louis

Maps:
SHOM 7032
IGN 0720ET

The commercial port of Kergroise in Lorient harbour.

Around Lorient

Landing fish at the harbour at Keroman.

● Lorient

THE HARBOUR OF LORIENT is at the confluence of three rivers: the Blavet, the Scorff and the Ter. A port city with a long working class history, Lorient has 5 harbours: naval, passenger terminal, yacht, the second largest fishing port in France and also the largest commercial port in Brittany. After saluting the tall dockyard cranes, paddle up the Blavet, explore the cemetery of Groix tuna boats, and follow fine meanders through the countryside to arrive at the quays of the medieval walled town of Hennebont. You are paddling in the footsteps of the English fleet of 1342.

Launching, Landing and Parking:

Port-Louis: harbour at La Pointe, large slipway used for careening boats, parking.

Locmiquélic: slipway in the harbour of Sainte-Catherine, limited parking.

Larmor-Plage: 1) Slipway near Kernével beach, large car park; 2) Slipway in Kernével harbour, in front of the harbour master's office, busy car park.

Hennebont: 1) Slipway Saint-Caradec, right bank above the town centre. Limited parking near a campsite. A peaceful spot for launching; 2) Slipway by the ramparts in the town centre, large car park, but often full, a good spot for a short stop; 3) Slipway in the upper harbour, right bank, at the end of the road, "Rue du Cabotage", in the Ty-Mor business park (*ZI* or *Zone Industrielle*).

Lanester (for direct access to the Blavet): 1) Le Plessis river, slipway near the bridge, easy parking; 2) Kayak club "Gilles Gahinet", near to the bridge Bonhomme, parking up the road.

Inside the ribcage of a boat in the ship graveyard at Kerhervy.

Leave on the flood tide, around mid-tide (Port Tudy) from the harbour of La Pointe, Port-Louis, head south of the island Saint-Michel (a military zone) and then towards Lorient. To the north, it is possible to go and have look at the fishing port of Keroman, the second largest in France by tonnage landed.

Skirt the commercial quays of Kergroise, the silos and cranes are visible from a long way away, then turn left into the yacht harbour in the town centre, noting the tower, La Découverte, an attractive old lighthouse in the Arsenal district of the town. The mouth of the Scorff is a military area; paddle back up the Blavet, the northwest bank is more industrialised, but less silted up, to Lanester. The small harbour of Saint-Guénaël and its surroundings mark the start of the rural Blavet. The Bonhomme bridge is modern, but stands next to two old bridge pillars, with statues at the top: a Breton man on one side and a Bretonne woman on the other.

The next bend, very silted up, shelters the boat cemetery of Kerhervy and a small open air theatre. If the tide is high enough you can paddle inside the rib-cages of these ancient boats and examine their

The fishing harbour at Keroman.

Around Lorient

construction timbers, slowly rotting with seaweed, mosses and lichens. Some of these are old tuna boats from Groix.

A glimpse of the Château de Locguénolé, and the forest closes in again on the steep banks. Each bend in the river reveals more old hulks, sunk deep in the mud or covered in vegetation.

After the road bridge of Locoyarn, some dockyards, a small marina and finally the railway viaduct mark the entrance into Hennebont. After a low bridge, a small stone slipway allows you to get out straight on the city walls. Once you have climbed these, surprise, surprise, they are protecting a very modern town. German positions in the town were bombed in August 1944 destroying much of the medieval city.

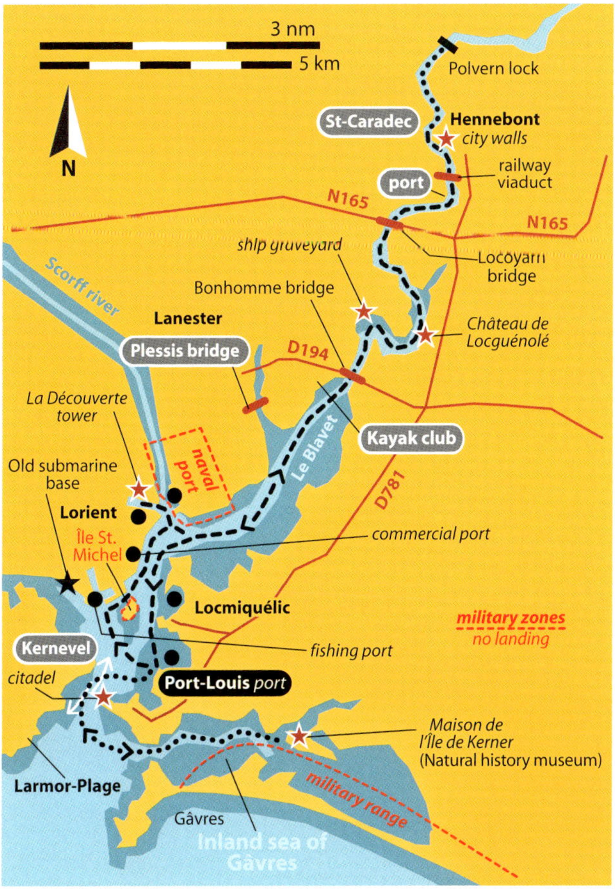

Learn more

Brittany's maritime vocation

Whilst paddling in Brittany you will meet professional seafarers.
The main fishing ports are Lorient, Concarneau and Le Guilvinec. Seventeen ports are equipped with cranes for fish landing. Large scale industrial fishing has long been in decline, local small scale fishing now represents ¾ of the trade. It is heavily regulated to preserve stocks. Each seagoer supports 4 jobs on land. Processing is usually done close to the ports, but some ports import fish to keep the canneries going.
Oyster farming, very evident in the estuaries and bays is in decline due to disease, but mussel farming and other shellfish production is doing well. Seaweed collection is covered in more detail on page 198. It may be a growth sector for the future. There are numerous marine research organisations scattered over about 30 sites, the best known being the French Research Institute for Exploitation of the Sea, IFREMER.
Brittany has five principal commercial ports; Saint-Nazaire, Lorient, Brest, Saint-Brieuc-le-Légué and Saint-Malo. Roscoff and Saint-Malo are ferry ports for cross-channel and Irish services, whilst many local ports and ferry operators serve the Breton islands.

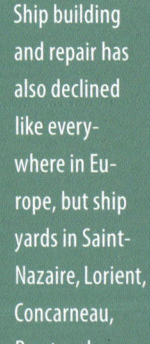

Ship building and repair has also declined like everywhere in Europe, but ship yards in Saint-Nazaire, Lorient, Concarneau, Brest and Saint-Malo are still active. Coming to our sport, the kayak construction companies; Plasmor, Polyform and Kerlo have been based in Brittany for the last 30 years.
Four national marine sport training centres are based in Brittany. *Pôles France* at Port-La-Forêt and Brest, and the National Sailing School (ENV) at Saint-Pierre-de-Quiberon are for sailing. Whilst a kayaking centre is to be found at Brest. ■

Around Lorient

Quartier Saint-Caradec at Hennebont.

Joanna of Flanders was about to give in to the French besieging the city in 1342, when she saw the English fleet sailing up the river from her window and ended negotiations. Stories about this feisty lady might have influenced Joan of Arc a century later. She is still celebrated in Breton culture.

Another slipway near the chapel of Saint-Caradec and a cafe mark the end of the trip. There is a small municipal camp site. It is possible to paddle a little further upstream but the lock is not far. The return makes use of the ebb tide and you can visit the harbour at Locmiquélic before returning to Saint-Louis.

Alternatives: Two shorter paddles could be made: 1) The tour of Lorient Harbour; 2) The paddle up the tidal Blavet from Lanester or Locmiquélic. Another good trip would be up the inland sea of Gâvres (Petite mer de Gâvres), east of Port Louis. You need high water to paddle around the lagoon. The island of Kerner has an old oyster farmer's house converted into a museum of the natural history of the lagoon. It is well worth visiting and is a good place for bird watching. The south of the lagoon is a military range — to be avoided! ∎

WEATHER, TIDE AND SAFETY

Expect heavy boat traffic around Lorient and watch out for shallow water and silt along the banks of the Blavet particularly below the Bonhomme bridge.
Make use of the tide in both directions. Between the citadel of Port-Louis and Larmor-Plage the current can reach 4kt. HW at Lorient is the same as Port Tudy.

108 — Sea Kayaking Guide — **Brittany**

16

The Island of Groix

Difficulty: ✖ ✖ ✖ / ✖ ✖ ✖

Distance: 18 nautical miles (2 days)

Leaving and Arriving: Port-Blanc

Maps:
SHOM 7031 / 7032
Navicarte 544
IGN 0720ET

Arriving in Port Tudy harbour.

Around Lorient

Locmaria.

Groix

FROM THE MAINLAND, the wild cliffs and hidden harbours of the island of Groix beckon the kayaker. In good weather the circumnavigation makes an excellent first "offshore" paddle with little tidal flow to worry about. Best undertaken in a group, this is not a trip to be hurried.

Launching, Landing and Parking:

Port Blanc slipway: near the village of Kerroch, 7km west of Larmor-Plage. Plenty of parking and a friendly slipway.

Perello Beach: sheltered in a west wind, parking with a portage.

Lomener Port: parking difficult during the summer.

It is also possible to launch further east, this is a longer crossing and a watch must be kept for large shipping using the port of Lorient:

Port-Louis: La Pointe harbour, slipway and parking.

Ban-Gâvres: slipway and adjacent parking.

Larmor-Plage : 1) Slipway near Kernével beach, large parking area; 2) The port of Kernével slipway, in front of the harbour master's office, limited parking.

The translator in Port Saint-Nicolas. Photo R. Bate

Leave Port Blanc a little before HW to make use of the light tidal flow towards the island. The crossing will take ¾ to 1 hour in good conditions. Aim towards the coastguard look-out on Groix and then follow the coast westward to Pen Men. This is a good place to reassess conditions as the swell height and wind will become evident. There is no shame in turning back and enjoying the lovely north coast of the island. If you are happy to go on, follow the dramatic cliffs and spray drenched rocks around to Port Saint-Nicolas. These cliffs are the most impressive of the island, resembling the bow of a tuna fishing boat, emblem of the island at the start of the 20th century.

Like Belle-Île, Groix is a steep sided raised plateau. On the western end, there are no possible landing spots between Port Melin and Port Saint-Nicolas. The almost hidden entrance of Port Saint-Nicolas and the calm waters will seem like an oasis amidst the rocks and swell. Eastward the jumble of rocks and cliffs continue with local names like Hell Hole and Thunder Hole giving an idea of what it would be like in stormy weather.

Beyond Pointe de L'Enfer (Hell Point) the coast starts to drop with several sandy beaches between the rocks; landing may be possible depending upon the swell. However, watch out for reefs and the swell or breakers around them even far out to sea. Locmaria is a good place for stretching your legs with its narrow streets, white houses and pink hollyhocks. This coast is the only geological nature reserve in France; collecting or removing any of the fascinating rocks or pebbles is forbidden.

Do not be taken in by the Pointe des Chats, despite its friendly small lighthouse, groups of trees and tiny beaches, it can be the most tricky part of the circumnavigation. Rock ledges lead to breaking swell far out to sea, closing-out inshore passages as the tide drops. Once round, the east coast is a mix of cliffs and beaches leading on to Les

Grands Sables. This vast convex beach formed by storms, tides and currents, alters from year to year and features on all the postcards of the island. Port Tudy has 3 yacht basins, one with a lock. Watch out for other boats and the ferry. This is the largest settlement on the island if you need to go shopping.

Beyond Port Tudy the coast becomes a series of ledges running out to sea, ideal for some fun rock-hopping. Port Lay is a charming little harbour and anchorage with boats moored fore and aft in lines. After some more rock-hopping, the obvious dam wall at Port Melin is the point at which to bid farewell to the Island. Looking across towards the mainland, large white blotches, kaolin mines NW of Port Blanc, give something to aim at. Little by little the coast will become clearer. The entry to Port Blanc is west of the little red tower, behind the high sea wall. ■

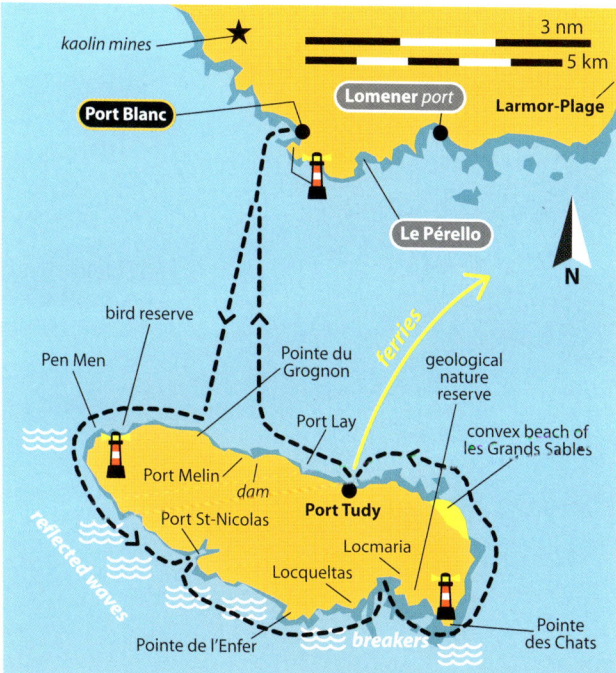

WEATHER, TIDE AND SAFETY

Think twice before tackling the west and south of the island. There can be severe clapotis close inshore and swell breaking far out to sea. In bad conditions the only landing places are at Port Saint-Nicolas and Locmaria (and here only at HW in swell). Tidal flow is weak in the sound (max 0.3kt) but make use of the compass or a transit to keep you on course during the crossing. An eastbound drift starts around HW -5 (Port Tudy), turns offshore from HW to +2 and then westbound from +3. Short lived peak flows along the southern coast of Groix may reach 1kt westbound around HW -6 and eastbound at HW -2. Apart from this, flows are negligible.

Sea Kayaking Guide — Brittany

17 The Laïta

Difficulty: ✗ ✗ ✗

Distance: 9 nautical miles

Leaving: Quimperlé — **Arriving:** Le Pouldu

Maps:
SHOM 7031
Navicarte 544
IGN 0620ET

Sand banks above Saint-Maurice

Around Lorient

● Quimperlé

The bar at the mouth of the Laïta, low water.

FOLLOWING a secret valley, the waters of the Laïta roll out like a dark carpet fringed with reedbeds. A chateau emerges from the forest canopy. A leaping salmon is frozen in a constellation of sparkling water drops. Twisted oak branches touch the water's surface. Lower down, golden sandbanks emerge from the dappled waters.

Leaving Quimperlé, the railway viaduct.

Launching, Landing and Parking:

Quimperlé town centre: left bank, slipway from the Surcouf quay, parking.
Towards low water, launching is difficult from the town centre, numerous gravel banks impede navigation until you reach the railway viaduct.
Quimperlé, on D49, right bank, below the kayak club, parking in a field, with direct launching possible.
Le Pouldu: this little harbour has a handy slipway and adequate parking.
Beach below Le Pouldu: large car park behind the beach.
If you are making a one way trip, the shuttle to Le Pouldu is shorter than that to Guidel on the opposite side of the estuary.
Harbour at Guidel-Plages: opposite Le Pouldu, parking.

Ducking under oak branches at Carnoët.

Leave Quimperlé at HW +3 (Port Tudy). The river takes you under a fine railway viaduct and the four-lane road bridge. The dark colour of the water is striking; this is not due to pollution, in fact more and more salmon are appearing in the river and there are signs of otters. The colour is due to peat washing out of the reed beds which fringe the river.

On the right bank, the forest of Carnoët and on the left a series of large country houses guarantee that the banks are very unfrequented. The only access to the banks is by a few small footpaths and occasionally, where the reed beds thin out, the GR34. You will not find many stopping places between Quimperlé and the bridge at Saint-Maurice, unless you like stumbling about in the reeds. The first possible spot for a break is after passing a small wooden boat house on the left bank where a stone quay marks the Pointe de Véchène. On the right bank, you pass the only house opening directly on to the river, near the ruins of the old Château de Carnoët. Geese are fattened here. The forested valley sides close in, but a gap in the reeds where the river Frout enters from the right offers a chance to explore inside the reed beds. Paddle up as far as you can, the reeds caressing your hair; or slapping your face!

Shortly after rejoining the main river, a meadow,

Around Lorient

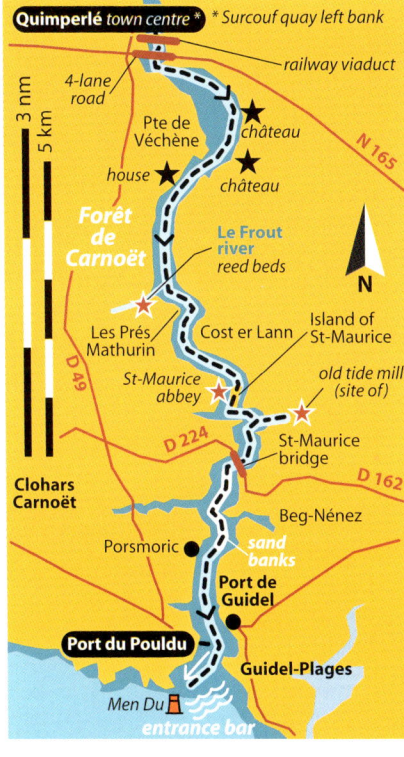

completely surrounded by reeds and forest, the Pré Mathurin, offers a picnic spot on the right bank, there is a choice between this and the meadow of Cost er Lann on the left bank. A post marks the administrative limit between what is considered to be seawater and what river water. This takes no account of the tides. At the next meander, sandbanks here and there force detours to find deep water. From the Île aux Vaches, you can explore an inlet through a gate in the dyke, this was the site of the defunct tide mill of Benoal.

After the Saint-Maurice bridge the current becomes stronger and the smell of the sea is in the air. You can take a detour into the muddy arms of Beg Nénez inlet. A straight section and then you are at Porsmoric which rises steeply from the river, Le Pouldu is not far away. If you like you can paddle down to the mouth of the river with its entrance bar. If the surf is not too high, this can be a good place for a spot of play; a fine way to round off a good day out. ■

WEATHER, TIDE AND SAFETY

This paddle presents no major difficulties and a two-way trip would be equally possible. If you want to make use of the rising tide leave a couple of hours after the tide turns before starting back upstream. The paddle could be done in the reverse direction. Passing the Abbey of Saint-Maurice near HW would allow a visit, the guide is very knowledgeable about bats, but also about other flora and fauna; however, at HW you will miss out on the sandbanks.

At Le Pouldu port the current can make paddling difficult amongst the moored boats: you could land at the small slipway upstream. The entrance can be a fine play spot, but could also be dangerous in large surf, have a look first.

18 The Cliffs of Clohars-Carnoët

Difficulty: ✗ ✗ ✗

Distance: 9 nautical miles

Leaving and Arriving: Brigneau

Maps:
SHOM 7031
Navicarte 544
IGN 0620ET

The mouth of the ria of Merrien.

The Quimper area 117

● Doëlan

*Passing in front of Doëlan.
Photo I. Leguérinel*

A WALL OF CLIFFS along the coast usually makes for an austere, not to say dangerous paddle, with no prospect of landing. Not so this section of coast, where numerous small inlets (*rias*) provide sheltered havens, lovely spots to make a halt; some with moorings providing a slalom course amongst the boat hulls, others giving the sensation of being the last person on earth.

Launching, Landing and Parking:

Slipway in Brigneau harbour: large slipway, car park 50m away.
Slipway in Merrien harbour: left bank, adjacent parking.
Doëlan harbour: much busier than the two options above, many slipways, but congested with difficult parking. The best is just below the green lighthouse on the Pointe de Cayenne which has two slipways (there is a charge for RIBS in summer) and a large car park. Another possiblity is the slipway at the far end of the harbour, access to water HW +/-2.

The entrance of Doëlan harbour.

Launch in the small harbour at Brigneau on the flood tide around mid-tide (Port Tudy). Paddle up to look around the forest lined estuary, the entrance is fairly wide and swell can be felt surprisingly far from the sea. A relic of the age of "blue gold" -the sardine-, the derelict Malachap cannery is perched on the breakwater at the entrance where they used to land fish.

Follow the coast east and after a quarter of a mile there is the first small inlet, marked by a white landmark on the cliffs; Poulguen. A customs house, high up beside the footpath has watched over this coast since 1790. The customs officers (*douaniers* or *gabelous* in French) paid a lot of attention to this coast, a paradise for English smugglers, with its hidden harbours. A long distance footpath, the GR34, skirts the coast in the footsteps of the *gabelous*.

The next inlet, Merrien is the longest, protected by a sharp bend in the entrance, with its navigation light half hidden in the trees. Well worth looking around, but watch out for raised oyster beds. The coast continues with a long headland of black cliffs, then a promontory protects Port Bali with its sheltered anchorage and half a mile further on its twin, Portec. Both these anchorages with their small beach and small stream could be far from civilisation on some distant isle, remote from the sound and fury of modern life.

Less than a mile of lovely cliffs further on is Doëlan, a delightful small harbour, slotted into a deep valley, cottages rising in tiers, fishing boats, two round towers… and the crowds of tourists! Have a good look around, the quays and harbours, the

The Quimper area 119

Port Bali.

red and green navigation lights amongst the cottages; paddle right up to the sheltered lagoon at the head of the valley. Then take the coast back to Brigneau again.

Alternatives: If you want a longer paddle, the coast between Kerfany-les-Pins and Le Pouldu is very beautiful. Between Doëlan and Le Pouldu, there are some lovely beaches below the cliffs and good rock-hopping. The wild coastline lends itself to multi-day trips and can be combined with Les Avens (paddle 19) and La Laïta (paddle 17). ■

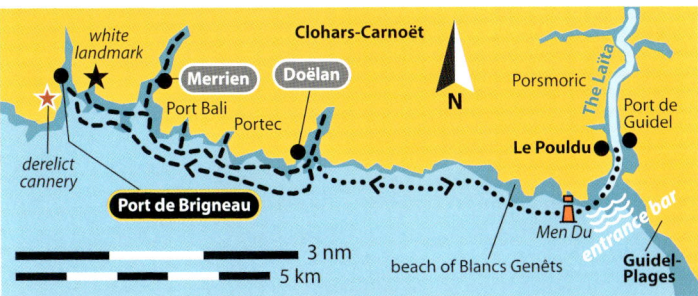

WEATHER, TIDE AND SAFETY

Brigneau Harbour, take care, swell can roll in a long way. There is very little tidal flow along the coast, but HW is needed to penetrate far up the inlets. Heavy swell will make this paddle more demanding. A double line of reefs between Brigneau and Merrien can create breakers. Consider the alternatives of paddles 17 or 19.

19 The Aven and the Belon

Difficulty: ✖ ✖ ✖

Distance: 12 nautical miles

Leaving and Arriving: Kerfany-les-Pins

Maps:
Navicarte 544
IGN 0620ET

Bélon Harbour.

The Quimper area

Pont-Aven.

FORMING THE LETTER "V", twin *rias* with forgotten corners, one is definitely "upmarket" and the other "downmarket". The beauty of Pont-Aven makes up for the former and the well known Belon oysters for the latter. Both are set deep in forest and lined with rounded boulders. Explore to your heart's content at high water but avoid the mud at low tide.

Paddling up the Aven.

● Pont-Aven

Launching, Landing and Parking:

It is easy to launch at the mouths of the two *avens*, Port Manech to the west and Kerfany-les-Pins to the east, but parking is difficult in summer.

Kerfany-les-Pins: ask if you can use the sailing school slipway, otherwise portage down to the beach.

Port Manech: launching from the beach is as easy as from the harbour.

On the Aven, two small ports face each other a mile upstream from the entrance: 1) Kerdruc, with a small slipway on the west side; 2) Rosbraz to the east, has two large slipways with limited parking in front of them.

Pont-Aven: launching only possible near HW, lots of parking, but very congested in summer.

On the Belon: 1) Left bank, near Moëlan-sur-mer, plenty of parking and 3 slipways, the one at the end of the harbour extends below LW; 2) Right bank, Riec-sur-Belon, near the seafood restaurant "Chez Jacky", parking up above.

Le château du Hénan on the Aven. Photo H. Le Flohic

Launch at HW -2 (Port Tudy) from Kerfany-les-Pins and round the point of Penquernéo to enter the Aven, then paddle past Port Manech with its small old fashioned beach and lines of white bathing huts. Up to Rosbraz, the Aven is all rocks and sand. On the right bank, the inlet of Poulguin with a fine chateau and rounded rocks at the entrance. A ship graveyard is to be found inside. The Aven is crowded with moorings from here to Rosbraz.

Above Kernéo, the Aven is very silted up, so much so that except right at HW it is wise to follow the buoyed channel. On the right bank, see the tall, slim silhouette of the chateau of Hénan -picnic spot and arboretum- then a tide mill belonging to the chateau. In olden times, the Lord of Heznant demanded a cask of wine and two *minot* (about 10kg) of salt from each barge which came up the river; today your bottle of Bordeaux is safe!

The course of the river narrows and becomes wilder, pine trees, rocks, still water. When you have the choice take the left channel to Pont-Aven. Round the next bend the dockyards and the first quays extend to the wooden pedestrian bridge (actually made of concrete) and beyond that a fine water wheel. Before it became famous for appearing in paintings, the town was known as "Pont-Aven, renowned town of fourteen mills, and fifteen grand houses". Today there is only a single mill and two biscuit makers; but crowds of artists and thousands of tourists!

Paddle back down the Aven to explore the Belon, often called Aven-Belon. The mouth is rocky and wild. At Beg Porz you will see 30 kayaks moored together with a

The Quimper area

strange longship. After a 90 degree bend, Bélon extends on both banks, if you get out on the left bank (your right), you will get a view of the river upstream. To the north of the inlet of Lapriot, steep stairs allow landing to visit the chambered cairn and woods of Kermeur Bihan. Stop here, or continue to paddle up the river: around Kermeur old quarries line the banks. The flat "Belon" oysters with their hazelnut taste are fattened in the famous oyster beds at Riec. Further on, there is the muddy creek of Penmor and after that the river becomes more and more silted up. Turn back towards Kerfany.

Alternatives: The itinerary given only extends about 0.6 nautical miles above Bélon, you can paddle much further; however, the deep water channel is narrow and twisting and is not buoyed. Don't get stuck in the mud as the tide drops. The river is navigable as far as the bridge at Pont Guily, the entire left bank above Bélon is a nature reserve. ■

WEATHER, TIDE AND SAFETY

Two things to watch out for: 1) The sea off the headland between the two Avens can be choppy; 2) Deep mud, even where the creeks look wide, the deep water channels are very narrow. Beware the falling tide.

If you descend either of the Avens (*aven*=jaw in Breton) with the tide, you may find a bar at the mouth. These bars of shifting sandbanks can have breaking waves if the wind and sea are running against an ebb tide.

124 — Sea Kayaking Guide — **Brittany**

20 Concarneau Bay

Maps:
SHOM 7146
Navicarte 543
IGN 0519ET

Difficulty: ✗ ✗ ✗

Distance: 16 nautical miles

Leaving and Arriving: La Forêt Fouesnant

Near the entrance of La Ville Close.

The Quimper area

● Concarneau

Low tide at the bay of Saint-Jean.

THIS TRIP MAKES a complete circuit of Concarneau Bay and, if you have time, allows a look-see at some of the side creeks: Pouldohan, almost unspoilt; historic Concarneau with its fine fortifications; the twin creeks of Saint-Jean and Saint-Laurent; then the entrance to La Forêt-Fouesnant. All of this under the watchful eye of the coastguard look-out of Beg Meil.

Launching, Landing and Parking:

La Forêt-Fouesnant: 1) The very large slipway south of Port-La-Forêt (signposted "Cale sud"); 2) More authentic, the old port (limited parking where you arrive at the port, just before the gangway).

Beg Meil: Kermil beach, parking and a portage to the sea.

Concarneau: 1) Les Sables Blancs (White Sands) beach, parking and portage; 2) The town centre, north-east of la Ville Close (the walled town on an island), two slipways (commercial users and emergency services) and a large parking area, congested in summer.

Trégunc: Pouldohan beach, slightly off the route of the paddle, but very handy.

The Concarneau water-bus.

Cabellou Fort. Photo I. Leguérinel

Leave at HW -3 (Port Tudy) from the old port of La Forêt-Fouesnant or the slipway to the south of Port-la-Forêt, very close to each other by sea, but a long drive apart. Paddle along the Cap Coz beach, this is a very popular and built up tourist spot; but the north-south oriented coast after this is altogether more rural with a succession of small cliffs and beaches backed by trees. Below the coastguard lookout at Beg Meil, turn to the east and paddle straight across the bay to the headland of Cabellou with its small fort (2.5nm). Follow the southern coast of the headland to visit the bay of Pouldohan. The narrow north branch ends at a tidal mill. Head back around the headland; north of this the rounded rock piled pell-mell is something to savour. Then head for Concarneau.

The town developed around the island of the Citadelle which formed a natural defensive point in case of attack. Early wooden walls were replaced by stone ramparts. The economy of the town was based on sardines, packed in barrels for delivery inland. Later, canneries replaced the traditional pickling in barrels; at the start of the 20th century, the town had 7,000 inhabitants of which 2,000 were women workers in the 30 canneries. After the catastrophic disappearance of the sardines from the shores of Brittany, the town turned to tuna fishing (becoming the third most important port in France) and ship building. Behind the port the shipyards compete for any space available.

The impressive ramparts of the walled town testify to its importance in the past. You can explore these, particularly the draw-bridges guarding the entry and

The Quimper area

the small clock tower decorated by a sundial which has become the emblem of the town. To the north a succession of ports; small fishing boats, then larger boats and dockyards. A small passenger water-bus shuttles constantly back and forth between the east of the walled town and the east of Concarneau.

Turning to the west and leaving the port, you pass the "Marinarium" (sea life centre), then the odd small lighthouse of La Croix (The Cross) in the centre of the town. Continue along the promenade, bordered by small beaches which ends at the beach of Sables Blancs (White Sands beach). The road turns inland and the cliffs start. The tiny beach of the Trois Sardines (Three Sardines) is a good place for a break before heading up the twin inlets of Saint-Jean and Saint-Laurent, both with forested shores and deep mud at low water. Saint-Jean is the shorter, Saint-Laurent is spoilt by a huge campsite that disfigures the western shore, but it ends at an interesting mariners cemetery. Skirt the long beach of Kerleven back to the start point.

Alternatives: It is possible to explore other inlets and creeks; the bay of Penfoulic, the marshes of La Forêt-Fouesnant (only at high water), other branches of the bay of Pouldohan or either side of the beach at Cabellou. ∎

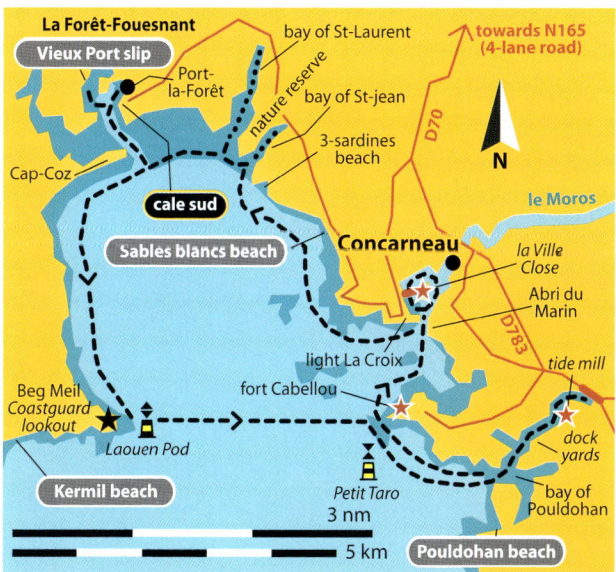

WEATHER, TIDE AND SAFETY

This stretch of water is relatively sheltered; nevertheless, swell can generate surf between the bay of Saint-Jean and the beach of Cap Coz, especially at low tide, and could create rough conditions off the points. There are numerous rocks near Beg Meil, the headland at Cabellou and along the promenade at Concarneau.
Don't be left high and dry by the ebbing tide in the creeks of St-Jean and St-Laurent.

21 The Glénan Islands

Difficulty: ✗ ✗ ✗

Distance: 25 nautical miles (2 days)

Leaving and Arriving: Pointe de Mousterlin

Maps:
SHOM 7146
Navicarte 543
IGN 0519ET

A small bay at Penfret.

The Quimper area

Glénan

Bird watching on the Île aux Moutons.

A break on the sand bank at Guiriden, opposite Penfret.
Photo E Julé

THE GLÉNAN ARCHIPELAGO, made up of six main islands and a multiplicity of rocks and reefs, surrounds a lagoon known as La Chambre. Sheltered from the prevailing winds this is a magical spot with its shallow azure waters, white sand and marl. The famous sailing school "Les Glénans" is based here. Started in 1947 its philosophy is self-sufficiency, taking responsibility and working together. Its courses are accessible to all. The best selling book; *Le Cours des Glénans* is an exceptional resource for all sailors. It has been translated into English many times; *The Glénans Sailing Manual*, *The New Glénans Sailing Manual*, etc.

Launching, Landing and Parking:

Pointe de Mousterlin (the headland between Bénodet and Concarneau): slipway to the east of the point, handier than the one near the hotel; parking at an angle along the road; portage, a trolley might be useful at low water.

Two other possibilities, these routes are slightly shorter as they take you directly across, missing out the Île aux Moutons: 1) West of the beach at Lesconil; near the sailing school, large parking area; 2) East of the port of Trévignon: slipway and large parking area.

The "Glénan blues" near Guiriden. Photo Y. Dodard

Leave around HW (Port Tudy) from the Pointe de Mousterlin, east slipway. Leaving the last of the rounded rocks behind, heading due south, the crossing to the Île aux Moutons (Island of Sheep), with its small lighthouse, will take about one hour. This will be a welcome stop. Land on the north beach with its two rusting cannons. However, access to the lighthouse is prohibited from April to August when the terns are nesting. "Bretagne Vivante" (Living Brittany) who manage the island have a volunteer stationed on the island who sleeps in the small concrete bunker built to shelter anyone shipwrecked here. His role is to look after and point out the birds and other animals, notably lizards, check that no dogs or predators disembark and remind people that it is a protected area. During the 1930s a Mr and Mrs Quéméré and their 11 children lived here and looked after the light. A lovely scattering of rocks leads eastwards from the island.

Continue due south towards the island of Saint-Nicolas, then head east to Bananec, an island of sand dunes which is connected by a sandy spit; then along to Guiriden, a miniscule rock radiating long spits of immaculate sand, very photogenic, and thus visited by motor boats and their barbecues if there is the slightest ray of sunshine!

Herring gull chick, Penfret.

The Quimper area

Continue on to the northern tip of Penfret, you can paddle around the outside, or take the lagoon on the inside. The rocky northern tip with its lighthouse is the abode of the herring gull, the rest of the island the sandy domain of the Glénans Sailing School. An ancient lookout on the southern tip surveys rocks much visited by divers. Continue to explore the lagoon, heading towards a chimney, the remains of an old soda factory, on Île du Loc'h. The north beach of this island, the sandy beach of your dreams, is visited by yachtsmen and kite surfers. If the west wind is not too strong, continue around the island to the bay on the west, this marks the

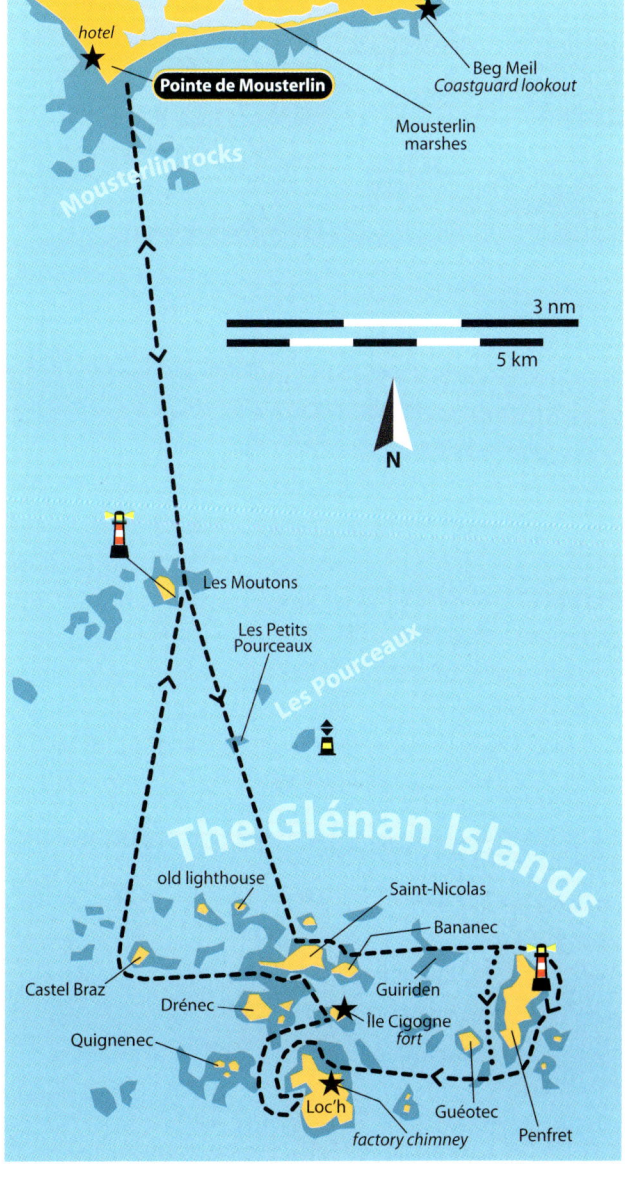

Bivouac on Île du Loc'h.

boundary between the land of men to the north and the land of the herring gull to the south. *Stop press: as of 2012 the island has been fenced and a watchman installed, this does not affect access to the beaches.*

Take a short break on Île Cigogne (Stork Island), the tower on the fort of this island is a central landmark of the archipelago, then a pause on Saint-Nicolas. This island is where the tourist ferries arrive. The smallest nature reserve in France is found here; a small patch of grass where the rare Glénan narcissus grows. The west of the archipelago is comprised of small islets and castles of rocks. Castel Braz, the most impressive is well worth a detour before setting off back. The return journey should be made starting near low water, heading first to the Île aux Moutons and from there towards a white square amongst the trees on a heading of 350 degrees. Bit by bit this turns out to be the hotel and the Pointe de Mousterlin.

WEATHER, TIDE AND SAFETY

Swell may make this trip more challenging. Mid way between the Moutons and Saint-Nicolas, two groups of rocks, the Grands and Petits Pourceaux (large and small feral pigs) can generate rollers and breakers. If the sea is too rough on the return to Mousterlin, try the slipway near the hotel. The tidal flows have only limited effect on this route, but need to be taken into account if you are leaving from Lesconil or Trévignon. If you plan to bivouac on an island managed by the Glénans Sailing School, contact them first. (The Glénans, Concarneau. Tel. 02 98 97 14 84).

Learn more

The Abri du Marin *east of Concarneau.*

The *Abris du Marin*

At the end of the 19th century Jacques de Thézac, a man of private means and passionate about sailing and photography decided to help seafarers. This was in response to him seeing the harsh conditions they lived under; lives marked by alcoholism, poverty and tuberculosis. He did this in two ways:

1) The annual publication of *L'Almanach du Marin Breton* (The Breton Nautical Almanac) a true encyclopaedia of sailing which was an immediate success and is currently in its 115th edition (2013). It contains a mine of information for seafarers, both leisure and professional. Today the *Almanach* is edited by "L'Œuvre du marin Breton". This association helps seafarers and their families who fall into financial hardship by offering interest-free loans and grants.

2) Building *Abris du Marin* (Seaman's Shelters). Houses built to welcome seamen, painted pink and managed by local associations with the aim of giving visiting seafarers dormitories, libraries, games and meeting halls and access to equipment needed for maintenance and repair. Fifteen *Abris* were built between 1899 and 1950 from Roscoff, the most northerly, to Île d'Yeu. There are two at Concarneau. The most well-known being that at Douarnenez (see paddle 27). ∎

22 The Odet

Difficulty: ✗ ✗ ✗

Maps:
SHOM 7146
Navicarte 543
IGN 0519OT

Distance: 13 nautical miles

Leaving and Arriving: Pors Meillou

The Chateau at Rossulien.

The Quimper area

● Quimper

Pors Meillou.

THE ODET, a beautiful tidal river. Its famous chateaux, their lawns stretching down to the water. The narrow winding passage of Vire-Court with its swift tides. Tiny ports and secret side branches to explore on either side all the way down to the mouth of the river.

In May and June the rhododendrons form a cascading blaze of pink and purple along the forested banks.

The entrance of the side branch of Combrit.

Launching, Landing and Parking:

Bénodet: 1) Slipway Penfoul port, large car park; 2) Other slipways, but access and parking difficult in summer.

Sainte-Marine: 1) Avoid the foot passenger port it is too narrow and crowded; 2) Kermor beach, outside the estuary, parking.

Pont de Cornouaille: launching possible on both sides of the bridge near the bridge supports, access from the north.

In the middle of the trip: 1) Pors Keraign, small car park and campsite; 2) Right bank, slipway at Rossulien, not very handy; 3) Pors Meillou, a good place to park and launch, but the limited parking area is inundated at high spring tides (coefficient greater than 100).

Quimper: 1) Downstream, slipway of Creac'h Gwen, left bank; 2) Also downstream, Cale Neuve (New Slipway), right bank, from the towpath, access from "Rue de la Cale Neuve", limited parking; 3) In the town centre, left bank, slipway near the faienceries Henriot, parking nearby unless there is a festival on.

The colourful cascade of rhododendrons in May. Photo I. Leguérinel

Leave from Pors Meillou, HW +1.5 (Port Tudy), explore the two hidden inlets of the anse de Toulven, upstream and against the tide on the left bank; secret moorings, twisted branches of old oaks caressing the river, small boulders along the banks, pine groves. Turn back towards Pors Meillou and paddle on downstream to the slipway at Rossulien before taking the famous passage of Vire-Court. Here, the river is squeezed into a narrow channel and the current can reach 6kt on springs. You are going in the right direction, so enjoy the magic carpet ride.

Downstream of this, look out for a promontory on the right bank: land here to look at some Roman remains recently excavated and restored. The banks are thickly wooded, cut here and there by a narrow valley or the glimpse of an ostentatious chateau. These country houses were built in the 18th and 19th centuries and, hidden behind their screens of trees, they now prevent the humble kayaker from landing. Port Keraign, an attractive small slipway on the left bank, is an oasis where the common man can land, picnic and cock a snook at the Chateau of Kerouzien opposite. A campsite is about 200m up the track from the slipway.

The river bed starts to widen, and you cross the entrance of the side branch of Combrit; pretty and full of promise. The arch of the Cornouaille road bridge marks the return to civilisation. The two ports where the estuary

The Odet by canoe.

The Quimper area

narrows are a complete contrast: Bénodet, left bank, is a yacht marina in an urban environment with a succession of sandy beaches, whilst Sainte-Marine opposite has a tiny port, a minuscule chapel and an *Abri du Marin* in pink, now a museum run by "L'Œuvre du Marin Breton". Visiting this will give the tide time to change direction to help you back up the river.

In May and June the wall of forest along the banks takes on a psychedelic air as the rhododendron bushes break into pink and purple. This alien shrub was very popular in gardens in the past and has managed to colonise most of the slopes of the valley.

Pors Meillou is easy to recognise by the strange little façade of brick and dressed stone at the edge of the forest.

Alternatives: It is possible to make the trip from Bénodet to Quimper and back, or the opposite, as the current dictates. However, the large and muddy open stretch of water at Kérogan is not very interesting and feels a long way as you are paddling. Still more possibilities; explore the side branch of Combrit, quite long, muddy, but very pretty, paddle this around HW leaving from Bénodet or Pors Keraïgn. ■

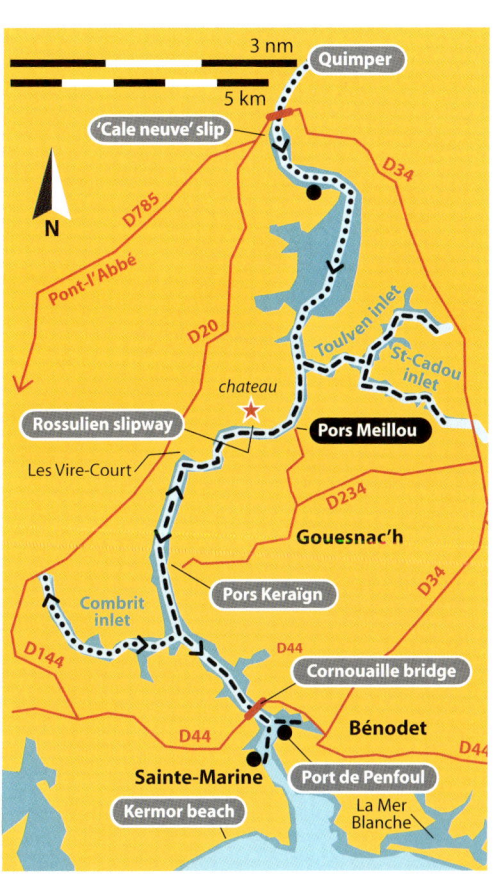

WEATHER, TIDE AND SAFETY

Spring tides are essential to get to the deepest reaches of the creeks. The slipways have sign boards informing water users of good practice. These say that kayakers should keep to the left bank of the river (looking downstream) from Quimper to Pors Meillou and to the right bank from Pors Meillou to the mouth of the estuary. The water can be very busy in summer, so look ahead and keep well out of the channels.

23 Towards Pont-l'Abbé

Maps:
SHOM 7146
Navicarte 543
IGN 0519OT

Difficulty: ✗ ✗ ✗

Distance: 15 nautical miles

Leaving and Arriving: Lesconil

Arriving near the chateau at Pont-l'Abbé at HW coefficient 111.

The Quimper area

● Pont-l'Abbé

The Perdrix light at Loctudy.

A LOW LYING COAST, with alternating rocks and haloes of fine sand, that give way, after passing beyond the black and white chequered light, the Perdrix (Partridge), to a little world of channels, mud flats and islands. This small natural harbour where the tide swirls this way and that, extends off in a narrow long arm, leading to a proud historic town which was the centre of the Breton revolt against the brutal hand of France in 1675.

The standing stone at Penglaouic at HW.

Launching, Landing and Parking:

Lesconil: slipway down to the beach near the sailing centre, large car park.

Poulluen slipway, at Prat an Asquel: 1.5 miles from Lesconil, parking tricky and a portage at low water.

Port of Loctudy: 1) Small beach at the end of "Rue du port", park diagonally along the road; 2) Yacht slipway, paying throughout the year; 3) Langoz beach, parking difficult in the summer.

Île Tudy: 1) If you are lucky you might find a parking spot near the ferry slipway; 2) Theren beach at l'Ile Tudy, slipway near the sailing centre.

Pont-l'Abbé: 1) Right bank, at the bottom end of the quay Saint-Laurent, just before the tow-path starts, slipway and parking; 2) Quay at Pors Moro, left bank, slipway usable if the tide is high enough and parking.

Around the Île Chevalier, portage over the bridge.
Photo I. Leguérinel

Leave from the beach near the sailing centre at Lesconil on the flood tide at about mid-tide. Paddle outside of the Enizan rocks, in good conditions the waves turn this area into a sparkling playground for the kayaker. Say hello to the Glénan Islands, just visible on the horizon. Continue along the coast heading north-east, a succession of headlands and sandy beaches. After the ledges at Doubennec, a halt is possible at Poulluen. The headland of Kérafédé has rocks extending out to sea as far as Karek Hir, an east cardinal. From here one can see the beach and lighthouse at Langoz.

The coast turns west and a nice black and white chequered light, Les Perdrix (The Partridge) marks the boundary of local rivals; Loctudy to the left and Île Tudy (actually a peninsula) in front of you. Let the tide carry you past the attractive stone cottages of Île Tudy.

You are in the tidal river of Pont-l'Abbé, the island of Garo is nearby and further away the imposing Île Chevalier, which divides the bay in two: the Anse du Pouldon to the east and the river leading to Pont-l'Abbé to the west. The tide will carry you past the buoys along the channel to the west of Île Chevalier. Your course will take you close to the island of Queffren and the island of Rats and along the beach on Île Chevalier. The standing stone of Penglaouic, now in the water is on the other, very muddy, bank. This marks the administrative boundary between Loctudy and Pont-l'Abbé.

The Quimper area

Following a long bank, the channel heads west, becoming narrower with a tow-path on the right bank. Pine trees…and the town approaches. You'll see an isolated mill on the left bank, then the dockyards, the quays and the buildings on the bridge, whose large arches mark the end of the port, and finally the silhouette of the chateau.

The return trip to Lesconil gives you another chance to admire the scenery, travelling from inland to the open sea.

Alternatives: Circumnavigating Île Chevalier is possible on a spring tide, but the Anse du Pouldon is an important winter bird habitat so only do this in the summer months and take care not to disturb the birds even then. Portage the bridge.

If you want to explore upstream of Lesconil in the estuary Le Ster, don't paddle underneath the bridge with its dangerous obstructions, portage around it. ∎

WEATHER, TIDE AND SAFETY

A flood tide is necessary to avoid the mud and adverse currents. At mid-tide, the current can reach 3kt in the channel towards Pont-l'Abbé. Numerous ledges between Lesconil and Langoz lighthouse can make paddling tricky if there is any swell.

24 The Étocs

Difficulty: ✗ ✗ ✗ / ✗ ✗ ✗

Maps:
SHOM 7146
Navicarte 543
IGN 05190T

Distance: 19 nautical miles (1 or 2 days)

Leaving and Arriving: Pors Carn

Le Guilvinec harbour.

The Quimper area

● Saint-Guénolé

A seal.
Photo L. Malthieux

A LEGENDARY COAST, a coast sloping gently into the sea, a sea flecked with white, omnipresent rocks, fishermen who take pride in their trade. Seals basking on their favourite rocks, why, sometimes even the tourists can catch a few rays of sunshine. The lighthouse of Eckmühl stands, tall and thin, over this savage domain of rock and sea.

Launching, Landing and Parking:

Anse de Pors Carn: large car park on the south side of the bay.
Port Saint-Pierre: beach between two slipways to the east of the Eckmuhl lighthouse, limited parking.
Port de Kérity: a handy slipway and good parking, but the sea goes out a long way at low tide.
Le Guilvinec: 1) Ster beach, outside the harbour to the west, near the lifeboat station; 2) Slipway inside the fishing port (beside the fire station), large car park; 3) Coast south-east of Guilvinec harbour, (Léchiagat) below the bridge, slipway and large car park.

The Étocs at low water. Photo L. Malthieux

A seal and a kayaker. Photo L. Malthieux

Leave from the south of the beach at Pors Carn at HW -3 (Port Tudy). This is the end of the famous surf beach of La Torche. Looking at the surf gives you a chance to assess sea conditions…and maybe turn back.

This is a coast of rolling and breaking waves, it can be extremely rough. The land is low, bordered by low cottages. Go past the "Rocher du Préfet" (Prefect's Rock) where, in 1850, that official saw his entire family disappear, carried away by a freak wave. You won't need a French dictionary to get the sense of the sinister names of rocks nearby; "Le trou de l'enfer", "La roche des victimes" and "Le bénitier du diable". (just in case…"Hell Hole", "Victims Rock", "Devil's baptism font")

To get around to Saint-Guénolé you need to give the islets and rocks a wide berth, the sea may be continuously breaking between the headland at Penmarc'h and the island of Conq. Saint-Guénolé was the most important sardine port in France, but it is a difficult harbour, two boats can barely pass each other in the entrance.

If the tide is high enough, slip along inside the ledges, you will see the Chapel of Notre-Dame de la Joie (Our Lady of Joy); then the two towers, striped black and white with a fluorescent red top which mark the headland of Saint-Pierre, or Eckmühl, where the big lighthouse stands alongside another older lighthouse. A tower, a chapel and an old lifeboat station lead along to Saint-Pierre harbour. Inside this, the boat house contains a historical monument, the *Papa Poydenot* a lifeboat launched in 1901, unsinkable, self-righting and self-bailing. It is still maintained in working condition by an army of volunteers. There is also an exhibition of the

The Quimper area

history of lifeboats and life-saving at sea. Penmarc'h is the only town in France to have three lifeboat stations; one for each of the distinct zones of Kérity, Saint-Pierre and Saint-Guénolé.

It is time to have a look at the 120 Étocs (pronounced Eto [eto]). A short crossing takes you in amongst the rocks which protect the coast inside from the swell. A seal or two will say "*bonjour*" and basking sharks are found here in spring. Head towards Le Guilvinec on a bearing of 70 degrees and take the time to look around this harbour, the foremost port for small-scale fishermen in France. You'll pass workshops and dockyards, the fish market(s) and warehouses. Under the fish market, "Haliotika" is an interactive museum of the fishing industry and its products.

Paddle out past the lifeboat station, along the beach at Ster and zig-zag amongst the rocks to the harbour at Kérity. The sleepy atmosphere of this port completely hides its history as the most important port in the region during the 16th and 17th centuries. Boats waited here for good conditions to weather the Pointe du Raz. Paddle back from here, unless you have organised a shuttle (very feasible) between Kérity and Pors Carn.

Alternatives : It would be possible to cover the same ground in several shorter paddles (Kérity to Les Étocs; Le Guilvinec to Saint-Guénolé; Pors Carn to Kérity), to do it in the opposite direction or to organise a shuttle. ■

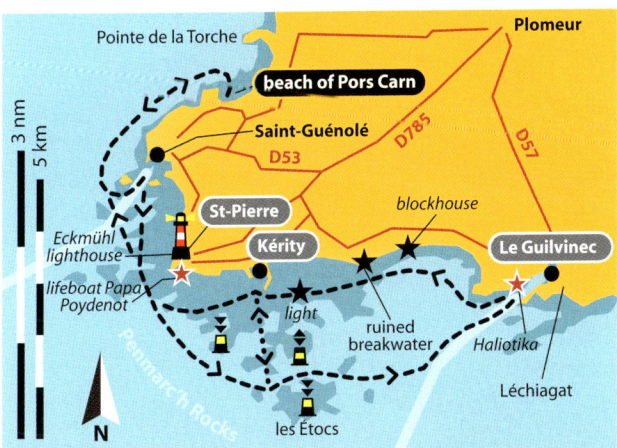

WEATHER, TIDE AND SAFETY

This trip is feasible in good weather with a swell of 1m or less. Strong winds may cause problems. Low water reveals a series of flat ledges running far out to sea, changing the nature of the coast. Nevertheless, Kérity and much of the Étocs are protected from the westerly swell by the outlying rocks. At Le Guilvinec and Saint-Guénolé watch out for the succession of fishing boats returning one after another from 16.00 to 18.30. Enjoy looking at them from a distance or better still from one of the quays, it is a lovely sight.

25 The Pointe du Raz

Difficulty: ✗ ✗ ✗

Distance: 6 nautical miles

Leaving and Arriving: Baie des Trépassés

Maps:
SHOM 7148 / 7147
Navicarte 541
IGN 0419ET

Sea Kayaking Guide **Brittany**

The lighthouse La Vieille with the Pointe du Raz behind.

Around Douarnenez

Pointe du Raz

La Plate.

THE POINTE DU RAZ is the French Cape Horn. Kayakers can pass through after careful planning, or go and play to test their mettle.

Even when the sea is calm, experience of tide races is a pre-requisite: when the wind and surf are up, it is something else again! Reserved for small groups of good paddlers confident in their rolling and rescue skills.

The Raz at mid flood tide.

Arriving at the lighthouse La Vieille.

Launching, Landing and Parking:

There is only one close access point, the beach at the **Baie des Trépassés**, there is parking on both sides of the bay. The tide goes out a long way, a trolley might be useful.

Surf in the Baie des Trépassés.

Launch at HW +6 (Audierne, Brest -20mins), trips often start with a spot of surfing and it may be necessary to punch out through breaking waves. Once through the break, you are in the infamous Baie des Trépassés (Bay of the Dead). This is not as bad as it sounds, as it is a translation from Breton. The original Breton name Boe an Aon (Bay of the River) became the similar sounding Boe an Anoan (Bay of Souls). However, many of those lost at sea in the Raz de Sein were washed up here (the Sein tide race was often deadly in the days of sailing ships).

There is little tidal flow in the bay and it is well worth exploring close along the cliffs, if there is little swell, there are some nice caves to explore. The first gap, between the headland and the Trouziard rock is an easy passage at slack water, useful if you need to pass the Point. Slack water arrives here first (around HW -6 Brest) and then moves further offshore, it lasts about 15 minutes.

The "classic" route is between Trouziard and the imposing mass of Gorle Greiz. As long as there isn't any swell, the flood tide running north-east generates "gentle" standing waves, and the passage is an enjoyable series of surfing down the waves. As the tide starts to run faster, the waves become steeper with breaking sections and menacing boils. Behind the rocks the back eddies are equally ferocious.

Between Gorle Greiz and the lighthouse La Vieille and then the cardinal La Plate, the waves are longer and more stable and easier to manage. There is a very strong back eddy behind La Vieille and depending on the swell it may be possible to land here and climb to the base of the lighthouse. The rock is called Gorlebella. In 1927 the lighthouse keepers were marooned for several months by continuous storms,

Around Douarnenez

they were not seen between December and February and were feared dead after the light became extinguished. Eventually, local fishermen swam a line ashore to rescue them. Landing at La Plate is more difficult; this is not a place to linger as conditions can change rapidly.

Good group control and awareness is necessary, although the current rapidly washes any casualty out of the roughest water. Once satisfied, ferry glide back to Gorle Greiz and then take the tide across the bay to Pointe du Van. This is a wild and impressive coast. A chapel keeps watch from the cliffs. In good conditions there is excellent rock-hopping to be had here. The steep slipway at Vorlen and to and fro manoeuvring needed by fishing boats to anchor in safety, bear testament to the determination of Breton fishermen to use any shelter on this inhospitable coast. The line fishermen who fish the sea bass in the Raz land their catches here.

Back at the beach, there is just the surf landing to look forward to!

Alternatives: it is possible to go and have a look at the race without being sucked in and then head directly down-tide to the headland of Van. ■

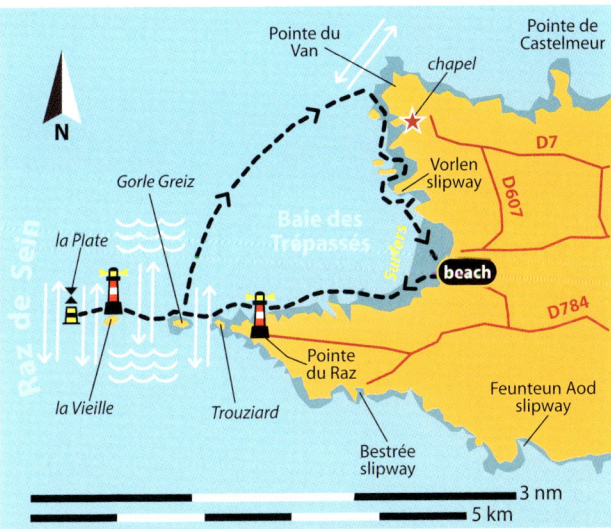

WEATHER, TIDE AND SAFETY

This is a paddle for an experienced group, try it first in neap tides and in good weather. Wind against tide or heavy swell can give rise to chaotic and dangerous seas. Plan carefully and once the tide starts running fast, play closer inshore. Between Pointe du Van and the beach there are numerous rocks and reefs, except around the port of Vorlen. Until recently, large shipping was forbidden to use the Raz, but with improvements in electronic navigation, the Portsmouth-Bilbao and Santander ferries have been given permission to pass between La Plate and the island of Sein. There are only a few sailings a week.

150 | Sea Kayaking Guide **Brittany**

26 The Bird Cliffs of Cap Sizun

Difficulty: ✗ ✗ ✗

Distance: 7 nautical miles

Leaving: Penharn—Arriving: Pors Lanvers

Maps:
SHOM 7121
Navicarte 542
IGN 0419ET

View from the headland of Trénaouret; in the distance, Le cap de la Chèvre.

Around Douarnenez

Cap-Sizun

Fishing hut.

Rock-hopping. Photo I. Leguérinel

THIS COAST IS RUGGED and so beautiful! Facing Cap de la Chèvre, it is the southern limit of the bay of Douarnenez. A coast of fractals, from a distance apparently smooth, but becoming more and more indented and folded as you zoom in and change from scale to scale. Facing an often stormy sea, it could be the coast of an offshore island, it is so wild and little visited.

Launching, Landing and Parking:

There is only one certain access point, **Pors Lanvers**: slipway and beach, small parking area reserved for regular users, but more parking higher up on the grass. Can be busy in summer.
Other access: 1) Pors Péron beach, frequent shore break; 2) Lesven beach, very rocky from mid to high tide; 3) Penharn beach, only at low water, difficult access down a track and then a portage down a steep slope; 4) Beach and slipway at Théolen, west of the headland of Brézellec.

Swell and rock-hopping.

Rough landing on the beach at Lesven at mid-tide.

Sort out the shuttle and leave at HW +6 from the beach at Penharn. Head west, to look at the little harbour of Porz Loédec, about 500m away, with a small slipway accessed by a staircase down the cliffs. Turn back towards the east, this will be your direction from now on. Narrow gulleys, caves and spume-covered rocks are a constant distraction, just keep an eye on the time.

You are passing the nature reserve of Goulien-Cap-Sizun. The coast of steep cliffs and rocky islets is particularly rich in nesting sea birds, guillemots (*guillemot de Troïl*), fulmars (*fulmar boréal*) and kittiwakes (*mouette tridactyle*) which are comparatively rare in France, are common here. Shags (*cormoran huppé*) and herring gulls are also common and the reserve, grazed by sheep, makes the cliffs a good habitat for the red-billed choughs.

Paddle past the Danou rocks then the Grand Crom, the coast turns south-east and becomes less rough, this is the bay of Lesven with an accessible beach at low water, a good place for a break.

The rocks of Cap Sizun were laid down as lava 456 million years ago several kilometres under the earth. Uncovered by erosion, the hard rock still resists the incessant swell day after day. North-west

Choughs with their red bills. Photo A. Audevard

Around Douarnenez

Porz Loédec.

facing facets are sharply sliced into little coves and caves. Leaving Lesven you pass just such a tormented zone. Once past the point at Luguénez the long thin headland of Beuzec-Kastel Koz comes into view. This promontory was used as a strong point for settlers from the Iron Age onwards. During the epoch of the Gauls, a double defensive wall (oppidum) on the landward end protected a village of 200 houses.

If you have not spent too long rock-hopping, you are now near the superb beach of Trénaouret and the headland of the same name. Further away is the headland of Millier with its small lighthouse and inland, the wind turbine, which dominates Pors Lanvers.

Another stretch of less eroded coast. Look out for the rustic fishing hut made out of bits and pieces, a modern cliff dweller? An islet close beside the cliff hides and protects Pors Lanvers, your arrival point.

Alternatives: From Pors Lanvers you could paddle to and around the headland at Millier to land east of it (see paddle 27), or even paddle as far as Douarnenez. ∎

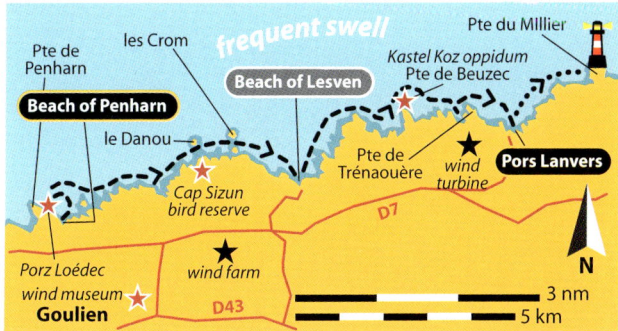

WEATHER, TIDE AND SAFETY

There is little tidal flow along this coast, but many other considerations; swell, few landing places and strong local down-draughts from the cliffs. At low water there are a few beaches suitable for short stops, hidden in the folds of rock.

A swell height of more than 1m will make it necessary to stay well offshore and render the trip more difficult. In these conditions landing may become very tricky or even dangerous.

27 Douarnenez

Difficulty: ✗ ✗ ✗

Maps:
SHOM 7121
Navicarte 542
IGN 0518OT

Distance: 7 nautical miles

Leaving and Arriving: Port de Rosmeur

The lightship at Port-Rhu, the flower at the heart of the Harbour museum.

Around Douarnenez

 Douarnenez

The sardine lady.

UNDERNEATH its sprinkling of modern yachts, Douarnenez has a character tempered in the forge of a long history of the fishing industry. From Roman times until the 19th century the sardine was the source of prosperity. Women workers in the canneries gained the name "*Penn Sardin*" (Sardine-head in Breton) and this became the name of all the inhabitants. After the collapse of the sardine fishery, it was the turn of lobsters and tuna. The Port-Musée (Harbour museum) with its floating exhibits and exhibitions on the quay celebrates the maritime past and present. Douarnenez is a paddle through history in the footsteps of Tristan and Isolde.

The curved slipway.

Launching, Landing and Parking:

Douarnenez: Rosmeur harbour, three sheltered slipways, large car park near the fish market.
Tréboul: 1) Harbour, slipway and parking; 2) Beach at Sables Blancs, parking in the road "Rue du Rheun" to access the ramp to the beach.

Inside Rosmeur harbour.

Launch into the harbour at Rosmeur and look out to sea. The mythical island town of Ys, which was swallowed by the sea after its princess was seduced by the Devil, is said to be out there somewhere. It is claimed that the city's bells can still be heard on a calm day at sea.

Head east towards the beach of Ry, past Plomarc'h gardens, where you can see the vats used for making *garum* a Roman fish-based sauce. Now head back west and into old Rosmeur harbour. Seafront buildings still carry the names of the ancient sardine canneries. In 1924 there was a memorable strike by cannery workers, the *"Penn Sardin"*. Look at the curved quay and slipway and try to imagine the harbour filled with over a thousand sardine skiffs.

Dominating the end of the harbour, the pink-coloured *Abri du Marin* is now the headquarters of the *Chasse-Marée* a well known magazine celebrating and documenting the maritime heritage of France. In the middle of the 20th century reclaimed land was used to build a new fish-market beside the modern port. Fish canning continued after the decline of the sardine industry with tuna and lobster,

Douarnenez, a maritime town.

Around Douarnenez

but nowadays fishing activity is limited to landing and selling the catch.

In 1997 the Coastal Conservancy acquired the island of Tristan. The name comes from the historical association of Douarnenez with the legend of Tristan and Isolde. You can land on the southern part of the island, where there is an exhibition about the history of the island open to the public but the rest of the island, botanic garden, lighthouse etc. can only be visited on guided trips. The droll statue, half woman, half sardine between Tristan and the quay marks the site of the old island of Saint-Michel. This was targeted and blown up in the war, a mistake, as it was only an old cannery.

In front of you is the harbour of Port Rhu, famous for its Harbour museum. At high water the lock gates are open allowing you access to admire the five historic vessels and the lightship. Have a look at the ship graveyard on the left bank and make a short tour of the marina of Tréboul, you can then head along to the beach at Sables Blancs for a stop. Return to Rosmeur, staying offshore.

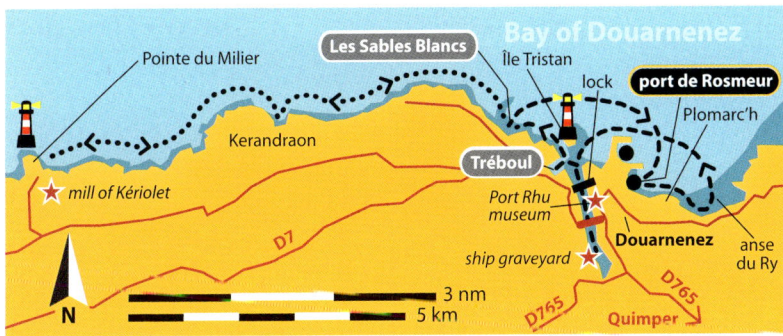

Alternatives: An extra 10 nautical miles, difficulty XX. Carry on from the Sables Blancs beach and explore the coast to the west, granite below and heathland above. Paddle as far as the light at Millier. In good weather conditions it is possible to land at the base of the headland to visit the water mill of Kériolet. From here you can walk out to the end of the headland to enjoy the view of the sea and rest, before heading back. Another possible landing place is in the bay of Kerandraon. ■

WEATHER, TIDE AND SAFETY

The basic paddle is in sheltered waters, out of the swell. The lock basin at Port-Rhu which contains the Port-Museum is open from HW -1hr 30min to +1hr 30 min on springs and HW +/-1 on neaps (Douarnenez)

The alternative coastal paddle should only be undertaken by experienced groups, landing places are few and far between; probably only possible at Kerandraon and just before the headland of Millier. Just beyond the headland at Millier it is sometimes possible to land on a small beach at low water.

158 — Sea Kayaking Guide — Brittany

28 The Caves of Morgat

Difficulty: ✖ ✖ ✖

Distance: 13 nautical miles

Leaving and Arriving: Morgat

Maps:
SHOM 7121
Navicarte 542
IGN 0418ET

Morgat caves.

The Crozon peninsula

Morgat

A low cave.

A coast with a Mediterranean look.

A LAND FORMED by the incessant ocean waves, carving caves deep into the cliffs. A journey to the centre of the Earth, an invitation to explore inside the 330 million year old rock, folded into pleats or wild contortions. Amazing colours, dark corners, splashes of light, sun rays filter through the water. The hollow crashing and gurgling, loud in the enclosed space, of the waves, still enlarging the deepest reaches.

Launching, Landing and Parking:

Morgat: at the south side of the harbour, launch outside the breakwater if the sea is calm, or use the slipway inside in front of the sailing school. Plenty of car parking, but congested in summer.

Crozon: Plage (beach) de l'Aber, long portage at low water.

The cliffs of Morgat from the island of Aber.

"Roundabout" arch.

Launch from the harbour at Morgat HW -1 (Brest) with a waterproof torch to hand. Head north-east to visit the the first caves, those that the tourist boats can enter, these have been a visitor attraction since at least the 19th century. The Pointe des Grottes has, amongst others, the spectacular Grotte de l'Autel, 80 metres deep, with a large rock in the middle. Turn back across the bay to the coast just south of the original departure point and carry on south-west past the launch point. In the season there will be numerous tourist boats and kayaks in the largest caves, but as you go further they will become fewer and fewer.

The weather and sea conditions will determine how closely and deeply you will be able to explore, in good conditions every little crevice can be examined, every rock hopped! Pointe de Saint-Hernot has a cave with numerous entries (only accessible at HW). The shingle beach, much visited, is the only landing place, when the tide is up, between Morgat and Cap de la Chèvre. At low water, the small rock or shingle beaches that appear here and there at the base of the cliffs can make idyllic landings.

Carry on along the coast, checking out any spot that looks paddle-able, a tiny crack may lead to a massive cave, an impressive entrance may peter out to nothing in a few yards. The red colour of the rocks inside the caves is due to oxidation, but close to the water level, encrusting plants and animals, specific to the tide height and light intensity, make layers of other colours. Don't be in a hurry to put on your torch, give your eyes a few minutes to adjust. Backing into a cave is sometimes easier and the light carries further than if you paddle in forwards. Enjoy the weird gurgling, sloshing and banging sounds emanating from deep, light-less recesses and reverberating around the cave.

Cap de la Chèvre (Goat Cape) with its 100m high cliffs preceded by a series of

The Crozon peninsula

large blocks rising up from the sea is an impressive place; even after all the delights of the coast you have already seen. This headland is swept by current and swell. The strata in the rocks are beautifully engraved. In good conditions at low water, there is superb rock-hopping amongst the ledges.

Paddle back the same way, you will see different things and the height of the tide will dictate whether you enter caves again or not. In any case you can still appreciate the exceptional beauty of this coast.

Alternatives: 1) You can prolong the paddle by heading east as far as the ravishingly beautiful Aber bay, which is backed by sand dunes and protected by Aber island, (2 miles beyond Pointe des Grottes); 2) You could continue around Cap de la Chèvre to land at the beach at Plage de la Palue if there is no swell or only a slight swell from the west - this is a surf beach. (4km shuttle to the car). ■

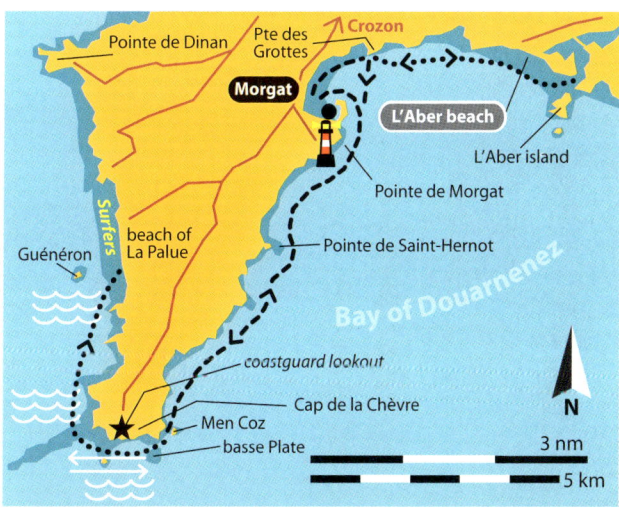

WEATHER, TIDE AND SAFETY

You do not want swell for this paddle! Sunny weather will enhance the colours. The morning light is good for the caves from Morgat to the Pointe de la Chèvre and the afternoon light favours the coast eastwards. For entering the caves, go in groups of 3 or so with one person staying outside to shout warnings of approaching swell (or tourist boats). Although the distance is short, the to and fro and tight turning will make this a tiring trip. Being confident at vertical paddling strokes such as the bow rudder, paddling on one side, prys and sculls will maximise enjoyment and minimise gelcoat loss. Flexibility around the waist to allow backwards paddling whilst looking backwards is also a useful skill. Even if it is too rough to enter the caves, the cliffs make a lovely paddle. The tidal flow is weak except near the Cap de la Chèvre where it runs north from HW -6 and south from HW (Brest), keeping close inshore will avoid much of the flow.

162 | Sea Kayaking Guide **Brittany**

29 The Tas de Pois

Difficulty: ✖ ✖ ✖ / ✖ ✖ ✖

Maps:
SHOM 7148
Navicarte 542
IGN 0418ET

Distance: 18 nautical miles

Leaving and Arriving: Camaret

The Tas de Pois.

The Crozon peninsula

● Camaret

Arrival on Pen Hir beach.

A NATURAL SPECTACLE guaranteed, some swell will make it even more exciting; steep cliffs, fine beaches, small and large caves and the unique scenery of the Tas de Pois; the piles of peas. As if this wilderness is not enough, Camaret is one of the most attractive harbours of Brittany.

Launching, Landing and Parking:

Camaret: 1) Port Vauban slipway, a nice slipway but difficult to park in summer; 2) Correjou beach, outside the large breakwater, congested parking close by in summer; 3) Inside the port, parking as for the beach, best around high water; 4) Southern end of the port, near the fish market, slipway used by fishermen and the sailing school.

Near Camaret: 1) Beach at Mort Anglaise, east of the Pointe Sainte-Barbe, limited parking; 2) Trez Rouz beach, limited parking).

Beaches in the bay of Dinan: 1) Goulien, south side of the bay, limited parking, long portage; 2) Kerloc'h, north side of the bay, parking up above, long portage.

Camaret.

The caves of Dinan at low water.

Launch from Camaret, timing is not critical, but access to the caves is generally easier near HW. Skirt the sea wall and head west. At the Pointe du Grand Gouin, the sea is likely to become rougher, but it is only at the lovely Pointe de Touliguet that the full sea conditions will become apparent. There is nearly always some swell on this coast.

Between the Grand Gouin headland and the headland at Toulinguet, the first arches and caves appear, with the scars of recent rock falls on the cliffs and large blocks in the water at their foot giving a dramatic touch. Erosion is always going on.

Once past the headland with its coastguard lookout, a marvellous cliff-scape lies ahead. The surf beach of Pen Hat, has the strange silhouette of the ruins of the house of the poet Saint-Pol-Roux above it. Next there are vertiginous indented cliffs ending in a line of rocks leading out to sea, the Tas de Pois (piles of peas), formerly called the Tas de Foin, (haystacks). A large cross of Lorraine can be seen on the headland of Pen Hir, a monument to the Breton contribution to the Free French Army. This is a popular spot for rock climbers. Take time to study the steep cliff faces and the progress of parties of climbers up them.

The gaps between the Tas de Pois are often choppy, so take care and keep the group together, but have fun looking at all of them. The "Tas" appear very big and imposing from the deck of a kayak! This is also a popular spot for laying crab pots and was formerly a sardine fishery.

Once through the Tas de Pois, the sea state may be much calmer. Pen Hir is a

The Crozon peninsula

long and lovely surf beach ending in more rocky cliffs and caves. From the Pointe de Portzen, head straight across the Bay of Dinan to visit the caves on the Pointe de Dinan. Go through the massive arch that you will have seen from a long way out to sea, then go back around the north of the headland to explore the linked caves. At low tide these can be explored on foot, but take care, the seaweed is very slippery.

Landing may be possible on the beach of the Bay of Dinan, this is a surf beach and it can give very good sea kayak surfing on long slow breaking waves. The return trip can take in the outlying rocks of Toulinguet which are about ½ mile off the point. Can you get through the arch? Once past the Point, the sea will ease off, giving you a chance to admire the port of Camaret from calmer waters.

The magnificent red-plastered Tour Vauban (Vauban's Tower) on the breakwater is a UNESCO heritage site. Close by is the chapel of Notre-Dame de Rocamadour and a boat graveyard. The seafront is an attractive mix of architecture with many small bistros. ∎

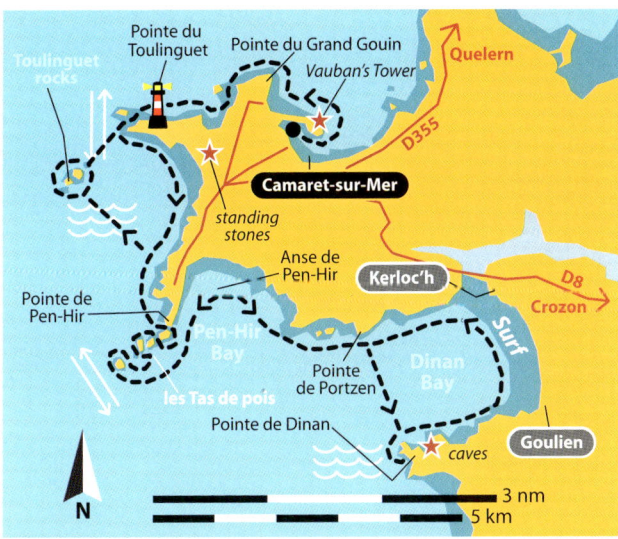

WEATHER, TIDE AND SAFETY

The tides are only strong near the Pointe de Toulinguet and between Les Tas de Pois (northbound from HW -6 and southbound from HW). If you are paddling against the tide then keep inshore and avoid going out to the Rocks of Toulinguet or out beyond the final islet of the Tas de Pois. This coast is often washed by swell, assess conditions before going too far. Wind and swell against the tide can give patches of very choppy water where the currents are strong. The flat profile of the beach at Dinan can give rise to breakers far out to sea. It would be possible to organise a shuttle to Kerloc'h or Goulien for a one-way trip.

30 Islands of Île des Morts and Trébéro

Difficulty: ✖ ✖ ✖ / ✖ ✖ ✖

Distance: 18.5 nautical miles

Leaving and Arriving: Camaret

Maps:
SHOM 7401
Navicarte 542
IGN 0418ET

The islands of Île des Morts and Trébéron, landing prohibited.

The Crozon peninsula

Camaret

Current near the Cormorandière.

TESTAMENTS to the military history and the defence of Brest and its entrance. What an astonishing variety of stonework, steel and concrete structures have colonised the rocks of this strategic port.

High cliffs, strong currents. Still a military area with landing restrictions; your only halt: Roscanvel.

Launching, Landing and Parking:

Camaret: 1) Port Vauban slipway, a nice slipway but difficult to park in summer; 2) Correjou beach, outside the large breakwater, congested parking close by in summer; 3) Inside the port, parking as for the beach, best around high water; 4) Southern end of the port, near the fish market, slipway used by fishermen and sailing school.

Near Camaret: 1) Beach at Mort Anglaise, east of the Pointe Sainte-Barbe, limited parking; 2) Trez Rouz beach, limited parking).

Roscanvel Port: a good spot with parking.

Slipway at Quélern: at the end of a lane, limited parking.

The fort of the Capucins with its access bridge at the entrance of the Goulet.

The remains of a pontoon near the Pointe des Espagnols.

Leave Camaret at HW -3 (Brest). Follow the coast towards the north, along the military base of the Roscanvel peninsula. In the distance the fort on the Île des Capucins (Franciscan monks) can be seen in silhouette, linked to the mainland by a bridge. This, together with the lighthouse Petit-Minou opposite, indicates the start of the Goulet de Brest (*goulet*=entrance channel).

This has been a strategic site since the earliest years but was further developed by Vauban (Vauban, 1633-1707, a self-made man from a modest background, was the foremost military engineer in Europe and responsible for defensive works all over France.) and during WW II. The cliffs are covered in fortifications, indicating the importance of protecting and controlling access to the strategic port of Brest.

Once past the fort, you are in the south channel, only just a mile wide, the current will help you along at up to 4kt on spring tides. The buoys separating the north and south channels will flash past. The Pointe des Espagnols (Spaniards Point) is named after an episode in 1594. Philip of Spain had built a fort defended by 400 Spanish troops to help the Duke of Mercœur a prominent catholic who had declared independence from Henry 4th of France. A combined force of

Landing in Camaret bay.

The Crozon peninsula

The Petit Minou (Little Pussy Cat) lighthouse in the Goulet.

3,000 French and 2,000 English took a month to take the fort with a death toll of 3,000. The 400 Spanish were massacred when the fort fell. The 60m high point is prolonged to the north-east by the rock known as The Cormorandière (Cormorant Rock). The tide flows very fast here, stay out, a strong back eddy forms along the shore. Keeping a heading of 110 degrees towards the point, Pointe de l'Armorique, for 15 minutes and then 5 minutes on 170 degrees towards the north end of Île Longue will make most use of the tide. Head towards the east side of Île Trébéron and the tide will carry you westward towards it. Take care not to approach Île Longue, this is a base for nuclear submarines, you can be sure that your movements are being followed and that any attempt to land on Île Trébéron or Île des Morts will be spotted.

Trébéron was a quarantine hospital for many many years. If the inmates died they were buried on Île des Morts (Island of the Dead). Both islands are managed by the Coastal Conservancy as reserves, but still guarded by the military, so do not land!

You can, however, land at Roscanvel on the peninsula. Once you have stretched your legs, take the ebb tide along the coast back to the start point. Between the Pointe Robert and the Pointe des Capucins the ebb may generate a strong back eddy along the cliffs, so it is advisable to go out a bit along this section.

In 1694 a combined English and Dutch force comprising 82 ships and

Blockhouse on the south side of the Goulet.

10,000 troops sent by William of Orange attempted an amphibious landing at Camaret, but were repulsed by Vauban. (This was part of the power struggle between William and James II, who was being supported by Louis 14th of France). Despite the fact that the French fleet had sailed to help capture Barcelona, and being very severely out-numbered, Vauban had confidence in his defences. A landing party of 1500 Englishmen, were cut to pieces by expert gunnery. The ebbing tide had left their boats stranded on the beach, so no retreat was possible. The beach, stained with blood, has since been known as Trez-Rouz (red beach in Breton) and the point at which their commander, Tollemache, was himself killed by a cannonball; Maro ar saozon or La Mort Anglaise; The Englishman's death. ■

WEATHER, TIDE AND SAFETY

Wind against tide can create a rough confused sea in the Goulet. The flood tide creates a clockwise eddy 1.5 nautical miles in diameter from the Pointe des Espagnols to Île Longue from HW -3 to HW. Do not attempt to land on the islands under any pretext, you will be arrested and interrogated at length.

It is possible to do the paddle in the opposite direction from Roscanvel or to make a one way trip with a short shuttle from Camaret to Roscanvel. It would be equally possible to make a short paddle to visit the islands from Roscanvel. Leaving from Brest (Sainte-Anne-du-Portzic) to visit the islands is another possibility. In this case take care of large shipping when crossing the Goulet, maintain a listening watch on "Brest Approche" on channel 8 (coastguard lookout at Portzic) and warn any oncoming shipping of your presence in good time.

Breton Lighthouses

Brittany is a huge peninsula which has to be sailed around to enter the English Channel. Burning beacons were the first navigation marks (at Saint-Mathieu, the monks from the Abbey were responsible for keeping them burning). In the 17th century Colbert dotted the French coast with day and night landmarks. New sites were lit such as Cape Fréhel. During the 19th century there was a big increase in shipping. Fresnel invented the lens system that bears his name and a rotating mechanism for the new brighter and lighter lights. The new lighthouses could be seen at greater distances and distinguished from one another by the type of light, fixed, flashing, coloured sectors and different patterns of flashes. Most of the existing lighthouses were built between 1830 and 1880; often in epic or heroic conditions (the lighthouses of des Héaux, Ar Men etc.). A dramatic fall in ship wrecks followed.

Most were built with public funding; however, Kéréon and La Jument which mark le Fromveur and the surroundings of Ushant (Ouessant) and d'Eckmühl near Penmarc'h were built from legacies left in wills. The lighthouse keepers often lived in very harsh conditions, but in some places they lived a family life, the family on the Île aux Moutons in the 1930s had 11 children of which 7 were born on the island.

The lighthouse keepers classified the lighthouses: those on land were "heaven", those on the islands "purgatory" and those at sea, which could only be reached in good weather, "hell".

But what is a lighthouse (*phare*)? The French definition* is a structure with a height above ground of more than 20m and a light intensity greater than 100,000 candelas. Other structures are merely lights (*feux*), even if they are often called lighthouses. There are 46 lighthouses and a great number of "lights" around the Brittany coast.

At the end of the 20th century electronic navigation started to develop and lighthouses became progressively more and more automated and their keepers were retired. The future of lighthouses is now in question as GPS and other methods become the norm. ■

Île Vierge. Photo P. Bisset

*In the UK, Trinity House does not seem to have a precise definition of what they consider to be a "lighthouse", they maintain 68 lighthouses of various shapes and sizes.

31 Brest Harbour–The Aulne

Difficulty: ✘ ✘ ✘ / ✘ ✘ ✘

Distance: 18 nautical miles

Leaving and Arriving: Logonna-Daoulas, Pointe du Bindy

Maps:
SHOM 7400
Navicarte 542
IGN 0517OT / 0518OT

The Sillon des Anglais at HW.

Around Brest

● Logonna-Daoulas

Paddling in the warship graveyard. Photo A. Antúnez Vitales

DEEP IN THE SHELTERED waters of Brest Harbour, the Plougastel peninsula, dissected with numerous inlets, is where the sea becomes land. Sea, mud, sand and soil are intimately interlaced.

On the far side, the Crozon peninsula with its dark wooded slopes and gravel strands, a wilder meeting of land and sea. The abbey at Landévennec and the warship graveyard on a bend in the river Aulne testify to very different elements of man's history.

Launching, Landing and Parking:

Plougastel peninsula: slipways in the port of Tinduff, bay of Daoulas, parking.

Logonna-Daoulas: 1) Pors Beac'h (pronounced Porse Ber), left bank of the river Daoulas, parking, slipway used by mussel farmers; 2) Yelen beach, to the right before arriving at Bindy, parking near water; 3) Pointe du Bindy, near Laogonna-Daoulas, parking with two beaches, one to the west and one to the south.

L'Hôpital-Camfrout: Island (actually a peninsula) of Tibidy, north east of Landévennec, parking and good access, but can be difficult to find.

Aulne, left bank (south side): 1) Slipway and beach at Landévennec, busy in summer (departure point for boat trips); 2) Slipway at the tidal mill situated in the forest of Landévennec, some parking; 3) Slipways at the small port of Tregarvan, large car park.

Aulne, right bank (north side): beach at Seillou, less than 1km south west of Île d'Arun, between Faou and Île de Térénez, shorter drive than Landévennec.

Arrival at the west beach facing the isle of Bindy at LW.

Launch from the west side of the very attractive Pointe du Bindy at HW -4 (Brest) and make a tour of the islets. Follow the coast to the mouth of the Hôpital-Camfrout river and head south, directly across the sea, to arrive at the Sillon des Anglais, a strangely beautiful arrow-shaped gravel bank extending out into the sea. The low cliffs and dark forest along here put one in mind of a Canadian lake, especially in calm conditions. The town of Landévennec with its houses, its chapel and its famous abbey brings you back to humanity. The Abbey had many communities within its tutelage and was a force to be reckoned with in its prime.

Follow the course of the Aulne and on a sharp bend in the river, deep in the forest, a group of warships await their turn at the breaker's yard. Their sharp curving bows, the grey expanses of their sides, slowly giving in to rust, the massive anchor chains lead to thoughts of distant war, to the clamour of sailors on the decks, to sights they have seen in active service. Such a contrast to the peaceful progress of the kayaks past them.

Over there…did you see the osprey on its perch? You might also come across fishermen after smooth hounds, these members of the shark family eat crabs and can weigh up to 20 kg, they are sold as *émissole* in French markets.

Continue up the Aulne to admire the bridges at Térénez, the new one with its complex curves, the old one so straight; yet built side by side. When you've seen enough, turn around and paddle back down the river along the north bank. Keep north and head for the island of Tibidy, follow the shore west, around the Pointe

Around Brest

de Hanvec and up the river Hôpital-Camfrout (an extra 4 miles there and back). On the right side of the river you pass the site of a tide mill and the river cuts its way inland. This river was famous for the quarrying and shipping of a dense and finely marked grey basalt called "pierre de Kersanton". This was sought after for roadside crucifixes and monumental masonry, and was used to build the lighthouse on Île Vierge (see paddle 36). The quarrying brought fortune to the area, now all that remains are the old quays.

L'Hôpital-Camfrout is a beautiful village dominated by the elegant clock tower of its church, right on the water's edge. Make your way back and along to the Pointe du Bindy.

Alternatives: These waters offer many alternatives, here are some: paddle up the Aulne as far as Chateaulin where a lock gives access to the Nantes-Brest canal; explore the bay of Daoulas; paddle up the river Daoulas to visit the abbey, you will need to arrive there around high water; explore the coast of the Plougastel-Daoulas peninsula. ∎

WEATHER, TIDE AND SAFETY

This paddle does not present any particular difficulties as long as care is taken that the tide is high enough when you go up the rivers. Especially that it is still rising if you decide to paddle up to L'Hôpital-Camfrout. You must wear shoes if paddling in this area; the rocks and mud are thick with razor sharp oyster shells.

Sea Kayaking Guide **Brittany**

32

The Headland of Saint-Mathieu

Difficulty: ✗ ✗ ✗

Distance: 23 nautical miles

Leaving and Arriving: Trez-Hir

Maps:
SHOM 7149
Navicarte 540
IGN 0417ET

The Abbey at Pointe Saint-Mathieu with the old and new lighthouses.

Around Brest

Le Conquet

Breakers at the beach of Blancs-Sablons. Photo E. Ollivier

MAKE THE MOST of the currents of the Sea of Iroise. The ebb tide south through the Chenal du Four and the westbound flow out of Brest, telescope into each other at the headland of Saint-Mathieu. On the flood, it is here that the tide divides into two. One arm is swallowed by the Goulet to be lost in the distant reaches of Brest harbour. The other funnels north up towards the English Channel, which officially begins not far away, creating a huge, back eddy in the bay of Blancs-Sablons.

Launching, Landing and Parking:

Bay of Bertheaume: the beach of Trez-Hir is well-sheltered, parking nearby.
Le Conquet: entry to the harbour is reserved for ferry passengers and fishermen; 1) Old slipway in front of the "maison des Seigneurs" in the town, parking difficult in summer; 2) Kermorvan peninsula, a footpath down to Conquet harbour, large car park, good launch site; 3) Two beaches south of Conquet on the coast road, Portez and Porz Liogan, parking.
Blancs-Sablons bay: 1) Pors Illien beach, easy launching and parking; 2) Porsmoguer beach, parking.

Sign at the headland of Corsen.

Fort of Bertheaume.

Leave Trez-Hir, the western end of the bay of Bertheaume, at HW -3 (Brest). In a southerly wind, the shelter of the bay is relative; it can be choppy with breakers over the rocks. Fort Bertheaume on its islet marks the entrance of the bay. This islet has been inhabited since the stone age. The current fort, built by Vauban, is on the ruins of older castles, and is linked to the mainland by a narrow bridge. It is now a visitor centre putting on many events including adventurous outdoor activities.

On this first leg, the tide will be against you, keep in as tight as you can. The high cliffs exclude all thought of landing except in very calm weather, at low water, on the "kayak beaches" of Saint-Marzin and Kérautret.

The rugged headland of Saint-Mathieu has a strange hotchpotch of buildings from various epochs: the coastguard lookout, chapel, the abbey ruins, two lighthouses. As you paddle past, the perspective shifts giving complex ever-changing views, which explains why this place was a favourite subject for artists in the 18th century.

The tide, constricted by the shallow waters between Molène and the mainland, moves at speed in the Chenal du Four. Le Conquet and Kermorvan fly past and you are soon approaching the most western point of France; Cap Corsen. Resist the temptation to stay on the moving carpet and just glide past. Cap Corsen has the coastguard headquarters (CROSS) which manages emergency calls on Ch. 16, it is also the point at which the Atlantic Ocean meets the English Channel.

Just before the headland, paddle towards the shore and enter the back eddy which will help you all the way back across the bay of Blancs Sablons with its alternating cliffs and sandy beaches. There are often opportunities to catch a few waves whilst taking it easy, waiting for the tide to turn. Once the current slackens it is easy to paddle

Around Brest

back past the islet (L'Îlette) and around the Kermorvan headland to have a look at Le Conquet. You'll find a cliff studded with small caves, an attractive port, and a hidden arm to the north to explore. All that remains is to get back into the tide which will carry you south to Saint-Mathieu headland. The tide coming out of Brest will not be very strong, but keep along the shore back to Trez-Hir.

Alternatives: A one-way trip to Le Conquet, 7nm, leave at HW -2, don't miss the harbour entrance! A paddle to Saint-Mathieu and back, in this case make use of the ebb, then the flood tide. A circuit of the bay of Blancs-Sablons from Porsmoguer, leave at HW -3 and head south along the beach in the back eddy to Îlette, then catch the tide to Cap Corsen and the back-eddy back to the start. ∎

WEATHER, TIDE AND SAFETY

The sea of Iroise can be choppy in wind, swell or large spring tides, if you have more than one of these factors in play it can be a demanding paddle. From Saint-Mathieu to Kermorvan the tide runs at 5.2kt, mid tide on a good spring tide. Choose good conditions and a neap tide if you are not certain. The timings given will make for an easy paddle. Beware wind against tide. In heavy swell, leaving, and especially landing, in the bay of Bertheaume can be tricky due to numerous rocks creating a disorderly sea. From Fort of Bertheaume to the lighthouse at Kérautret, the cliffs fall straight into deep water, but near Saint-Mathieu the ledges and rocks of Les Rospects can give rise to breaking waves.

33 Molène Archipelago

Difficulty: ✘ ✘ ✘

Distance: 25 nautical miles (2 or 3 days)

Leaving and Arriving: Le Conquet

Maps:
SHOM 7149
Navicarte 540
IGN 0317OT

Balanec and Its pond, Ushant in the background (mid-tide).

Around Brest

Le Conquet

Seals near Morgol. Photo E. Julé

STRONG CURRENTS guard a necklace of delightful islands, the Molène archipelago demands chart-work the night before, but is well worth it. Marvel follows marvel, crystal clear water, underwater forests of weed, white sand, dark rocks and the sound of seal song. Molène deserves at least a two-day trip.

The camp site on Molène is the only authorised bivouac spot. Photo I. Leguérinel

Launching, Landing and Parking:

Le Conquet: entry to the harbour is reserved for ferry passengers and fishermen; 1) old slipway in front of the "maison des Seigneurs" in the town, parking difficult in summer; 2) Portez beach, south of Conquet on the coast road, Parking congested in summer: 3) Kermorvan peninsula, a footpath down to Conquet harbour, large car park, good launch site.
Blancs-Sablons bay, for a direct crossing to Molène: 1) Pors Illien beach, easy launching and parking; 2) Porsmoguer beach, parking.

The crossing in calm winter sunshine. Photo C. Meyer

Leave from the peninsula of Kermorvan half an hour before slack water, low tide (Brest +6), to make use of slack water in the Chenal du Four. The crossing to Béniguet should take about one hour in good conditions. Passing north of the island is good for bird watching, whilst dolphins are often seen off the southern tip. It is forbidden to go above the high water mark except near the guardian's hut, from where a permissive footpath leads across the island.

The start of the flood tide (Brest -5) will aid the crossing to the strange rock; Morgol. This is a high sharp triangle, split down one face and stained white with bird droppings. The lower round island nearby harbours a grey seal colony, don't disturb them, don't land.

Litiri, the next island, together with the island of Quéménès, enclose a lagoon fringed with sand. You can land on the beach at Litiri, but this is a private island, so no going above the high water mark. Quéménès has been managed by the Coastal Conservancy since 2007. There is a small traditional potato and sheep farm and a guest house, which is booked up months in advance. Landing is permitted on the east side and on the *lédénez* (the local

*Dolphins.
Photo L. Malthieux*

Around Brest

The lighthouse of Kéréon stands watch over the Fromveur.
Photo Y. Dodard

name for a tidal island attached to a bigger island). This has a fantastic beach.

The tide runs fast between Quéménès and Triélen, requiring an energetic ferry glide! Triélen is a bird nesting island and you are not allowed to leave the footpath during the nesting season. Triélen and its *lédénez*, the Île aux Chrétiens (no landing), are connected to Molène at extreme low water on exceptional spring tides. There are organised walks with local guides to take advantage of this.

Head on to Molène, the best landing place is on the south side near or on the lifeboat slipway. A trolley is useful if you are using the camp site which is 100m away to the south-west. This is the only authorised bivouac site on the islands. A toilet and water are available near the lifeboat station. If the camp site official comes around he will charge 8 euros a night (2012).

The next day there are three even more remote spots to visit; Balanec, breathtakingly beautiful (access prohibited during the bird season 1st April to 15 July); Bannec (access only below the HW mark except for authorised bird watchers); and the lighthouse of Kéréon. This latter is an almost legendary destination for the kayaker, time your visit for slack water. It stands guard over the Fromveur (Great Torrent) the sound between Molène archipelago and Ushant. The tides here can reach 11kt with heavy seas, dangerous to even large shipping if there is wind against tide.

Take time during your paddle to walk round Molène and find out about the church

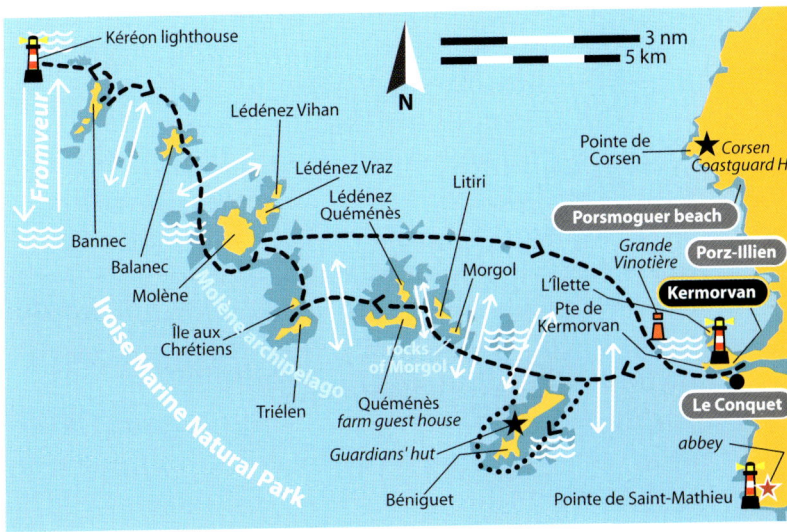

The "large islands" of the archipelago which have a loc'h (a brackish pond) were cultivated until WW2.

clock and the rain water collection system, a more practical reward offered by a grateful Queen Victoria to the islanders after the wreck of the Drummond Castle in 1896.

Alternatives: It is possible to make the paddle from Aber Ildut, some 6 miles north of Le Conquet. With careful planning to make use of the tide, this is no further "over the water" on a good spring tide. ■

WEATHER, TIDE AND SAFETY

Settled weather and neap tides are essential for this expedition, unless you plan to make use of a spring tide to start from Aber Ildut. Good experience of paddling in strong tides and using ferry glides is also essential. For the direct crossing given in this guide, stick to the timings and be sure that you cross the Chenal du Four and take a look at the Fromveur at slack water. For any alternatives, study of a detailed tidal atlas is absolutely vital. The timings and direction of the tidal flow is complex north of the archipelago. Very helpful if used well, but could be literally fatal if not, the tide can be too strong to paddle against. England-Spain car ferries now have permission to use the Chenal du Four and the Fromveur; there are not many sailings, but keep an eye open.

The camp site of Molène is the only bivouac site, it is a lovely "wild camping" spot beside the sea. If you have 3 days, you will find plenty to do and visit, even if leaving the beaches is forbidden on most islands. The north-facing coasts have most beaches, the south-west faces are steep, rocky, and wave swept. The paddle from Molène back to Le Conquet will take 2-3 hours non-stop.

Something to note; the passenger ferries serving the islands will absolutely NOT take kayaks, so the weather window must be long enough to get there and back under your own steam.

The Formation of the Abers

Learn more

by Alain Corre

The coast of the Abers developed during the ice-ages. Geologists are still exploring deposits dating back to previous ice ages, but the most recent ice age has left the greatest impression. The current coast is a flat littoral plain, spiked with islands, islets and reefs, dissected with deep cut valleys, *rias* or locally *abers*. The rounded rocks standing 20m or so high along the coast are a relic from when the sea was about 8m higher, 100,000 years ago. At that time they were reefs and the sea was eating into the base of the Léon plateau. The remains of old sea cliffs can be seen along the edge of this higher ground a few kilometres inland of the present coast. During the last glaciation, only 20,000 years ago, sea level was up to 120m lower than now. The English Channel was dry and groups of Magdalenian hunter-gatherers followed troops of reindeer and mammoths, a life style possibly similar to the traditional Inuit. Rivers dropping steeply to the lower sea level, cut valleys deep into the old land surface. With the melting of the ice, sea level rose again. About 6,500 years ago it stabilised more or less at the current level. The valleys were re-flooded producing the Abers.

At this time the coast was 2-3km further out than at present. Recent geology has been a history of steady erosion of the deposits left when sea level was lower. The current inter-tidal zone is a flat surface interlaced with deposits of sand and gravel around islets and reefs. Studies of old soil horizons under sand dunes and beaches show that these were once freshwater marshes and lakes. Traces of post holes under the sand at Guissény show that man lived beside these lakes. Ceral grains and cinders found at Plouguerneau are a witness to the start of farming and the more settled neolithic culture. Their chambered cairns and cromlechs are the most substantial monuments these people, not so dissimilar to ourselves, left behind. Many of these are now on islands where they have been well preserved; Guénioc and Venan are veritable open air archaeological museums. If you stop in the inter-tidal zone for a picnic, look around, small sharp flakes, worked by these people are fairly common and easily spotted amongst rounded pebbles. ■

34 — Aber Ildut to the Rocks of Portsall

Sea Kayaking Guide — Brittany

Difficulty: ✗ ✗ ✗ / ✗ ✗ ✗

Distance: 10 nautical miles (1 or 2 days)

Leaving: Porscave — **Arriving:** Portsall

Maps:
SHOM 7149
Navicarte 539 / 540
IGN 0416ET

*In front of the lighthouse, Le Four.
Photo A. Antúnez Vitales*

Around Brest

Portsall

Aber Ildut, the short side branch of Porscave at HW.

Moorings made of tree trunks in the port of Mazou.

A BROKEN COAST, where swell and a strong tidal flow amongst the outlying rocks and reefs can make navigation tricky.

In 1978 the rocks of Portsall were the scene of the wreck of the Amoco Cadiz, still by far the largest oil spill in Europe.

Three islands, each one charged with history; Melon, Yoc'h and Carn will impress you in different ways.

The Island of Carn. Photo P. Bisset

Launching, Landing and Parking:

Aber Ildut: 1) South side of the Aber in the harbour of Porscave, large car park, portage to slipway; 2) North side, Lanildut, beach near the quay where they land seaweed, the quay can be busy and congested, drop off quickly and park further up the hill; 3) Another little beach 150m to the west of the harbour, portage, limited parking.

Melon beach and slipway: very sheltered behind the island of Melon, the tide goes out a long way, parking.

Argenton: large slipway but limited parking, long portage at low water.

Portsall: 1) South side of the entrance to the bay at Trémazan, slipway and limited parking; 2) In the harbour, parking beside the "L'Ancre: An Eor" which has an exhibition about the Amoco Cadiz and a sailing centre. Beach near the lifeboat station.

Swell admidst the rocks of Argenton. Photo J.P. Van Obbergen

Launch from Porscave at HW -4 (Brest). Opposite is Lanildut, the premier port for the seaweed trade. The *Goémoniers*, the seaweed collecting boats, can be recognised by their screw devices the *scoubidou*. The kelp they collect is used in the pharmaceutical and food industries. Once out of the harbour, head north, rounded masses of pink granite make up the coast, the famous *granite rose*, there are lots of small inlets amongst them. The island of Melon is worth exploring with its chambered cairn and standing stones from neolithic times and more modern quarries and stone-lined trenches which were used to process seaweed at the turn of the 20th century. Nearby, but hard to find, are the mooring posts at Mazou, made by replanting tree trunks, roots and all, in the sand and gravel. This technology was cutting edge when it was introduced by Irish monks early in the Christian era.

The beautiful peninsula of Saint-Laurent hides the three well protected bays of Argenton. These dry completely at LW. The next island is that of Yoc'h. Two thousand years ago when it was still a peninsula, it had a thriving community. Its fine maritime turf, bordered by rocks sculptured into improbable, lichen-covered, shapes gives a grandstand view of the sea. At sea, the Four lighthouse marks the start of the channel of that name. On spring flood tides, a race can form all the way from the shore out to the rocks of Argenton near the lighthouse.

The deep sandy inlet of Lanhalles is sandwiched between the rock outcrops which slowly grow into cliffs, highest at the Pointe de Landunvez, and then drop away again towards the bay of Portsall. The entrance to Portsall is famously guarded by sharp and dangerous rocks; in a kayak you can easily slip amongst them. It is worth paddling on another mile to the island of Carn and landing on the little stony spit on the south end. The island is named after its chambered cairns, with piled stone vaulting dating to 6,000 years ago. It is possible to explore inside two of them (take a torch) and appreciate how well they were made. Mariners still use them as a landmark, not bad for something built so long ago. A German WW II blockhouse

Around Brest

on the west side of the island is unlikely to prove so long-lived.

Back at Portsall, the bay is sandy and shallow, surrounded by villages and countryside, dominated by a cross and a standing stone, two streams drain into it. At low water the beaches join up leaving a wide desert to cross.

Alternatives: The Aber Ildut makes an interesting, sheltered paddle, information panels and a historical quarry trail can be found if you land on the stone slipway on the south side about 0.5nm upstream. The Aber is cut deeper than seems possible by the current tiny stream, in geological ages past, the river Aulne drained through here rather than Brest. It is worth paddling out to the Four lighthouse if conditions permit. It would also be possible to paddle the other way along the coast on the ebb tide, or use the tide for a paddle there and back. ■

WEATHER, TIDE AND SAFETY

This coast is subject to strong tidal flows, swell and fog. Look at weather forecast and plan carefully. The most dangerous areas are between Melon and Argenton, and off Portsall where rocks and shallows can lead to breaking waves. The general tidal flow is north to north-east from HW -4 and south to south-west from HW +2 (Brest). Local HW is Brest + 0.10 minutes.

35 — Aber Benoît and the Island of Guénioc

Sea Kayaking Guide — Brittany

Difficulty: ✗ ✗ ✗

Distance: 14 nautical miles

Leaving and Arriving: Landéda, port du Vrill

Maps:
SHOM 7150
Navicarte 539
IGN 0416ET

Kayakers on Guénioc.

Around Brest

Saint-Pabu

The folly at Roch An Dioul.
Photo C. Magré

EXPLORE THE RECESSES of an *aber* dedicated to oyster farming which penetrates deep into the forest before loosing itself in winding muddy creeks. Then glide along with the ebb tide some way offshore to the island of Guénioc and its archaeological sites. They would surely be much more famous if they were not set on an isolated island.

Guénioc, rocking stone.
Photo R. Maclennan

Launching, Landing and Parking:

Aber Benoît: 1) Slipway in the harbour of Port Vrill, just inside the Aber on the north side, parking;
2) South side of the Aber, slipway of Saint-Pabu-Stellac'h, parking;
3) Slipway at Tréglonou beside the bridge over the Aber, accessible HW +/-2.

Towards the mouth of the Aber Benoît.

Halt on a saline meadow, Aber Benoît at HW. Photo R. Bate

Leave the harbour of Vrill at HW -1.30 (local HW=Roscoff -0.40 minutes) and paddle up the Aber, past the pretty houses and quays. The channel turns south into the territory of the oyster farmers. It is here that the famous oysters of Prat ar Coum are fattened up. On a bend two shallow bays open to the south-east and south-west, the main channel leads east in a steep-sided densely-wooded valley. After a long straight section, the sudden changes in perspective around some sharp bends are truly wonderful.

The folly on Roch An Dioul, then the bridge at Tréglonou…once the tide turns it is time to turn back. If you have time, carry on a bit further, the creeks finally end just under the road bridges at Tariec and there is a water mill at Kerilien.

Leave the mouth of the Aber and head towards the island of Garo and then north-west to Guénioc. Guénioc is no longer ever accessible on foot, although it was in former times. The best landing place, near the "rocking stone", at the south-east point can still be difficult; huge blocks of stone and rounded boulders barely class as a beach and the swell can be a serious killjoy.

Looking north from Guénioc at low water. Photo P. Bisset

Around Brest

A rock pile oriented north-west/south-east and cutting the island in two, turns out to be man-made. This long cairn contains a series of round chambers, many missing their roofs and accessed by tight passages roofed with large slabs. These date from different periods, but the most ancient are 6,000 years old. On the north side of the island, a clearly visible round enclosure of flat slabs on end indicates the site of a mediaeval village, there are other vestiges nearby. At the southern end a standing stone stands guard over the "rocking stone". Stand on it and try rocking, maybe I am not heavy enough! These are impressive archaeological remains and the isolated site, surrounded by the sea, makes them even more special, look after it.

If landing at Guénioc proves too difficult, it is worth visiting the Tariec islands nearby. These two islands are connected to the mainland at low water. Little Tariec has a nice beach, but Great Tariec is more interesting with its ruined chapel. Return to Vrill harbour by the same route.

Alternatives: At high water it is possible to follow the coast inshore around the peninsula of Sainte-Marguerite, by mid tide it is frequently a frustrating case of trying to find a route amongst the rocks and sandbanks. The sea is very shallow indeed north of Garo. ■

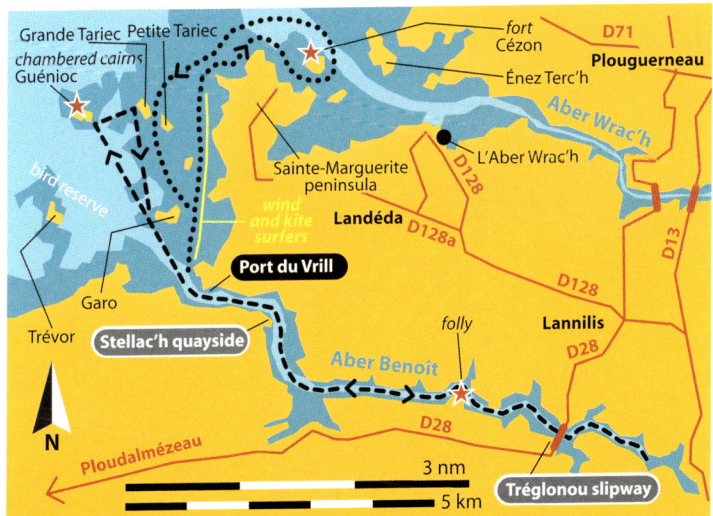

WEATHER, TIDE AND SAFETY

This paddle can be divided into two. The only enemy to navigation in the Aber is mud, the tide runs strongly enough in places to slow you down as well, for an easy life, make good use of the tides. There are back eddies between Garo and Guénioc, and Garo and Vrill, which make the paddle back against the ebb tide easy. Heavy swell can prevent landing on Guénioc. The tide can run fast between Guénioc and Tariec.

Sea Kayaking Guide **Brittany**

36 Aber Wrac'h and L'île Vierge

Difficulty: ✗ ✗ ✗

Maps:
SHOM 7150
Navicarte 539
IGN 0416ET

Distance: 9 nautical miles

Leaving and Arriving: The harbour of Aber Wrac'h

Landing at low water at Stagadon.

Around Brest

● Landéda

The spiral staircase of the lighthouse on Île Vierge. Photo R. Bate

BETWEEN THE LAND and the deep blue sea there is a whole world…

A sparkling pattern of islets lies between Aber Wrac'h and Île Vierge, dominated by the lighthouse the tallest in Europe and the tallest purpose-built lighthouse in the world. Each islet is a microcosm of character and history.

To be enjoyed with the emerald light of clear sea playing over white sand and tide-combed seaweed strands.

The smiling landmark on Fort Cézon.

Launching, Landing and Parking:

Ste-Marguerite peninsula: the beach facing the island of Cézon, beside the Penn-Enez campsite, a small car park, but very quiet.

Slipway in the harbour of Kastell Arc'h in Lilia: north side of the Aber and embarkation point for Île Vierge, parking.

Aber Wrac'h: 1) Harbour of Aber Wrac'h, south side of the Aber, the most easterly slipway has a large car park and space for trailers;
2) Perros slipway, north side of the Aber, limited parking; 3) Port of Paluden, slipway on the south side of the Aber downstream of the bridge of the same name.

Panorama looking south from the lighthouse on Île Vierge. Photo S. Earl

Launch at HW -1 (local HW=Roscoff -0.30 minutes), cross the main channel and head north-west. During WW II, the islands of Cézon, Île Longue (Enez Vihan) and Enez Terc'h (also called d'Erhe) were occupied by the Germans, who left a system of blockhouses and trenches. Enez Terc'h had already been an American seaplane base during WW I, and is sometimes called "Île aux Américains". All three are now densely covered in undergrowth.

Paddle between Enez Terc'h and the mainland (only possible near HW) and set your sights on the island of Wrac'h, easily recognisable by the fluorescent red light tower. This has a lovely beach, a good place for a pause. In summer a local association organises art exhibitions in the garden at the base of the light.

The tide will be dropping fast by now, have a good look to check if you can still cross the isthmus north-east of you into the small bay of Lilia (otherwise paddle around to the north). Pass the slipway used by the boat trips out to Île Vierge and continue north-east to Enez ar Vir and Enez Venan (you will have gathered by now that enez means island in Breton). Then north to Île Vierge, to the lighthouse which has been calling you throughout the paddle. Land on the south side near the harbour wall. In summer the lighthouse is sometimes open to visitors; if you can manage the 365 stairs! The reward is a magnificent view, not only of the sea and coast all around, but also of the sinuous coils of the staircase itself. Study the sea and decide if the outside of the islets in the breakers and swell, or the sheltered inside passage is for you.

Around Brest

Make your way from rock to rock in short ferry glides to the south-west to the island of Stagadon. This is used by a centre run by Father Jaouen working with disadvantaged young adults; "victims of shipwreck on land". It is a lovely island but can be busy with both water-sports run by the centre and other visitors. The centre has a guest house on the island.

Head across the channel to Île de la Croix and then along in the shallow water to Île Cézon with its smiling pirate land mark painted on the fort. There are some interesting tunnels to be found if you can brave the undergrowth. Skirt Île Longue to arrive back at Aber Wrac'h.

Alternatives: 1) East of Enez Venan the coast is less broken, but nevertheless an enjoyable paddle as far as the harbour at Le Correjou (2.5nm); 2) Exploration of Aber Wrac'h which is navigable at HW as far as Le Diouris, although the last mile or so is more like a river running in a steep wooded ravine, is a good bad-weather option. ∎

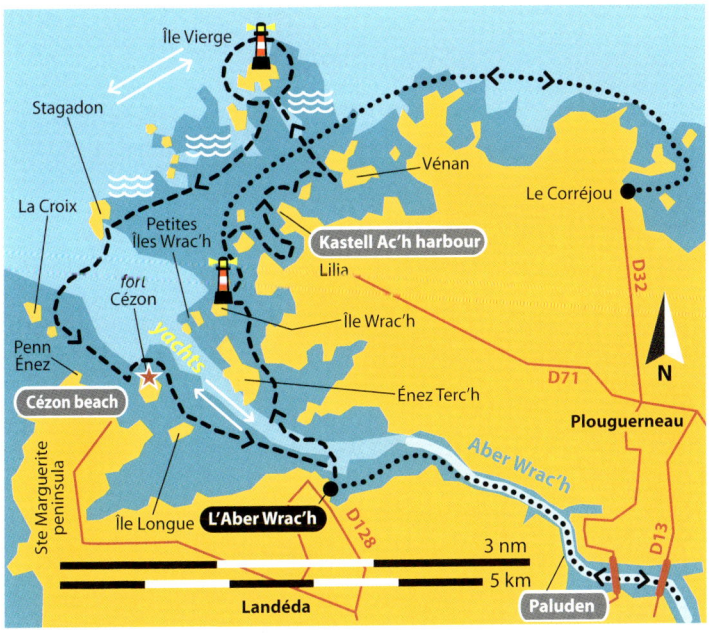

WEATHER, TIDE AND SAFETY

The paddle will take 3 hours without stops, keep an eye on the falling tide, not to be left stranded. Neap tides allow longer exploration around the islets.
In heavy swell there can be breaking waves all the way across the channel caused by tide against wind and waves, watch out, the ebb will be sweeping you down into this rough water. The open sea outside is usually calmer. At around mid-tide, reefs between Lilia and Île Vierge can stir-up surf very close to the rocks -take care.

It's scoubidou *folded over the harvest of kelp, a heavily laden* goémonier *returns to port. Photo C. Magré*

Learn more

The *Goémoniers*

Goémon means any seaweed which has a use. Seaweed has been vital to the economy of this coast since the earliest times, used as; fuel, animal feed, for soil improvement, a source of chemicals and even stuffing mattresses. Without the fertility it brings, the island of Sein, for instance, would be a sandy wasteland.

The *Goémoniers* (those who collect *goémon*) were mainly drawn from the poor coastal and island inhabitants of Finistère. They practised two sorts of collection; drifting weed thrown up by storms (*goémon d'épave*) and cut weed (*goémon de coupe*) which was harvested using sickles on poles. A complex assemblage of very localised laws and customs regulated the harvest to ensure fairness and a minimum of disputes. The seaweed was collected in boats, by horses and carts or in wicker baskets. Communities cut footpaths and steps down the rocks and opened up tracks for carts. In at least one case, a system of one way circulation was enforced on the beach to avoid traffic jams! It is estimated that an industrious family of five or six could harvest 5 tonnes or more of wet seaweed on a single tide at the start of the cutting season when weed was abundant.

Learn more

Once ashore, the weed was transported to farmland or processed for chemicals. To extract chemicals it was spread out to dry on the sand, gathered into piles and burnt in long ovens. These were trenches lined with stones, with a system for dividing the trench into sections. Once you have your eye in, these ovens, now grass covered, can be frequently spotted, maybe even near your tent on the camp-site.

Goémon *oven, Pointe de la Croix, Brignogan.*

The ash was collected and used for soda for glass manufacture (18th century) and in the 19th and 20th centuries became important for iodine used in pharmacy and the photographic industry. By the middle of the 20th century, the chemicals could be obtained more cheaply elsewhere and the industry declined.

Seaweed then became important again as a source of texture agents for cosmetics and foodstuffs. The *scoubidou*, invented in 1969, a mechanical screw mounted on a boat allowed semi-mechanised collection and it is these which now provide the 35,000 tonnes landed annually at Lanildut, half of total French production. Ninety percent of the production is in Brittany, but seaweed stocks are declining in the south. There is a limit of 75 *scoubidou* boats to try to ensure a sustainable harvest.

Much more recently, seaweed cultivation has been started, with production on lines in the sea to meet demand from top chefs for Japanese cuisine. Seaweed is still collected for fertiliser, for example on the island of Batz. ∎

The seaweed on your plate

A small type of red seaweed, locally known as *pioka* is the same as the "carrageen" used in Ireland and Wales. This is used to solidify milk in traditional recipes, but also appears as E 407 in commercial preparations. The numbers 400 to 408, all based on seaweed, are some of the more benign of the dreaded "E" numbers.

37

The Pagan Coast

Difficulty: ✗ ✗ ✗

Distance: 8 nautical miles

Leaving and Arriving: Ménez-Ham

Maps:
SHOM 7150
Navicarte 539
IGN 0416ET / 0515ET

Ménez-Ham, wooden tender.

Around Brest

Brignogan

Sea kale, a rare and protected plant.

Customs cottage at Ménez-Ham. Photo R. Maclennan

LONG BEACHES of immaculate sand, here is paradise… In front of them rocks shaped by the waves, scattered at random or piled together in chaotic heaps. They form small harbours, mysterious castles, channels that divide and rejoin, provoking currents, breakers and boils. You are on the Pagan coast where numerous shipwrecks, coupled with the extreme poverty of the inhabitants created the legend of the wreckers.

Launching, Landing and Parking:

Pontusval lighthouse: on the headland of Beg-Pol, slipway down to the beach, parking.
Ménez-Ham village: beach, slipway and large car park.
Neiz Vran headland, beach and small car park on the west side.
Between Ménez-Ham and Neiz Vran, numerous beaches with access from the coast road.
Brignogan-Plage: slipways only accesssible near HW, not recommended.

Port of Ménez-Ham.

The port of Ménez-Ham is a shelter in the midst of the rocks.

Leave from the slipway in the quaint village (very touristy) of smallholders -*goémoniers*- fishermen of Ménez-Ham and find a path between the rocks and out towards the west. Keep an eye on your progress; the bell-tower of Kervizouarn and the point of the island Enez Amann ar Rouz near Neiz Vran are the most obvious landmarks on the map. However, with care you should be able to identify the prominent rocks which mark certain harbours and hidden channels.

The rock of Kastell, then the large flat rocks of Karreg Hir (or Carreg Hir), followed by 3 small sheltered inlets show the way to Enez Amann Ar Rouz. This small island of earth and rocks is extraordinary: a close cropped turf, swept by winds and rocks eroded into bizarre shapes. This extremely poor patch of ground could barely nourish a family, and needed to be fertilised with seaweed. No wonder the "Pagans" were said to welcome the riches brought by shipwrecks.

These granite rocks formed 300 million years ago were twisted into place during the tertiary period and then sculpted by freshwater flows and the sea level changes of the quaternary ice ages to give the strange landscape of today.

Paddling back east, the bell tower and château

After harvest the seaweed was stacked in piles.

Around Brest

of Kerlouan and the massed rocks which defend the village of Ménez-Ham serve as landmarks. Continue past the entrance to Ménez-Ham, after skirting some more massive rocks, the lighthouse of Pontusval (18m high, visible at 10nm) on the headland of Beg-Pol will come into view, its little beach is a welcome haven.

Turn back again to Ménez-Ham, this is a good place to paddle at low water with multiple anastomosing kelp-lined channels. It feels as if you are flying at low altitude over the kelp. This is a place where *pioka*, carragheen, is collected. The small red fern-like fronds are blanched, dried and used as a source of texturiser in cosmetics and foodstuffs. At high water you can paddle closer in to the beaches or play amongst the rocks and reefs.

The lighthouse of Beg-Pol.

Alternatives: At high water, explore the natural harbour of Tresseny, a long sandy inlet extending as far as Guissény. ■

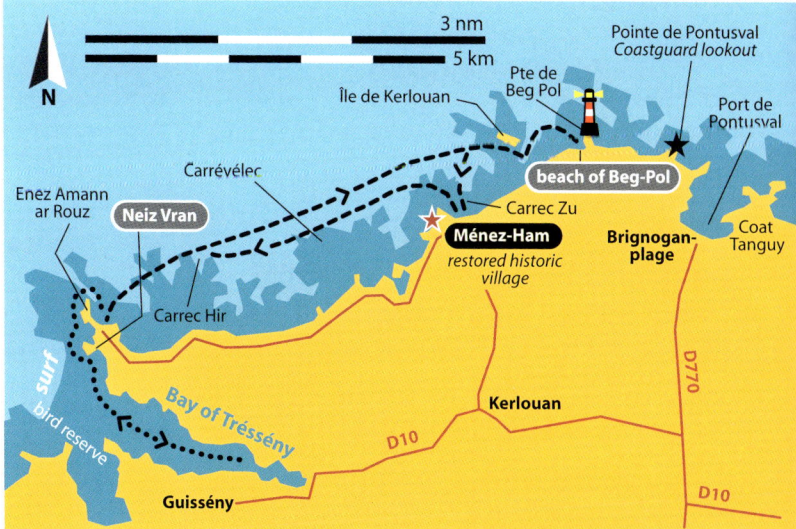

WEATHER, TIDE AND SAFETY

A trip for calm weather or little swell. A heavy swell will mean paddling further out to sea. Tidal flows are not a major issue, so the paddle can be done at any stage of the tide. The only point to watch is that Pontusval harbour in Brignogan Bay dries completely at low water.

204 | Sea Kayaking Guide | **Brittany**

38 The Dunes of Keremma

Difficulty: ✖ ✖ ✖

Distance: 10 nautical miles

Leaving and Arriving: Plounéour-Trez

Maps:
SHOM 7150
Navicarte 539
IGN 0515ET

The chambered cairn at Kernic at mid-tide.

Around Brest

● Plounéour-Trez

Reed beds deep in the bay at Goulven.

THE NATURAL harbours of Goulven and Kernic, extend far into the low-lying coast. They are so flat that at low water they have been used for horse racing. Partially bordered by reclaimed polders, the ecologically important sand dunes of Keremma separate the two. Offshore, banks of odd shaped rocks help protect the harbours from the assaults of the sea.

Launching, Landing and Parking:

Lividic beach: parking near the football stadium, a long portage at low water.

Goulven bay: the beach at Plounéour-Trez on the eastern entrance of the bay is usable HW +/-3.

Guinirvit harbour: north shore of the natural harbour of Kernic, car park, the strong tidal flows in and out of Kernic restrict the use of this charming port, but it is a good stopping place at HW, or a base to explore inside Kernic.

Porz Guen: the harbour of Plouescat, near the sailing centre, limited parking, difficult access at low tide.

Brignogan-Plage: the slipways are only usable near HW, not recommended.

Entrance of the bay of Goulven, low water.

Erosion of the sand dunes at Penn ar Chleuz, bay of Goulven at HW.

Leave Lividic beach at HW -1.30 (local HW=Roscoff -15 minutes), follow the coast as it bends south until you can see the bell tower of Goulven.

The natural harbour of Goulven is extremely flat and surrounded by sand dunes and reclaimed polders, the rocky coast of Finistère feels a long way away. To be caught by the falling tide could mean a portage or trolley of many kilometres; or a prolonged chance to bird watch in this ornithological reserve! Cut across the entrance of the bay at Treigueiller as the inlet is a quiet area for birds.

After leaving the harbour, follow the superb beaches of Keremma. Louis Rousseau, a prominent utopian socialist and originator of the Christian socialist movement founded the village of Keremma (named after his wife Emma) as a socialist commune in 1823, he improved the sea defences to protect the reclaimed land from flooding and some farms were established.

Not far offshore, the twin rocks of Roc'h Vran and Méan Mélen make good landmarks. From the sea, the coast looks flat and dull, but the dunes are spectacular once you land and walk inland. This is a European conservation area for rare plants including the Fen Orchid. The site belongs to the Coastal Conservancy and there is a visitor centre. The dunes extend on to the long promontory closing off the harbour of Kernic. A house was illegally built here in the 1960s but demolished. However, you can appreciate why someone would want to live here.

The tide will be ebbing through the narrow entrance…paddle harder!… It will be worth it. Kernic is a mixture of flat sand and salt marshes, contrasting with the rocks around the small harbour of Guinirvit (or Kernivilit). The chambered cairn (*allée couverte*) now only uncovered at mid-tide was on dry land when it was built

Around Brest

Entrance of the harbour of Kernic.

4,500 years ago and sea level 10m lower. It was originally roofed with rock slabs and covered by a large mound. Kernic is as flat as Goulven. The inland end was formerly an air field and now houses a sand yacht centre. Calcareous sand had been extracted from the bay on a small scale for land improvement since time immemorial, but larger scale extraction in the 1980s resulted in a change from net accretion to net sand loss and the still evident erosion of the dune system. Attempts are being made to control the invasive *Spartina anglica*, the spikey grass just flooded at HW springs. Kernic is an important ornithological site, avoid paddling into the depths of the bay and scaring birds into the air, particularly in winter.

Turn back and take the current out of the entrance and head back westward. Go some way out to sea to avoid the shallow water and rocks which emerge as the tide drops. These form gulleys and channels, and strangely shaped eroded rocks appear. Watch out, from time to time a breaking wave can erupt, even if the area seems to be protected from the Channel swell. The return to the beach at Lividic is a case of winding your way between the sand banks and rocks; not too difficult, as you have the flood-lights of the football stadium as a guide.

Alternatives: 1) Harbour of Goulven from Lividic; 2) Kernic from Porz Guen. ■

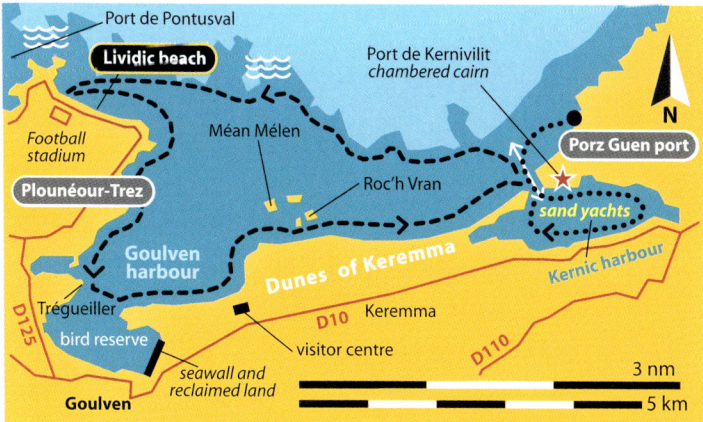

WEATHER, TIDE AND SAFETY

These two bays do not present any particular problems. Swell can roll into the bay, especially near Kernic and then there is the strong current in the entrance (arrive before HW +1 to avoid a hard paddle). Take care not to be left high and dry by the ebb tide. Arriving back at Lividic at low water will mean a long portage.

208 — Sea Kayaking Guide **Brittany**

39 The Island of Siec

Difficulty: ✘ ✘ ✘ / ✘ ✘ ✘

Distance: 9 nautical miles

Leaving and Arriving: Port Neuf

Maps:
SHOM 7151
Navicarte 538
IGN 0515ET

Ruined cottage on the island of Siec.

The Morlaix area

Santec

Dossen beach and Siec at low water.

TWO LITTLE ESTUARIES, a spectacular and well known surf beach, a small island and it's farm, a coast paved with rocks, sandy spits or tombolos, all drying at low water; this is on the way out.

The way back, the same; but transformed by the tide.

Surf at Moguériec. Photo L. Malthieux

Launching, Landing and Parking:

Port Neuf: slipway, sandy bay and parking.

Moguériec: beach north-west of the harbour breakwater, or inside the harbour if the tide is high enough, parking 150m away in the town centre.

Dossen Beach: near the entrance to the Dunes camp-site, large car park, portage, (this camp-site is very handy for Roscoff ferry port).

Dossen village: opposite Siec island, slipway to beach and neaby car park (used by twice weekly markets in summer).

Guillec estuary: slipway, "Rue de Guillec" at Tévenn, limited parking, accessible HW +/-3.

Portage at Port Neuf.

Launch from Port Neuf at HW -1.30 (Roscoff), paddle past Moguériec and paddle up the estuary of Guillec with the tide. This is a wild valley, bounded by sand and forest, which meanders 2 km inland.

Follow the same path back and, watching out for the rocks around the entrance, paddle up the sister estuary of the river Horn, this is less easy to navigate, but you can go past a village and look at the forest and sand dunes of Dossen. In 1699 a great storm swept far inland, taking away 250ha of farm land and menacing the town of Saint-Pol-de-Léon. Constant attempts to stabilise the sand dunes ended in afforestation of the area with pines in 1862. The sandy soil inland is good for root vegetables; carrots, lettuce, and the local speciality; the pink onions of Roscoff. We are in the centre of the golden belt of Léon where the vegetable is king.

Dossen beach, according to sea conditions can be a fabulous surf spot, or a flat sandy beach for the family with buckets and spades. The island of Siec closes out the horizon to the north. Paddle between Siec and Dossen on the mainland, the waves sweep over the tombolo from both directions; keep your eyes open. Now the island of Batz and its lighthouse come into view.

North of Siec is a domain of rocks and swell, content yourself with paddling around Siec and then into the harbour on the south side. This was one of the rare Channel harbours to be involved in sardine fishing and had a cannery. You can stop and have a look around, the island is privately owned, but access on foot is allowed. It is an attractive place, the ruins on the west end have a Celtic feel, rather like Ireland, -especially in the rain!

The bar near the slipway at Dossen village is run by one of the French onion sellers who used to be a common sight in England with their strings of onions, and black bicycles. You will be amazed by how many onions these Roscoff agricultural labourers managed to shift! Ask to see his letter from the Queen, a favourable reply to a request asking her to stop police harrassment of Breton onion sellers. You may also learn something of Breton nationalism along the way. Roscoff has a small museum dedicated to these beret clad onion sellers.

The Morlaix area

Two options for the paddle back to Port Neuf: go and play in the surf on the way back; or paddle straight back across the bay. The small bay at Port Neuf dries out at low water, but you can portage the kayaks to the point and bring the car down to collect them.

Alternatives: If sea conditions allow, it is possible to continue to the island of Batz, heading towards the lighthouse. Keep outside of the breakers and then ferry glide across the main channel, which is close in to Batz. If you want to make it an overnight trip, there is a simple camp-site, just above the beach below the lighthouse, near where you land. ∎

WEATHER, TIDE AND SAFETY

High water is needed to paddle up the estuaries. The surf at Dossen can be excellent, but you may not be alone, watch out for board surfers, kite surfers…and other kayakers. The coast beween Siec and the channel across to Batz can be rough with heaped-up swell, it is open to any waves and is shallow with outlying rocks and reefs. Look carefully and think twice. However, it can be great fun in amongst the rocks. It is up to you.

40 The Island of Batz

Difficulty: ✗ ✗ ✗

Distance: 10 nautical miles

Leaving and Arriving: Roscoff

Maps:
SHOM 7151
Navicarte 538
IGN 0515ET

View from the lighthouse, north coast of Batz.

The Morlaix area

Roscoff

Campsite on Batz.

Pink onion harvest in front of the lighthouse.

A TRADITIONAL farming village thrown into the sea. An island which doubles in size at low water; immense fields of rocks and surf uncovered on the north coast. To the east, beaches and the folds of sandbanks. To the south, the channel, with its swirling tidal flows, separating the island from Roscoff. To the west, swell swept rocks.

Launching, Landing and Parking:

Roscoff: 1) The small beach below the chapel of Sainte Barbe, this dries less than the port of Roscoff, is closer to the channel and has a slipway down to the beach; limited parking; 2) Bloscon port, currently under renovation, access uncertain; 3) The beach at Traon Erc'h, south of Bloscon, near the jardin colonial (botanic garden), limited parking.

Landing stage for the ferries to Batz at Roscoff at LW.

Arrival at Porz Kernok on Batz.

Leave from the beach at Sainte-Barbe at HW -2 (Roscoff) and ferry glide out to the island of Ti Soazon, various navigation marks indicate the channel and the current may be swift in places. Ti Soazon translates as the English House and the island boasts a smugglers hole known as Toul ar Butun (tobacco hole), maybe the names are related. From Ti Soazon, a vista of rock, sand and sea lead the eye towards Batz. At low water, all of this area is dry land, beaches of fine sand stretch along the coast.

Beyond Pointe Bilvidic the extensive beach of Grève Blanche (White Strand) comes into view with the coastguard look-out and lighthouse behind. These will be useful reference points throughout the paddle. The shore becomes more and more rocky beyond the Pointe de Porzcaréou. Inland, the island has small long and thin sandy fields surrounded by high protective hedges, here and there a tethered milk cow or horse. The patchwork quilt of 25 smallholdings, many of them organic, farm a total of 160ha and make use of every inch of cultivable land. The warm micro-climate means that early potatoes, cauliflowers, and the famous pink onions (see paddle 39), sold under the label "Île de Batz", are a month ahead of those on the mainland just across the channel. Part of the charm is that this is a working island, not just a tourist destination.

Tethered cow on Batz.

The Morlaix area

Once around the wild west coast, either of the twin sandy bays at Porz Retter makes a good stopping place. The island campsite is just above the beach, sandy grassland with a shower and toilet block. Walk up to the lighthouse to stretch your legs. This is open to the public in summer and provides a fine aerial view of the rocks you have just paddled through. Back on the water, the tide will be running against you at up to 3.5kt, keep along the shore to make use of back eddies. After the lifeboat station, the long quay of Porz Kernok marks the place where the ferries shuttling back and forth to Roscoff, land. Take care of these busy working boats and another long landing stage which is often partially submerged. Once back near Ti Soazon, ferry glide back to the start. ■

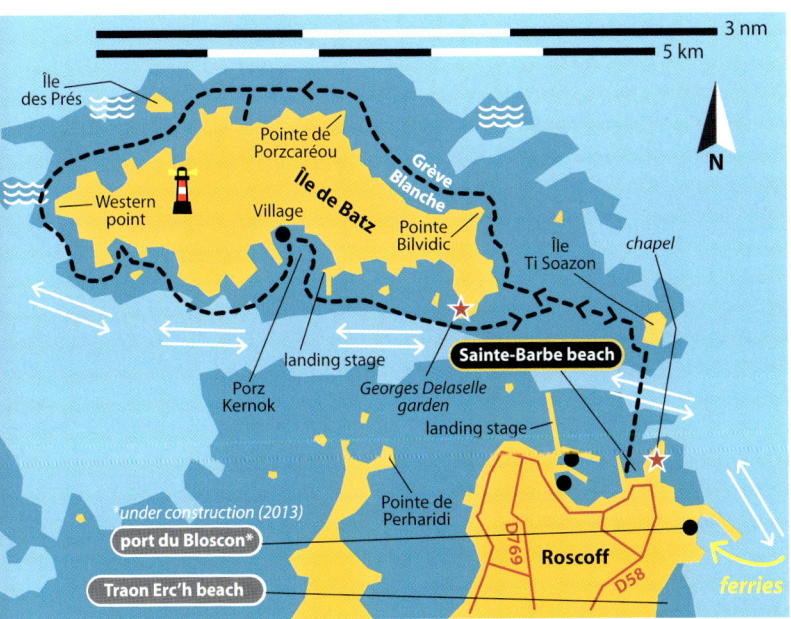

WEATHER, TIDE AND SAFETY

The east, north and west can be dangerous with large surf breaking over the rocks and reefs. Low tide doubles the size of the island and can make landing near impossible along these coasts. Swell may make it necessary to stay well offshore. Good weather and high water are recommended for the circumnavigation. The channel is more sheltered, but wind against tide can raise a substantial sea around mid-tide when the current is strongest. The westbound (ebb) tide starts running in the channel at HW (Roscoff) and eastbound (flood) at LW, it is strongest (max 3.5kt) at mid-tide. The tide outside of the island starts about an hour later, westbound HW +1 and eastbound HW -5 and is generally weak; however, locally strong sets can be encountered amongst the rocks at mid-tide.

41 — The Bay of Morlaix

Sea Kayaking Guide — Brittany

216

Maps:
SHOM 7151
Navicarte 538
IGN 0615ET

Difficulty: ✘ ✘ ✘ / ✘ ✘ ✘

Distance: 15 nautical miles

Leaving and Arriving: Plougasnou

Le Taureau castle (the Bull).

The Morlaix area

Morlaix

Beach on the north-west of the island of Callot.

THE CONFLUENCE of the estuaries of the rivers Morlaix and Penzé forms the vast Bay of Morlaix, dotted with rocks and islands; one with a fort, two with lighthouses, one linked by a tidal causeway, one with a secret tunnel, many are bird reserves. The tides run strongly, the rocks stand boldly; delicious edible seaweeds and shellfish...are we in paradise?

Launching, Landing and Parking:

Roscoff: 1) Bloscon port, under renovation until 2013; 2) The beach at Traon Erc'h, south of Bloscon, near the jardin colonial (botanic garden), limited parking.

Pempoul port: this is the port of St-Pol-de-Léon, right at the end of the breakwater, large slipway and parking area. This port dries completely at LW and launching can be tricky from the end of the slipway due to the current.

The bridge over the Penzé (D58) Pont de la Corde, near Henvic; just south of the bridge on the east side, slipway all the way to LW. Some of the parking area floods on spring tides. Muddy at extreme LW. Toilets and a nice chapel.

Térénez port: very busy and congested during the summer, slipways to both the harbour and the beach, find a parking spot first.

Port of Diben: the best slipway is the one near the end of the embankment, large parking area.

Hill and chapel on the island of Callot.

The island of Louët.

Leave Diben at HW -2 and pass the succession of small inlets along the coast towards the south. Once near Térénez, turn west and go between the island of Stérec and Barnenez headland with its well known chambered cairn, a National Monument and said to be the largest megalithic mausoleum in Europe. Next pass to the north of Île Noire (the Black Isle). You will find neither a castle nor a gorilla (only Tintin fans will appreciate this!), but an old square towered lighthouse which marks the entry of the Morlaix river. Head towards the next islet with its castle, Le Taureau (the Bull), which stands proud beside the main channel. This was built in the 17th century to protect the important port of Morlaix from English corsairs. It is open to the public, but only for those on organised boat trips from Carantec.

Once you have admired the castle (from the outside), head west-south-west. The rocky cliffs of the island of Louët with their nesting herring gulls, hide the picture postcard lighthouse found on the east side. The lighthouse keeper's cottage with its garden is now a tourist lodge for up to 10 persons. Continue along past Carantec, the water is shallow here so you will need to keep well offshore. Look out for the Grand Cochon (Large Pig) with its green navigation mark. Another rock is painted white. Ahead of you is the causeway across to the island of Callot, this is dry for much of the tide, but if you have paddled at a reasonable speed, you will still have sufficient water in the Passe aux Moutons (Passage of the Sheep) to paddle through it to the Penzé river side of the bay. Just mind the curving concrete causeway. Saint-Pol-de-Léon is in front of you, and far off to the north-west, Bloscon and the port of Roscoff.

The Morlaix area

Follow the west coast of Callot, rocks, little beaches, cottages. The island is inhabited, but still lovely, a succession of rocky spurs linked by pinky sand beaches. Stop near the northern end, choosing whichever beach, east or the west, is out of the wind. The promontory has a compass table detailing the panoramic views, a short walk towards the chapel will give you an idea of the layout of the island.

The route back is through the islands and rocks of the bird reserve, from Île Verte (Green island) to Île Ricard, this island has nesting egrets, but having no trees they nest amongst the purple mallows. It is forbidden to even approach the islands and no landing is allowed. Yellow buoys mark the limit to which you can approach. Wardens look after the birds and will be happy to tell you more about them if you ask. A series of ferry glides letting the tide carry you north will take you back to Diben.

Alternatives: Explore either estuary, Morlaix or the Penzé and its forested side valley, the Dourduff, go up with the tide and back on the ebb. ∎

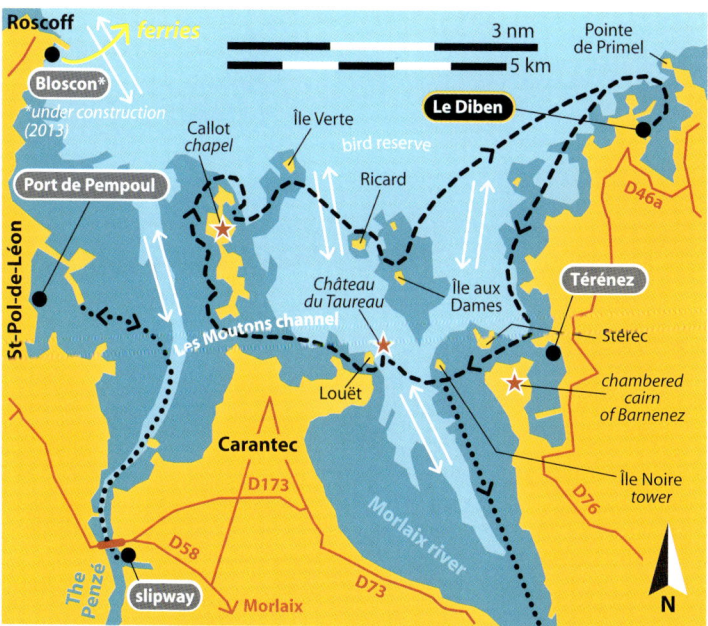

WEATHER, TIDE AND SAFETY

The Bay is generally well sheltered, but a northerly swell can penetrate amongst the islands. Finding the way is easy, but check on prominent landmarks from time to time. Watch out for strong rivers of water in the main channels at mid-tide. Low water here has its own charm with local people collecting seaweed and shellfish, you can make the same paddle many times and see different things each time. HW in the bay corresponds to HW Roscoff, with a southbound flow during the flood tide and a northerly flow during the ebb. HW far up the rivers will be slightly later.

42 — Primel and the Heather Coast

Difficulty: ✖ ✖ ✖ / ✖ ✖ ✖

Distance: 11 nautical miles

Leaving: Le Diben — Arriving: Toul an Héry

Maps:
SHOM 7151
Navicarte 538
IGN 0615ET

Sea Kayaking Guide — Brittany

You can see all of Diben from the Customs cottage.

The Morlaix area

Locquirec

The heather coast (Côte des Bruyères) deserves its name.

THE ROUGH AND MAJESTIC headland of Primel is the gateway to this paddle. Interspersed with only a few sandy beaches, this coast is dominated by cliff faces with the rocks at their feet giving good rock hopping at low water. Between Beg an Fry and Locquirec the beaches start to gain the upper hand — and may give the chance of some surfing!

This coast is exposed to the wind and swell. Photo E. Julé

Launching, Landing and Parking:

Diben: slipway near the end of the harbour breakwater, large car park.
Primel-Trégastel beach: to avoid paddling around the headland in bad conditions, parking.
Moulin de la Rive beach: half-way between Beg an Fry and Locquirec, sandy beach, limited parking.
Locquirec Harbour: dries at low water, risk of breaking waves in the entrance.
Beg Douar, harbour of Plestin-les-Grèves: slipway in the north-west of the bay of Saint-Michel-en-Grève, parking.
Toul an Hery harbour (estuary of the Douron): difficult at low water, the tide goes out a long way.

Near the Pointe de Locquirec.

Arrange the shuttle to Toul an Héry and then leave from Diben at HW -4 (Roscoff) and paddle around the headland of Primel. This has strong currents and is the most tricky, but equally the most interesting, part of the paddle. It is a natural fortress marking the boundary between the Bay of Morlaix and the Heather Coast, and is topped with a standing stone and customs cottage. Skirt Primel beach and the bay of Saint-Jean-du-Doigt.

From this point on, high cliffs become the norm. The sea below is festooned in rocks, just perfect for rock-hopping if conditions are right. The cliffs are topped with bracken, brown in winter and bright green in summer; at other times of year, tinged purple by the heather, or splashed yellow by gorse and broom.

After rounding a small point, you are at Beg an Fry. There is a grassy picnic spot just up the track, where a monument commemorates the French Resistance in WW II. A Breton group the "Var" used this place to land allied agents and evacuate escapees. It is a lovely walk up the valley to the Trobodec restored water mill with its water wheel and internal machinery in working order. This area is owned by the Coastal Conservancy and grazed by

Rocky coastline at Beg an Fry.

The Morlaix area

Taking a break at Locquirec at mid-tide.

long haired Highland cattle to maintain the meadows. On the way back make a circuit along the cliff tops. The reward will be panoramic views towards Locquirec.

Between Beg an Fry and Locquirec there are some nice beaches, why not stop for a swim? The famous "CapLan and Co", much more than a book shop and publisher is to be found above the beach of Poul Rodou (the first beach east of Beg an Fry). You can browse the shelves of books, drink a coffee, buy Greek specialities, or eat Greek food and drink Retsina to your heart's content.

The next stage is around the rocky promontory of Locquirec. There is a sheltered landing just around the point if you need to take a break. Surf entering the bay can make for seething waters, once on the east side, stop just before the narrowest point of the inlet. The remains of the Hogolo Roman baths are near here, a unique site in Brittany. Upstream, the delightful harbour of Toul an Hery is always a calm spot.

Alternative: The estuary of the Douron, timed to paddle with the tide, is an enjoyable bad weather or beginners trip. ∎

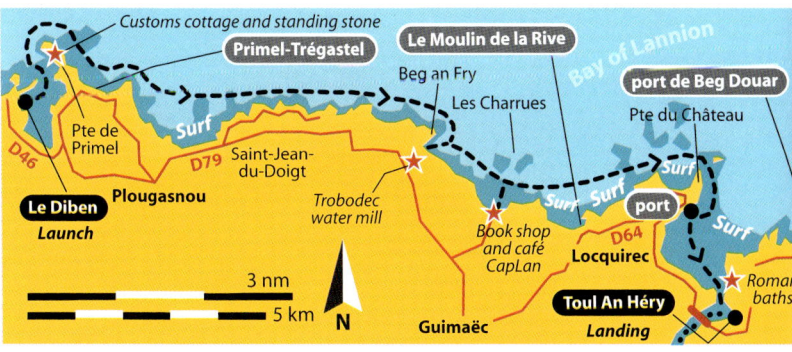

WEATHER, TIDE AND SAFETY

Watch out for the strong tides and exposed coast of the Primel headland. Except for Diben, surf may be encountered on all the beaches and landing spots. A long portage may be necessary at low water. The cliff sections can be dangerous in a heavy swell with a north wind. It would be possible to make this a return trip with a bivouac. Make use of the tidal flow, the eastbound flow starts at HW -5 and the westbound HW +1 (Roscoff), flows build up and ease off gradually. Beg an Fry can be a worthwhile destination from either Diben or Locquirec depending on the tide.

43 Trébeurden and Île Grande

Sea Kayaking Guide — Brittany

Difficulty: ✘ ✘ ✘ / ✘ ✘ ✘

Distance: 10 nautical miles

Leaving and Arriving: Trébeurden

Maps:
SHOM 7151 / 7152
Navicarte 538
IGN 07140T

Standing stone on the island of Losquet.

The Pink Granite Coast

Trébeurden

Old quarry on Île Grande.
Photo F. de Ravel

FROM THE DELIGHTFUL island of Millau, to the holiday honey-pot island of Île Grande, taking in the picture postcard beach of the small island of Molène, the islands lay a protective arm around Trébeurden. Outside, the sea can be calm, but could also be a furious mix of swell and strong tides. The water flooding over Les Peignes (the Combs) could prove a kayaker's Cape Horn.

Paddling past the rock "Le Corbeau" (The Crow).

Rock rose on Aganton.

Launching, Landing and Parking:

Trébeurden: 1) Slipway at the north entrance of the harbour, outside the breakwater, large parking area, but often congested; 2) Slipways south of the harbour, very busy, regulated parking.
Île Grande: 1) Slipway and beach at Port Gélen on the north of the island, very congested in summer with a sailing school; 2) Slipway at Saint-Sauveur, south of the island, usable HW +/-4, an extremely long portage at LW, limited parking.

The restored homestead and cromlech on the island of Millau overlook the sandy beach of Ile Molène.

Leave Trébeurden at HW -3 (Trébeurden=Roscoff +5 minutes), head south and through the narrow gap between the island of Millau and the mainland with the rock, Le Castel, in the middle. Follow the south side of the island, windswept and bleak, this can be rough with wind and reflected swell. The north coast is lush and green, land at the first slipway. It is worth walking up to look at the restored homestead and the chambered cairn. The island, now owned by the Coastal Conservancy, was a summer retreat for the fashionable of Paris.

Head north, skirting any rocks that stick out of the water. Aganton is joined to Île Grande at low water by a rock sill. This can be a rough spot, but if conditions look OK, paddle through and around the rocks of the point of Toul ar Staon, to land in the bay of Porz-Guen. Walk along the beach to the north-east where you can join the coastal footpath next to a statue of a quarry worker. To the south the footpath leads to lovely viewpoints, heading towards the village you pass a chambered cairn. Continuing another 800m along the coastal path leads to a an ornithological centre with an exhibition and bird hospital (LPO). During the 19th century, quarrying moved from the Chausey islands to this area. Île Grande was the main centre with camps for stone extraction on Morvil, Aganton, Losquet, Fougère and Renard. You can see the ruins of houses, quarries and quays all over the area, and the debris left from cutting them into regular blocks. The dressed stone was transported by barge to Île Grande.

A series of hops along the inside edges of Aganton, Losquet and Molène form the way back. The south coast of Aganton facing Losquet has some superb sheltered sandy

The Pink Granite Coast

beaches. Losquet was extensively quarried and was the site of a fake airfield built by the Germans to deceive Allied forces during WW II. Later it housed a 200m mast for transatlantic communications. Now owned by Coastal Conservancy, it has returned to a wild state. Molène is the most popular islet for a day on the beach. There may be space for you to stop and join the sunbathers for a while. Then it is straight back to Trébeurden.

Alternatives: Paddling back outside the islands can be exciting, a race forms over Les Peignes and swell breaks far out to sea when the tide is running. On a large spring tide it is possible to circumnavigate Île Grande. It is shallow near the road bridge onto the island, so aim to arrive there very close to HW. Once it starts to dry, the beach grows as fast as you can portage a kayak, you will have to run to catch up! ■

WEATHER, TIDE AND SAFETY

This is a sheltered paddle as long as you stay inside the islands. High water is the time to visit this area as it dries to a remarkable extent at low water. Breaking swell can close-out the channels between the islands as the tide drops. Tidal flow is mainly weak and variable inside the islands, but can be very strong over Les Peignes and in some of the channels. The sill between Aganton and Île Grande can be a good play spot (helmet recommended) on spring tides soon after it is covered by the flood tide (HW -3) especially if there is some swell against tide. The tide runs north-east from HW -4 (Roscoff) and south-west from +2, a large eddy forms to the south of the islands on the ebb tide.

44 Trégastel

Maps:
SHOM 7151 / 7152
Navicarte 538
IGN 07140T

Difficulty: ✗ ✗ ✗ / ✗ ✗ ✗

Distance: 7 nautical miles

Leaving and Arriving: Trégastel

A secret channel.

The Pink Granite Coast

Trégastel

Grève Blanche beach, Trégastel. Photo Y. Dodard

Launching, Landing and Parking:

Île Renote (a peninsula): (north of Trégastel) beach and large car park, a carry down over large rocks. It is possible to by-pass the height barrier if you only have boats on the roof and are not a camper van.

Trégastel: 1) Forum beach (Coz Porz), not very practical, crowded, a portage from the car park; 2) Grève Blanche beach, parking 50m away, "Rue du roi Arthur"; 3) Grève Rose beach, limited parking.

Landrellec Harbour: accessible at HW, long portage at mid-tide, marathon portage at LW.

Île Grande: slipway and beach at Port Gélen on the north of the island, very congested in summer with a sailing school, a good spot out of season.

VISIT TWO WORLDS during this paddle. The famous pink granite (*granite rose*) interspersed with chic beach resorts, followed by grey rock strands and pebbles as the geology changes. Exploring the island of Morvil gives a good idea of the wild nature this place can have.

Huge blocks of granite rose. *Photo Y. Dodard*

The island of Morvil, view west towards the radar dome.

Leave Île Renote at HW (Roscoff +15 minutes), this way you will be able to explore numerous narrow channels between the rocks and reach places inaccessible at low water. The rosy sand of the beach at Île Renote sets the tone for the first part of the paddle, the famous "Côte de Granite rose", the Pink Granite Coast, with its massive rocks eroded into strange forms.

Turn the corner and salute the massive square rock Le Dé (The Dice), it does look like a dice, balanced ready to throw. Amongst the other rocks (can you recognise the Witch, the Pile of Pancakes, the Turtles?), you can see the slipway by the "Forum" a modern sea water spa and aquarium whose construction on this beautiful coast was very controversial; paddle on.

After the next headland, dominated by the rock "King Gradlon" (a mythical early Christian Breton leader), is the Grève Blanche with its beach huts. The west end of the beach has suffered storm erosion. A tombolo links the beach with the Île aux Lapins (Rabbit Island) at mid-tide; you should be able to paddle over it. The next island, Île de Seigle (Rye Island) is cut into three at HW. Erosion gives the rocks a randomly pleated and fluted look. Île Tanguy

Tombolo, island of Renote.

The Pink Granite Coast

(Tangi in Breton; a Saint and also a common name) is a complete contrast with its trees and greenery, it marks a change in the scenery.

There is a change in the geology, lower and more fertile inland with plum orchards, bordered by black rocks. Offshore, haphazard piles of rocks look as if they are the result of recent erosion. In fact they are the debris of quarrying in the 19th century which completely altered the coastline, gnawing away at the islands to pave cities and towns. If the tide is still high enough, go and have a look at the charming harbour of Landrellec, hidden behind Île Plate (Flat Island). The large tidal area behind this island is often a moonscape of rocks and sand. Land on the south-west of the island of Morvil, below a ruin. It is worth exploring this island, fertile to the north, but eaten in two by quarrying to the south. On the way back everything will look different because the tide will be lower, it will be as if you were seeing it for the first time.

Alternative: Paddle on past Le Corbeau (The Crow) and visit Île Grande before turning back. ■

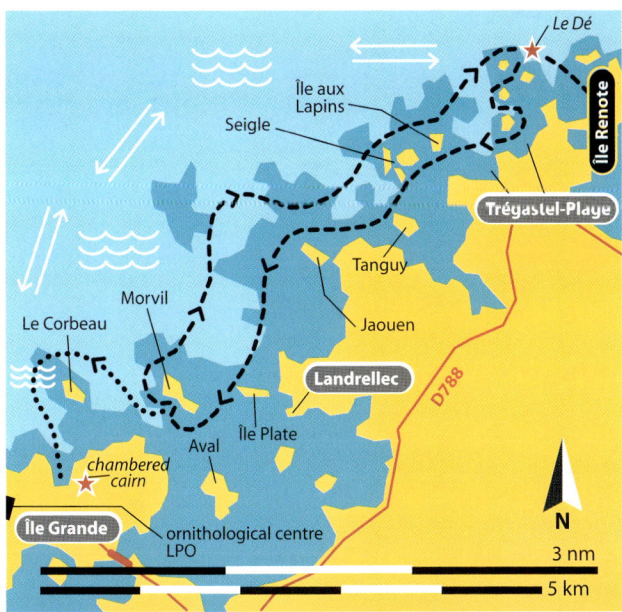

WEATHER, TIDE AND SAFETY

Sections of the paddle are exposed to the swell, especially between Île de Seigle and Île Morvil. Route finding can be difficult amongst the rocks. The tide runs quite strongly at mid-tide. The general flow is eastbound from HW -4 and westbound from HW +2 (Roscoff).

45

Pink Granite: La Côte de Granite Rose

Difficulty: ✘ ✘ ✘ / ✘ ✘ ✘

Distance: 7 nautical miles

Leaving and Arriving: Ploumanac'h

Maps:
SHOM 7152
Navicarte 537
IGN 0714OT

Cliffs near Porz Rolland.

The Pink Granite Coast

Ploumanac'h

Weird rocks line the shore.

GRANITE IS OFTEN thought of as a grey austere rock. Along here, apart from its warm orangey-pink colour, it evokes a whole menagerie of animals, any number of mythical figures and even everyday items. Pierced with windows, fluted, sometimes in precarious balance, no wonder it allows the imagination licence to wander. It is not so often that one paddles in a make-believe world. Rock dice, a castle of pink granite, a sweet little lighthouse, Men Ruz, and the three landmarks could illustrate a childhood story book.

Paddling near the rocks.

Launching, Landing and Parking:

Ploumanac'h harbour (sill 2.55m): 1) Slipway on the east side, sometimes congested, vehicle access only with permit, parking along the harbour side; 2) North-east slipway, limited parking, practical out of season.
Île Renote (a peninsula): (north of Trégastel) beach and large car park, a carry down over large rocks. It is possible to by-pass the height barrier.

Ploumanac'h lighthouse.

Launch from Ploumanac'h at HW -2, at the entrance of the harbour turn left and make your way through the chaotic maze of rock, sandy spits and channels of limpid water towards Trégastel. You will eventually arrive at the channel between the Île Renote peninsula and Costaérès Island. The fantasy mansion on the island was built at the end of the 19th century. The name *costaérès* in Breton means "the old drying place", a reference to its use for drying fish and seaweed in the more distant past. Have a look out at the open sea and check that the swell looks feasible for continuing. If it is too intimidating, exploring all the reaches of this sheltered bay makes a nice day out.

In front of you are the Sept Îles, the Seven Islands, (see paddle 46), head west and follow the coast around Île Renote, salute the improbably balanced square rock le Dé (the Dice), then turn back east towards the lighthouse of Men Ruz. Once past the lighthouse, take time to explore the inlets amongst the rocks one by one, starting with the one housing the lifeboat. When Perros-Guirec is in sight, look out for the end of the *granite rose* near the spectacular inlet of Porz Rolland. There is a sharp change in the geology, from the pink

Costaérès chateau.

The Pink Granite Coast

Kayaks on the sand. Photo D. Hottois

granite to the grey rock of Perros-Guirec. On the coastal footpath you can stand with one foot on the pink and one on the grey. This frontier marks the moment to turn back.

Paddling back with the tide now ebbing, enjoy the white water of swell breaking into surf over the rocks. Once past Men Ruz, take the channel in towards Ploumanac'h and turn into the beach of Saint-Guirec. The small monument, in the water or high and dry on the sand, according to the tide, shelters a statue of the saint. Local girls used to push a pin into the nose of the statue to predict if they were going to get married. If it stayed in place they would be married within the year, if not they would have a longer wait.

Paddle back into Ploumanac'h and enjoy the atmosphere of the harbour. ■

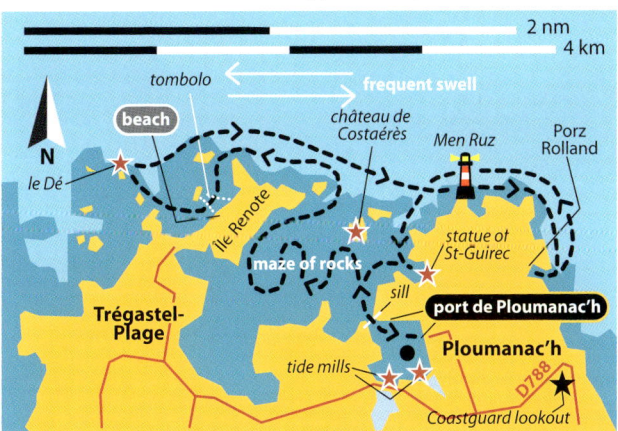

WEATHER, TIDE AND SAFETY

The tide runs at up to 3kt between Île Renote and Men Ruz, small races can form near Men Ruz around mid-tide. The general direction is eastbound from HW -4 and westbound from HW +2 (Roscoff). It is impossible to do this paddle at low water because the first part becomes dry land, and rocks and a tombolo close the passage between Île Renote and Le Gouffre. Swell is often a feature of the sea between Île Renote and the Sept Îles and can be very impressive, necessitating giving the rocks a wide berth. However, once clear of the rocks the sea drops into deep water without obstructions. A sill blocks the entrance to the harbour of Ploumanac'h at 2.55m above chart datum. It is possible, with some difficulty, to portage around this, but even the channel up this far is narrow, shallow and twisting at LW.

46 Les Sept Îles—The Seven Islands

Difficulty: ✗ ✗ ✗ / ✗ ✗ ✗

Distance: 7 nautical miles

Leaving and Arriving: Ploumanac'h

Maps:
SHOM 7152
Navicarte 537
IGN 0714OT

Beach on the Île des Maines with Île Bono in the background. Photo E. Julé

The Pink Granite Coast

Ploumanac'h

*A puffin.
Photo A. Audevard*

WIDE BLACK EYES are watching you, strident cries welcome you, swirling clouds of birds encircle and deafen you…you have reached the Seven Islands.

Savour the atmosphere and magic of the islands, islets and reefs, but respect nature.

Launching, Landing and Parking:

Ploumanac'h harbour (sill 2.55 m): 1) Slipway on the east side, sometimes congested, vehicle access only with permit, parking along the harbour side; 2) North-east slipway, limited parking, practical out of season.

Île Renote (a peninsula): (north of Tregastel) beach and large car park, a carry down over large rocks. It is possible to by-pass the height barrier.

Rouzic Arch. Photo P. Bisset

Rouzic.

Leave Ploumanac'h at HW -4 (Roscoff) and head north. It is worth consulting a detailed tidal atlas and doing the chart-work for the crossing. Slack water offshore is at HW -5 and at HW -4 it will be slack near the coast, but after taking an hour for the crossing, it will be eastbound at 2kts or even 3kts near the islands. Ferry glide to go west of the Île aux Moines (Monks' Island) and land on the north beach near the building called "La Caserne". If it proves difficult to make the ferry glide, land on the south side of the island near the passenger boat slipway.

Île aux Moines is the only permitted landing place in the archipelago. There are lots of points of interest, so it is worth going for a walk to see the lighthouse, the fort and the batteries, and of course the magnificent panoramic views. The footpaths are fringed with bracken and foxgloves. If you are quiet you will see one, two, half a dozen long-eared animals. With binoculars you can see seal pups on Île Plate in the springtime.

Back at the boats, paddle on past Île Bono and then Île Malban, which resembles a small volcano. Malban has a small colony of puffins nesting in burrows. In the 1930s they were hunted just for the fun of seeing them fall out of the sky! The few dozen pairs that are left are a small remnant of the thousands of that time.

From Malban to Rouzic, the tide sometimes eddies around as it is running north-south between the islands. A few gannets will soar past having a look at you, and then you are into the wheeling flocks around Rouzic. The entire north-east side of the island is a huge gannet colony, now estimated at 16,000 pairs. The nests

The Pink Granite Coast

are spreading into less favoured slopes due to population pressure. The first pairs appeared in the 1960s and the popularity of the island rapidly increased. Gannets spend all their time at sea unless breeding. You can rock-hop around the island looking at the wildlife, apart from the gannets there will be seals, razorbills, guillemots, shags and herring gulls.

Slackwater inside the archipelago is at HW +1 and starts westbound at HW +2. You can make use of the favourable tide to ferry glide down-tide back to Ploumanac'h. Before completing the crossing the westbound tide may have increased to exceed 2kts. Head for the obvious headland, by mid-crossing the lighthouse of Men Ruz will be clearly visible. Keep an eye open for brownish non-breeding skua (*labbe* in French), they live by forcing gannets to disgorge their catch and so are attracted to the area. They nest much further north and usually stay well offshore. ∎

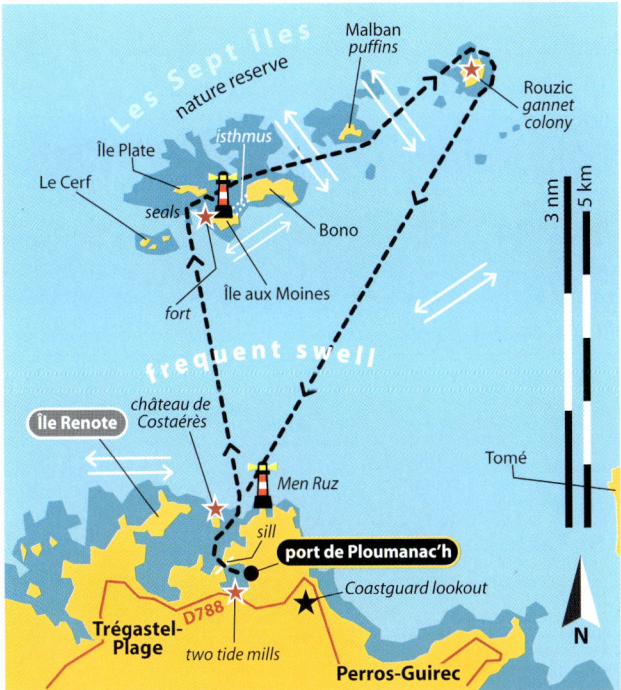

WEATHER, TIDE AND SAFETY

Swell is often to be found in this area, keep an eye open for rogue waves. Indications of the possible tidal flows are given in the description, but it is advisable to do your detailed chart-work for the crossings and work out the headings to paddle in advance. If you want a closer look at the nesting gannets, the bird observatory on Île Grande has close circuit television trained on nests from February to September. Do not be tempted to bivouac on Île aux Moines or anywhere in the archipelago. It is prohibited and conservation staff have the authority to issue spot fines and other penalties.

240 | Sea Kayaking Guide | **Brittany**

47

The Islands of Port Blanc

Difficulty: ✗ ✗ ✗

Distance: 6 nautical miles

Leaving and Arriving: Buguélès Harbour

Maps:
SHOM 7152
Navicarte 537
IGN 0714OT

A stop in the labyrinth of Port Blanc.

Around Paimpol 241

Port Blanc

Tide mill at Buguélès. Photo R. Bate

Amongst the rocks of Port Blanc. Photo E. Julé

A SERIES OF MASSIVE rocks mount guard over the coast of Port Blanc. Complex currents have created gravel spits and tombolos around them. Forming a complicated pattern of islands that protect the beautiful inshore lagoon. The water dwindles as the tide drops eventually becoming just a small pool in front of Port Blanc. An ever-shifting labyrinth to explore.

Launching, Landing and Parking:

Buguélès Harbour: slipway and large car park, it can be a long walk at low tide.

Port Blanc: 1) Slipway and beach facing Île aux-Femmes, small car park; 2) Sailing school slipway, large car park; 3) Slipway east of the light "Le Voleur", between Port Blanc beach and the bay of Pellinec, limited parking.

In the lagoon near Balanec. Photo L. Malthieux

The channel east of Saint-Gildas is open to mid-tide.

Leave Buguélès at HW -1 (Port Blanc=Roscoff +17 minutes) and head left into the lagoon. Take time to look at the tidal mill with its red roof, powered from a pool between Île Balanec and Île Ozach. Then head west.

The area before you get to Saint-Gildas is lovely and at high water you can explore around Île du Milieu to have a look at Île Iliec with its chateau. Rocks resembling a Japanese garden emerge from the lead you paddle through. The exit is a narrow opening in the gravel bars. This environment is in constant flux, gravel spits form and enclose the spaces between the islands, creating salt marshes, a sand bank, a patch of mud. It only needs the next storm to rearrange the pattern, creating channels where none existed before, a shifting patchwork of different habitats.

Some of the islands are left to run wild, others immaculately manicured; the serried houses on Balanec, jumbled cyprus trees on Milieu, the neat meadows on Saint-Gildas. Each year at Pentecost local people bring their horses to be blessed on Saint-Gildas, they cross at low tide from Buguélès following sunken causeways.

Back in the main lagoon, continue towards the west, Île des Femmes (Ladies Island) and Île du Château Neuf are less private and invite a landing, one has a handy tombolo to land on. A prominent navigation mark on Île du Château Neuf indicates the main access channel to the lagoon. This island takes its name from the castle-like rock on the east side.

Leave the lagoon, Île Tomé and the Sept Îles are on the western horizon, but turn back east. Follow the coast, enjoying the passages amongst the rocks, but

Around Paimpol

keep a weather-eye open, the water movements can be surprising. It is said that you need to watch at least 10 waves before taking a chance on a tight place. Even if you have been here several times it can be unrecognisable and disorienting as the rock walls disappear or emerge from the sea with the tide. The ringed plover makes its camouflaged nest on the gravel strands, don't land in the nesting season; you will tread on a nest or chicks before seeing them. If the tide is against you there are back eddies amongst the rocks to help you on your way. The channel into Buguélès is marked after Enez Inic, but you can often cut the corner. Arrival back at the slipway after a portage.

Alternatives: Continuing the paddle west to take in Île Tomé would make a long day out. There are nice white sand beaches on the way. Check your tidal planning. ■

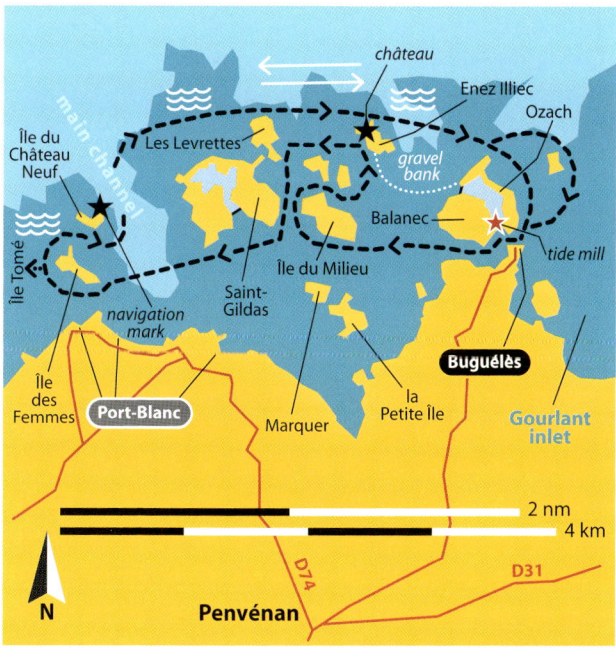

WEATHER, TIDE AND SAFETY

Much of the lagoon can be explored on foot at low water; make the paddle at high tide. Outside the islands the sea can be rough and confused around the rocks. The paddle could be made in either direction, but HW is good for the lagoon, the causeway to Balanec is the first spot to dry. Staying inside the lagoon would make an interesting beginners paddle.

On large spring tides an impressive race forms between Île des Femmes and the mainland at HW -3 to HW -1 especially if there is wind against tide (an easterly wind).

244 | Sea Kayaking Guide | **Brittany**

48 The Island of Er

Difficulty: ✗ ✗ ✗

Distance: 9 nautical miles

Leaving and Arriving: Plougrescant

Maps:
SHOM 7152
Navicarte 537
IGN 0814OT

The lagoon at low water

Around Paimpol   245

Plougrescant

Slipway at Beg ar Vilin.

Near the Pointe du Château at high water.

SOARING OVER a desert…the vast expanse of sand at low water between Plougrescant and the island of Er, punctuated by rocks like the Hoggar Mountains, an occasional oasis of greenery where some soil is retained on rocks above the tide mark, even a solitary tree. The IGN 1:25,000 zero contour line, indicating the tide height at mid-tide is a magical "open sesame" to help you find where the water lies. The tide transforms everything. In sunshine this has the air of a tropical paradise, with turquoise lagoons turning into rivers or even torrents with the rhythm of the tides. Once the tide falls it is time to explore this hidden landscape on foot.

Launching, Landing and Parking:

Plougrescant: 1) Slipway at Beg ar Vilin, parking beside a camp-site, very busy in summer; 2) Porz-Hir (Kericu) slipway, beach and parking.

La Roche Jaune: quay beside the Jaudy, limited parking, nice bar, the "Café Pesked".

East side of the Jaudy estuary (only near HW, HW +/-2): 1) Port Beni, beach and limited parking; 2) Port la Chaine, pebble beach, near the lighthouse facing Île Blanche, a lovely spot, but not ideal for launching.

Kayaks equipped with sails waiting for the tide in the lagoon.
Photo E. Ollivier

Leave from the slipway at Beg ar Vilin at HW -3 (local HW=Paimpol -20 minutes). Leave Île Loaven on your right and paddle north, the tide will be running against you, but by keeping inshore it is possible to keep out of it. Pass in front of Porz Hir (Kericu), shortly after this is the headland of Pointe du Château.

The open sea can be calm in good weather; however, wind, swell, breakers, tidal movements and the temptation to go rock hopping can create traps for the unwary. A local expression says; *"enfer de Plougrescant et paradis de Port Blanc"*; "hell at Plougrescant and heaven at Port Blanc". If conditions are good, enjoy paddling along the shore, but keep an eye open for rogue waves.

From its back and from the sea, the famous Castel Meur, "house in the rocks", shows only a glimpse to the elements. This has become the image of Brittany, so much so that the owners now have an injunction to prevent commercial use of photographs without permission. Nearby a visitor centre has exhibitions about the Gouffre nature reserve. The Gouffre comprises the high cliffs on the headland, a particularly wave-swept spot. Impressive to see in a storm.

Turn around and head back towards the northern point of the island of Er. Just before this point, a beach makes a good stopping place. Circle the island clockwise, in good conditions the granite sentinels, standing bravely against the waves, make fine play spots. A seal may be basking on its rock, let it sleep.

The north east of the island is equally exposed with plenty of rocks to avoid. Just before passing the very prominent navigation mark "Men Noblance", land

Around Paimpol

to look at the view; a panorama of the estuary and mouth of the Jaudy and the Sauvage peninsula, tipped by the long Sillon de Talbert. The island is only 50m wide here, so you can walk across to appreciate its crescent shape. Continue the circumnavigation, once past the southern point, take the channel up between Er and la Petite Île, this leads into a tranquil lagoon. Land to appreciate this exceptional spot: wild but welcoming. The islands are private but the owners manage them to preserve their wild nature.

Watch the tide! At HW +2 get on the water again, turn la Petite Île by the north and return, zigzagging between the higher ground as it emerges from the sea. Île Loaven and then Beg ar Vilin are your landmarks.

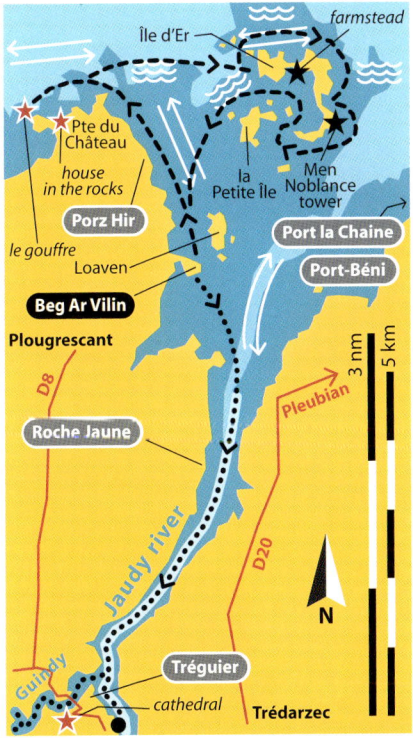

Alternatives: Explore the Jaudy estuary, HW at Tréguier is about 5 minutes later than at the mouth, it is possible to land just downstream of the marina to go and see the Cathedral and central square. The Guindy is also worth paddling and much longer than it looks if all the meanders are straightened out! The 17th century aqueduct, built to bring water to Tréguier is at its head. ∎

WEATHER, TIDE AND SAFETY

The tide goes out a long way between Er and the mainland, anticipate the rapid drying and don't get caught. Tidal streams can be fast…local rivers in the sea…, a northerly wind or swell combined with the shallow waters can cause heavy seas outside of la Petite Île. Take care on the headland of Pointe du Château, avoid the ebb tide as an incident can rapidly escalate as you are carried west out to sea or into the breaking waves around the outlying rocks. In bad weather, stay in sheltered water, in good conditions this is a single X grade paddle.

248 | Sea Kayaking Guide | **Brittany**

49

The Sillon de Talbert and Les Héaux

Difficulty: ✖ ✖ ✖ or ✖ ✖ ✖ / ✖ ✖ ✖

Distance: 5 or 13 nautical miles

Leaving and Arriving: Loguivy

Maps:
SHOM 7152 / 7153
Navicarte 537
IGN 0814OT

Les Héaux lighthouse. Photo E. Louet.

Around Paimpol

Loguivy

Bivouac on one of the islets at the end of the Sillon.

FROM THE SHELTERED estuary of the Trieux towards a reef far out to sea, watched over by the lighthouse of Les Héaux. As this trip develops it becomes more and more interesting. The Sillon de Talbert divides it into two; inside, calm water and shallow seas becoming a vast moonscape as the tide drops, outside, rocks, swell and the sometimes capricious channel of La Gaine.

A seal near Les Héaux lighthouse.
Photo R. Bate

Launching, Landing and Parking:

Loguivy: 1) Roc'h Hir (on the left; sand, on the right; gravel) parking 150m away up the hill, very congested in summer; 2) Further east, slipway in the bay of Gouern (locally pronounced Le Ouern) (camping), only accessible at HW +/-3, parking near the road; 3) Pointe de Traou Plat, (or signposted Beg Nod), between Loguivy and L'Arcouest, parking.

The currents sculpt the landscape of the Sillon.
Photo E. Louet

Bouchots *sheltered by the Sillon. Photo P. Mallard*

Option 1: Leave at HW -1 (Paimpol) from the beach of Roc'Hir. Cross the Trieux channel towards the Île à Bois. This is really a peninsula and in its dense undergrowth hides no less than 46 pillboxes of different types, some even converted into holiday homes. The Trieux was so strategic during WW II that the Germans thought of closing the entire estuary with chains.

The channel around the Île à Bois is a lovely place, it is worth paddling into the anse of Pommelin, completely sheltered and very attractive. At its head is the mouth of a small stream, a spot simply called "Le Paradis" (Paradise). Follow the succession of small bays towards the north-east, the island of Coalen has a chambered cairn, now part submerged, on the beach.

From the top of the island a panoramic view covers; Île à Bois, Île Modez, and the Sillon de Talbert. All of this area dries at low water, it is even possible to walk out to Île Modez. On the mainland opposite the island is the chapel of the Bonne-Nouvelle (Good News). Take the same route back to Loguivy.

Option 2: Leave at HW +3 (Paimpol), take the same course as option one, but don't linger, head straight north. Past the buildings of the seaweed processing works (*Centre d'Étude et de Valorisation des Algues – CEVA*), skirt the end of the Sillon Noir and then the Sillon de Talbert, passing over barely covered rocks and sand banks. From the end of the Sillon de Talbert, the normal route is to follow the rocky islands of Olonne and Roc'h Louet out to the north-east.

Around Paimpol

251

This can be a tricky area with currents between the unevenly arranged gravel banks. If the breaking swell permits, head north inside the last islet; Sark.

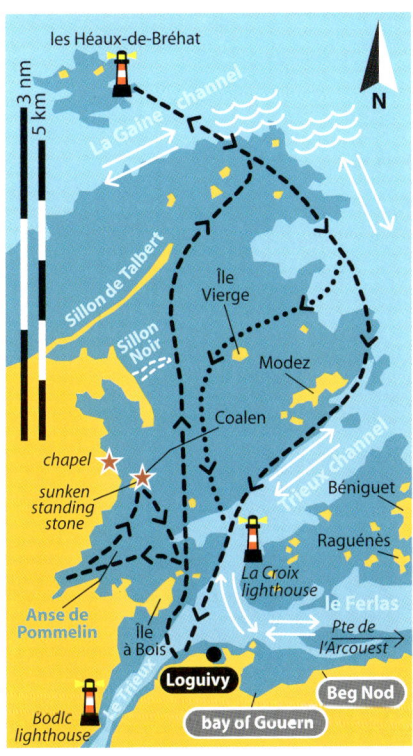

You are at the edge of the Gaine channel, there might be swell and strong currents. If conditions allow, ferry glide out to Les Héaux, the lighthouse is your guide. A small beach on the east of the rocks allows landing. There is a chaotic landscape of rock to surmount before reaching the foot of the lighthouse and the ruins of cottages used by the construction workers. Seals use the rocks for giving birth in spring, so do not wander around and disturb them.

Use the flood tide for the paddle back, east of Île Modez is a superb maze of rocks, there is a lagoon near the Trusques rocks; the island is private.

Return to Loguivy making use of the tide running up the Trieux channel, skirt the lighthouse La Croix, keep west of the sea-marks, the Vincre and the Vieille to arrive back.

Alternative: Use the tide and paddle to the west of Île Modez, it can be hard to find the way through, but it gets easier as the tide rises, this is a more leisurely course and just watch how fast the tide advances over the desert sands. ■

WEATHER, TIDE AND SAFETY

There is a serious risk of being left stranded by the dropping tide if the timetable given is not followed. Stay vigilant and practice a good ferry glide. Île Coalen; access only possible near HW. Crossing the Gaine can be exciting, the tide runs east from HW -6 (Paimpol) and west from HW (Paimpol). The tide in the Trieux is inbound from HW -6 and outbound from HW.

The view of islets and rocks from Saint-Michel's hill on Bréhat, Birlot tide mill in the foreground. Photo C. Magré

Learn more

The Bréhat Archipelag

You are hiking in a rocky, dissected Breton landscape. A magic spell means that the earth stays still, but the footpaths rise and fall to the height of a two storey building every six hours. No finger posts, no colour coded paint marks such as you find on the marked paths of Europe, no one to ask the way. Rocks in such bizarre formations that you turn your head at every step, interspersed with sensuous smooth curving virgin sand banks…it would lead you on forever.

It is the land of metamorphosis. Normally, views change as you move; here it is the scenery that transforms itself in front of your eyes. A strong tide race, there only a moment ago, calms itself and reverses. Sharp rocks barring your passage become an open stretch of water. That wide channel has become a labyrinth of narrow passages. The lighthouse, once so tall, shrinks and sets behind the rocks. The sky joins in, changing the lighting from one moment to another, colours brighten and fade, change hue. It all adds to the magic.

Imagine designing an ideal sea kayakers' planet for Antoine de Saint-Exupéry's Little Prince, everyone would have their own ideas about what would make it perfect, never the less there would be many things in common. One thing would be to never have to return by the same route.

Around Paimpol

Another would be challenging paddling for any level of kayaker. Bréhat is close to the ideal, it is also special and unique like the Prince's rose.

The tide washes around Bréhat and you can follow it around, never retracing your steps. You want some demanding rock-hopping; the north coast is just the place, with some swell to give it added zest. However, the long bank of the Sillon de Talbert serves as protection from excessively wild seas. You like playing in tide races; the north-east corner on a big tide is just the spot. Drifting dreamily on calm water more your scene; La Chambre, well named "the Bedroom", will fit the bill. Love limpid transparent water; behind Île Modez as far as the Sillon de Talbert, yellow sand is interspersed with brown and green weed, dark rocks and shiny shells. Jumping fish punctuate the voyage. Food for free on the agenda; shellfish, shrimps and crabs, just choose low water. Need to stretch your legs; Île Verte, Île Coalen and the footpath on Bréhat between the landmark of Rosédo, and the lighthouse Le Paon (The Peacock), offer lovely walks. Bad weather; there are always sheltered paddles in the welcoming estuary of the river Le Trieux.

Then once back on land there are the old salts beside their fishing boats moored in the harbours, fish markets selling local catches and of course the sea front seafarers' bars. ∎

Learn more

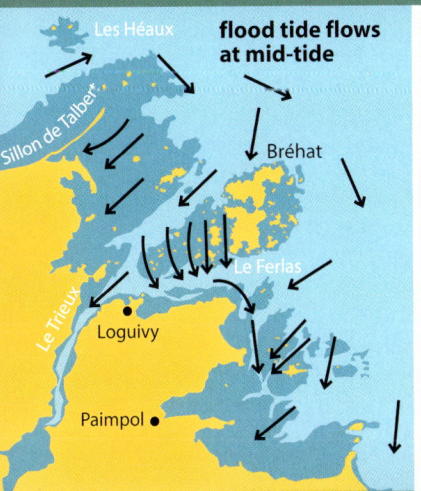

The tides around Bréhat.

The tide offshore is flowing from west to east offshore during the flood tide. This flow from the west divides into two southerly flows around Bréhat. The flows amongst the archipelago rotate anti-clockwise and finally reverse as the tide starts to ebb and the offshore flow becomes east to west. The tide is felt in the estuary of Le Trieux as far as Pontrieux.

254 | Sea Kayaking Guide | **Brittany**

50

The Rocky South West of Bréhat

Difficulty: ✘ ✘ ✘ / ✘ ✘ ✘

Distance: 8 nautical miles

Leaving and Arriving: Loguivy

Maps:
SHOM 7152 / 7153
Navicarte 537
IGN 0814OT

The lighthouse of La Croix (The Cross) is painted white on the seaward side but remains natural stone on the Trieux side.

Around Paimpol

Loguivy

THE LIGHTHOUSE of La Croix stands guard over the scattering of rocks like a comet's tail to the south west of Bréhat, washed by strong currents at mid-tide with passages opening up and closing all the time. It is very easy to get lost, but sooner or later you will end up in one of the three main channels that define this small world: the channel of Trieux, that of Kerpont and finally the channel of Ferlas. Rocks awash, bare rocks, rocks with a tuft of green vegetation, what defines an island?

Launching, Landing and Parking:

Loguivy: 1) Roc'h Hir (on the left; sand, on the right; gravel) parking 150m away up the hill, very congested in summer; 2) Further east, slipway in the bay of Gouern (locally pronounced Le Ouern) (camping), only accessible at HW +/-3, parking in the road; 3) Pointe de Traou Plat, (or signposted Beg Nod), between Loguivy and L'Arcouest, parking.
L'Arcouest: huge parking area on the grassy slopes for tourists heading for the ferry to Bréhat, on the left about 200m before L'Arcouest. Paying in summer. Height barrier 2m. Parking outside the barrier as well, but a longer walk to the sea.

The rocks of Bréhat at low water.

Sunset from the beach at Roc'h Hir.

Leave from Roc'h Hir, Loguivy at HW +1. The port, despite the uncertain future of fishing, has been renovated, but still keeps its roots with the sea-dogs of old. If it takes your fancy, set off with them in mind and paddle with the tide north-east. Leave the two navigation marks, La Vieille (The Old Lady) and Le Vincre (The Victor) to your right and head towards La Croix lighthouse. Leave the lighthouse to port and go between it and some rocks, Les Agneaux (The Lambs), then Les Trois Îles.

The next island, Île Verte (Green Island) has lost the old pine tree on its summit that served as a landmark, but a new one is growing, land on the gravel beach on the south side. The island is managed by The Glénans Sailing School and if they are there, ask permission to walk around, there is a superb view. The south-east of the island has the remains of a very ancient port.

Continue to follow the Trieux channel seaward, or dodge in and out of the rocks, it is up to you. The whole area becomes a lunar landscape at low water. Once past this area, head for the coastguard lookout on Bréhat. From here you have two options: 1) Exploration by land, land on the beach near the entrance of La Corderie bay and walk north-eastward to the white landmark of Rosédo, this is the wildest coast of Bréhat; 2) By sea, explore the bay of La Corderie, at HW it is possible to portage the narrow isthmus to the east coast of the island.

Turn southward through the channel Le Kerpont, Bréhat on the left and Béniguet on the right. Numerous back eddies on the Bréhat side make it easy to go against the tide. You pass the Birlot tide mill, then an old lifeboat ramp and a little

Around Paimpol 257

beach where you can land. A footpath leads upwards to the chapel of Saint-Michel and a lovely view. You might have to force your way through the bushes. Continue south, it is possible to stop at a slipway and have a look at the fort, now a glass works.

Once in Le Ferlas channel, head west, skirting Raguénès. This island's fine beach makes a nice spot to stop. The ebb tide will help you, but each gap between the islands has a north-easterly current, you will need to do a succession of ferry glides. Just before arriving, cross Le Ferlas at an angle back to Loguivy with its moored fishing boats and live-fish tanks in the market. To finish off this lovely paddle, why not have a drink at "Chez Gaud", the sailors' bar. ∎

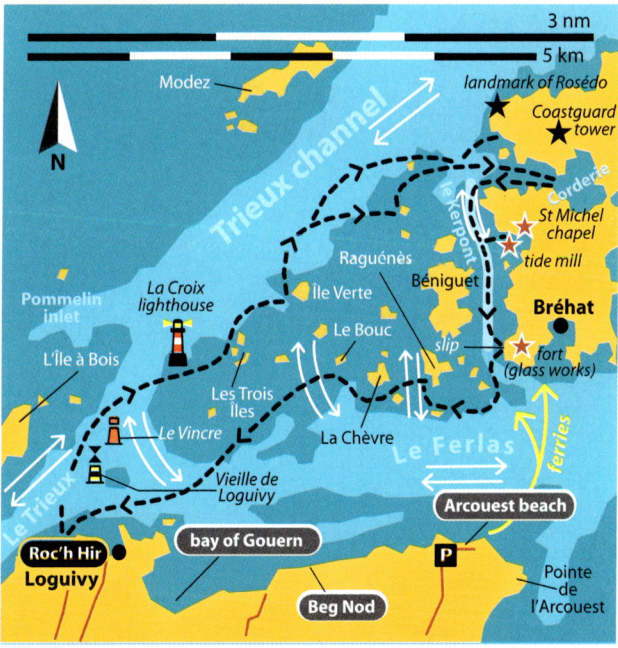

WEATHER, TIDE AND SAFETY

This stretch of water encourages and is excellent for random exploration, but some areas dry at low water. Points to watch; currents, keeping track of where you are and other traffic. The flood tide would allow doing the paddle in the opposite direction, but a short portage might be necessary on low spring tides as the Kerpont channel does dry in one place. For tides see the information pages on the Bréhat archipelago.

Sea Kayaking Guide — **Brittany**

51 Circumnavigating Bréhat

Difficulty: ✗ ✗ ✗ / ✗ ✗ ✗

Distance: 7.5 nautical miles

Leaving and Arriving: L'Arcouest

Maps:
SHOM 7152 / 7153
Navicarte 537
IGN 0814OT

The lighthouse of Le Paon (the Peacock). Photo C. Magré

Around Paimpol

Loguivy

The island of flowers.
Photo C. Magré

Birlot tide mill in Le Kerpont channel.
Photo H. Le Flohic

BRÉHAT, THE ISLAND of flowers and four distinct faces. On the west, Le Kerpont channel with its rocky archipelago; to the north a maze of granite walls with foam filled passages under the watchful eye of Le Paon lighthouse. On the east, La Chambre, an inland sea, the tide running quietly through numerous channels amongst the rocks. Then the south with its supernatural lighting reflecting the ochres and golds of its rocks and sand.

Launching, Landing and Parking:

Loguivy: 1) Roc'h Hir (on the left; sand, on the right; gravel) parking 150m away up the hill, very congested in summer; 2) Further east, slipway in the bay of Gouern (locally pronounced Le Ouern) (camping), only accessible at HW +/-3, parking in the road; 3) Pointe de Traou Plat, (or signposted Beg Nod), between Loguivy and L'Arcouest, parking.
L'Arcouest: huge parking area on the grassy slopes for tourists heading for the ferry to Bréhat, on the left about 200m before L'Arcouest. Paying at a hut in summer. Height barrier 2m. Parking outside the barrier as well, but a longer walk to the sea.

The north coast of Bréhat is a rock hopper's paradise.

Launch at HW +4.30 from L'Arcouest, cross Le Ferlas channel and follow Le Kerpont channel into the archipelago. To the right an old lifeboat ramp and a tiny bay, have a brief stop if necessary. Half a mile further on, a loving restored tide mill in working order, water stored at HW is run out from the lake behind the mill to turn its wheels. Above the mill, the neat Saint-Michel chapel, on the highest point of the island, offers superb views. Béniguet is a private island with holiday accommodation. Where Le Kerpont channel joins the Trieux channel, wind over tide can raise breaking waves, the bay of La Corderie (the rope maker), the old port of Bréhat, is a good place for a stop.

Once beyond the white landmark of Rosédo, check again if the conditions are suitable for the circumnavigation. From here to Le Paon the tide is not strong, but swell and reflected waves can raise white-water. Enjoy the rock hopping, but keep a weather-eye on the waves and swell. The coast becomes more and more rugged as the lighthouse approaches. From here, far out to sea, the lighthouse on the Horaine rocks, is visible. Four submerged tidal turbines were installed out there in 2012, at a depth of 35m, generating power for 3,000 homes from the 3kt flows.

The tide will carry you between the rocks and the lighthouse, but watch out for the water movements, this corner of the island catches the tide. Landing is possible on the hidden stony beach south of the island Ar-Morbic. You have two choices from here, depending on the state of the sea and tide: 1) Continue around the outside of the archipelago in the swell, three white landmarks on the islets of Ar-Morbic, Roc'h

Around Paimpol

Louet and Quistillic, will guide you around; 2) Explore La Chambre (the Bedroom) a sheltered anchorage inside the islets, by extension this name is used for all the sheltered east side of the Bréhat. Some spots dry at mid-tide and it becomes something of a labyrinth of islets. Head southwards as well as you can. Stopping in a small bay gives access to the attractive village centre.

At the southern entrance of La Chambre, the two routes come together again. Enjoy the form and colours of the south coast, reminiscent of the French Riviera. Paddle along past the navigation mark Men Joliguet and Port Clos (watch out for the ferries shuttling across between L'Arcouest and Bréhat) and once opposite Raguénès, cross the channel back to the start.

Alternatives: The area around Île Ar Morbic is a good play spot at mid-tide on springs. Go in a group, the flood tide offers a better chance of finding respite near the east coast of Bréhat if it picks up too much. ■

WEATHER, TIDE AND SAFETY

Study the tides around Bréhat before leaving. It is best to pass the Paon lighthouse with the tide or near slack water. It can be surprisingly hard to find your way in La Chambre. The circumnavigation can be made in either direction to fit in with the tides. Port Clos is very busy with ferries, avoid trying to land there.

52 | The Trieux Estuary

Difficulty: ✗ ✗ ✗

Distance: 16 nautical miles

Leaving and Arriving: Loguivy

Maps:
SHOM 7152
Navicarte 537
IGN 0814OT

The Château de la Roche Jagu dominates the Trieux.

Around Paimpol

The "Maison de l'Estuaire" is a visitor centre exploring the flora and fauna.

THE TRIEUX ESTUARY penetrates far inland. Up to the port and bridge of Lézardrieux it has a strong marine atmosphere. Above the bridge there is a wide expanse of shallow water.

The rail enthusiast will enjoy the sight, sound and smell of the Paimpol steam railway which skirts the banks as far as Pontrieux. Higher still, the narrow water course is squeezed tightly between the steeply wooded sides of the valley, crowned by the Château de la Roche Jagu.

Launching, Landing and Parking:

Loguivy: 1) Roc'h Hir (on the left; sand, on the right; gravel) parking 150m away up the hill, very congested in summer; 2) Further east, slipway in the bay of Gouern (locally pronounced Le Ouern) (camping), only accessible at HW +/-3, parking in the road; 3) Pointe de Traou Plat, (or signposted Beg Nod), between Loguivy and L'Arcouest, parking.

Lézardrieux: municipal campsite at Kermarquer, west bank above the bridge, direct access to the water.

La Roche Jagu: west bank, slipway and parking below the Chateau.

Pontrieux: below the weir, very tidal, access only near HW, parking.

Frinandour: below the railway viaduct, north bank of the Leff, access only near HW, parking.

Roc'h Hir beach.

Leave the beach at Roc'h Hir at HW +3 (Paimpol) and paddle close to the Roche aux Oiseaux, this offers an superb viewpoint if you scramble up to it, after this there are a series of attractive inlets. On the west bank, just before the Coatmer navigation light there is a ruined tide mill. On the east side is a Glénans Sailing School centre and traditional sailing boats (gréements) on their moorings. The port of Lézardrieux is on the west bank after passing Brassens' beach (Brassens was a 1950s French singer famous for songs with a dark humour but bouncy rhythm). Lézardrieux is famous for its yacht marinas, but also a port for sand and gravel dredgers. The tide can run fast under the lovely metal bridge at Lézardrieux creating a play spot.

The river then opens into a wide expanse of water called the Lédano. This is mainly shallow over mud banks, the main channel runs near the west bank. The municipal camp-site of Kermarquer has direct access to a beach on the west bank a couple of hundred metres above the bridge. Depending on the tide, it may be possible to land near Camarel about 1km further on to have a look at the chapel of Goz Illiz. As the banks draw in, a small creek leads to the tide mill of Traou Meur. The river is now in a steep sided, tree-lined valley. The steam railway runs along half way up the slopes on the east bank. After two gentle meanders, a wooden landing stage allows a stop to

The port of Kerblouc'h far up the Trieux.

Around Paimpol

visit the Maison Seznec. This is now a visitor centre with an exhibition about the flora and fauna of the area. In 1923 it was the scene of a murder mystery, unsolved to this day. Guillaume Seznec was sentenced to transportation after the crew of a dredger, waiting for the tide, heard shots at the remote house. However, the body of the victim was never found. Seznec returned to France in 1947 but was pushed under a lorry. A skull was said to have been found in the mud of the river in 1953. In 2001 the case was re-opened, but vital evidence had been removed from the file.

Around the next bend, the high point of the trip: the magnificent Chateau of Roche Jagu dominates the river high on the slopes overlooking a sharp bend. The original building dates from the 15th century, it is the only remnant of the 10 fortresses that used to defend and control the river. The Great Storm of 1987 led to the rediscovery of the old ramparts and gardens, allowing restoration of delightful terraces overlooking the river. It currently houses exhibitions and hosts cultural events. Enjoy looking around. Then take the tide back to Loguivy.

Alternatives: There are two possible continuations of the paddle; 1) Continue up the Trieux to the harbour at Goas Vilinic, 2km below Pontrieux, which has a camp-site beside the river. From Roche Jagu this is an extra 4 miles there and back; 2) From the railway viaduct at Frinandour (a lovely spot) paddle up the Leff as far as the road bridge le Houel, this is an extra 7 miles there and back. ∎

WEATHER, TIDE AND SAFETY

It is easy to plan alternative trips or to do the paddle in stages. The tide running under the bridge at Lézardrieux forms turbulence and boils, on a spring tide with wind against tide it can be a tricky spot. A strong wind running up or down the river can make this a long trip, consider a one way trip with a shuttle.

266 | Sea Kayaking Guide | **Brittany**

53 Porz Even and the Island of St-Rion

Difficulty: ✗ ✗ ✗ / ✗ ✗ ✗

Distance: 8 nautical miles

Leaving and Arriving: Porz Even

Maps:
SHOM 7152 / 7154
Navicarte 537
IGN 0814OT

Saint-Rion beach, view of the Mez du Goëlo.

Around Paimpol

The houses of Saint-Rion.

THE PRETTY ISLAND of Saint-Rion is worked by a farmer; a mix of potatoes and pasture. Facing it on the mainland a mile away is Porz Even. The bucolic scene echoes those of the other farmers, those who work the sea; their fields the oyster beds, their stock the oysters. They can only tend to their stock when the tide is out. All the way to Bréhat, low water reveals a world of sand, stones and seaweed, a moonscape to be explored.

Launching, Landing and Parking:

Ploubazlanec, Porz Even: 1) To the south, a large slipway reserved for commercial fishermen, a barrier prevents vehicle access; 2) Nearby a small slipway leads down to the foreshore, parking only possible in a few visitors parking places; 3) 150m to the east, beach and slipway, parking near the *viviers* (live-fish tanks), take care not to get in the way of the oyster farmers.

To make the paddle in the opposite direction: L'Arcouest: huge parking area on the grassy slopes for tourists heading for the ferry to Bréhat, on the left about 200m before L'Arcouest. Paying at a hut in summer. Height barrier 2m. Parking outside the barrier as well, but a longer walk to the sea.

Fishing boats in Porz Even at high water.

View from the top of Saint-Rion.

Launch from Porz Even at HW +4 (Paimpol) and paddle east across to the island of Saint-Rion. The beach on the south-west is a fine landing spot from which one can enjoy the low-lying landscape, the restored old village and the neighbouring islands of Mez de Goëlo. These islands, extending from the headland of Plouézec mark the limit of the Bay of Saint-Brieuc. Skirt the lovely southern shore of the island where a wall of dressed stone is topped with a tuft of grass or the silhouette of a horse. From the east point, the current will be running north. Ferry glide from rock to rock towards the Roho rocks, where a tiny beach is exposed as the tide drops.

Let yourself be carried north-west by the ebb tide, the tide runs strongly in every little channel, hop your way through the sand bars to Île Blanche (White Island), the northern limit of the shallow waters. From here Bréhat is clearly in view. Return keeping more to the west, passing the headland of l'Arcouest. This was home to many prominent academics including at least four Nobel prize winners, notably Pierre and Marie Curie.

Exploration on foot reveals more of the intertidal zone, its moonscape of rocks and sand washed into spits and tombolos looking devoid of life. Of course it is exactly the opposite if you look care-

Landing in the seaweed.

Around Paimpol

fully: this is one of the most diverse and busy habitats on Earth. A few steps away, evidence of man and the harsh life at sea; the Croix des Veuves (Widows' Cross) where the wives and daughters of fishermen went to pray for the safe return of their loved ones…and in the cemetery at Plouazlanec, the "Mur des Disparus en Mer" (Wall for those Lost at Sea) a memorial for those fishermen who never came back. Porz Even is one of the places which inspired French author Pierre Loti who wrote the novel *An Icelandic Fisherman* published in 1886. This portrays the harsh life of Breton fishermen who sailed each summer to the stormy seas of the Icelandic and Greenland fishing grounds.

Take care to avoid the oyster beds on the way back, and don't get in the way of the commercial fishermen as you portage back to the car. ■

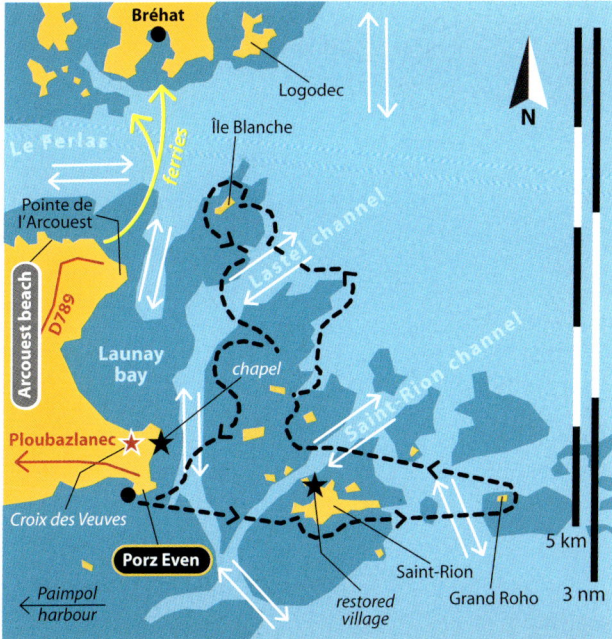

WEATHER, TIDE AND SAFETY

The problems: finding your way at low water and using the currents.
This paddle can also be made in the opposite direction. It is less interesting around HW because the lunar landscape is submerged.

54 The Cliffs of Bréhec

Difficulty: ✗ ✗ ✗

Distance: 14 nautical miles

Leaving and Arriving: Bréhec

Maps:
SHOM 7152 / 7154
Navicarte 536
IGN 0814OT

Bréhec Bay at high water.

Around Paimpol

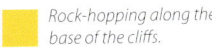

Rock-hopping along the base of the cliffs.

THÉODORE BOTREL, a well known Breton singer and songwriter around 1900, sang *"J'aime Paimpol et sa falaise"* (I love Paimpol and its cliff), apart from the harbour café called "La Falaise" there are no cliffs at Paimpol; however, only a few miles south, the cliffs of Bréhec are something to sing about. This stretch of coast has much to offer the kayaker; picturesque harbours, beaches of blue pebbles, the cliffs, rock-hopping and natural shelter. The long distance path GR34 which runs along the top of the cliffs offers another perspective if you don't want to paddle.

Iron rich rocks and blue pebbles.

Launching, Landing and Parking:

Port Lazo: south of the bay of Paimpol, suitable for doing the paddle in the opposite direction, the beach dries rapidly as the tide drops.

North of Bréhec: Porz Pin beach, a shingle beach, risk of dumping surf at high water, parking, portage.

Bréhec Harbour: slipway, sheltered beach and parking, can be congested.

Vieux Bréhec slipway: just south of Bréhec below the Tamaris camp-site, parking, slipway to beach, beach exposed to swell.

South of Bréhec: Bonaparte beach and Port Moguer harbour, two launch sites, susceptible to swell.

A fulmar soaring stiff winged. Photo A. Audevard

Leave Bréhec harbour at HW -4.30 (Paimpol) and head north-east. The flood tide will be strongly against you off each headland, but back eddies will make for easy paddling in each bay. The cliffs of schist, greywacke and sandstones have spectacular folding and are very varied all along the paddle. Sea birds, especially fulmars, recognisable by their grey colour and stiff wings nest along the cliffs. It is even possible to see the small tubes on top of their beaks used to expel excess salt, as they soar close to the kayak. This coast is good for rock-hopping, before Porz Pin, the rock strata have resulted in several long thin gulleys. Porz Pin with its steep beach of blue pebbles is a good place for a break. As you paddle along the cliffs, look out for tiny meadows amongst the crags where they used to cut hay. They sometimes look almost impossible to access.

The Pointe du Minard marks the limit of the bay of Saint-Brieuc and the tide swirls past, keep close in to avoid the flow, but watch out for anglers, this is a favourite spot. The next long bay, with its little beach of Porz Donan leads to the headland of Plouézec and the islands of Mez de Goëlo, which are the southern limit of the bay of Paimpol. The rock and lighthouse of L'Ost-Pic lie just off the further island. Strong currents run in the channels between the islands, sometimes giving standing waves. Having had a close look at L'Ost-Pic, turn back south, the tide will be in your favour and will help you rapidly back along the coast. Paddle straight past Bréhec, two miles further on is the harbour of Gwin Zegal, (rye whisky in Breton) protected by a peninsula of jagged rocks. The moorings are made of entire tree trunks, roots and all, replanted in the rocks, this technology was introduced by Irish missionaries in the Middle Ages.

Around Paimpol

Turn back, if you are tempted to paddle out to look at the bird rock "la Mauve", take care to ferry glide back, the tide runs strongly here. Follow the shore to keep out of the tide, past Port Moguer and then the lovely Bonaparte beach. This was famously used by the French Resistance during WW II. The resistance group "Shelburn" from Plouha organised the nocturnal escape of 135 allied airmen during 1944. If the tide is now high enough, you will be able to enter some of the caves along this section. Around the final headland, the Pointe de la Tour, there are some huge blocks of yellow sandstone veined with violet. All that remains is to paddle back to Bréhec. The beach at Vieux Bréhec has lovely lozenge shaped smooth ochre pebbles, a sign advises that it is strictly forbidden to collect them. ∎

WEATHER, TIDE AND SAFETY

This coast is protected by the cliffs from the prevailing south-west and west winds, so if you stay close inshore, can be a good option for windy weather. The swell curves round into this coast, giving a clean wave, look out for good breaks. However, if there is heavy swell there are few landing places except near low water: many beaches have a shore-break at high water. Watch out for divers, they often fish along this coast, look out for their brightly coloured floats. Back eddies make it easy to paddle against the tide, but expect the need for a short burst of paddling past each headland. The tide runs south from HW -5 and north from HW +1 (Paimpol).

Sea Kayaking Guide   **Brittany**

55 The Islands of Saint-Quay

Difficulty: ✗ ✗ ✗

Distance: 8 nautical miles

Leaving and Arriving: Tréveneuc

Maps:
SHOM 7154
Navicarte 536
IGN 0916OT

Harbour Island at high water.

Around Paimpol

Saint-Quay-Portrieux

The coastguard lookout at Saint-Quay.

HOW MANY are there of these islands? At high water only two, at low tide, impossible to say. What will one see? A small lighthouse with a red star, an army of limpets, the vestiges of a botanic garden, the last figs of the season...

And on the cliff of Saint-Quay? A Byzantine palace, and a coastguard lookout covering Bréhat to Erquy.

Launching, Landing and Parking:

Plouha: slipway at the Palus beach, large car park.
Tréveneuc: Saint-Marc beach, large car park, but still congested in summer, in front of a shell-fish kiosk.
Saint-Quay-Portrieux: La Comtesse beach, access via the harbour car park.
Binic or Étables-sur-mer: a good launch site to make use of the tide, but access only above mid-tide. (Binic: slipways inside the harbour and outside, La Blanche beach, car parks; Étables: Godelins beach, parking some way away.

The Saint-Quay rocks and islands at low water.

The "Ottoman Palace" facing the Île de la Comtesse (on the right).

Launch from Saint-Marc at HW +4 (Paimpol) and head out to sea, due east, ferry glide across the ebb tide which will be pushing you north. About 2 miles out, near the east cardinal "les Madeux", a back eddy will take you south-east towards the rocks of Saint-Quay.

At high water, only the island of Harbour with its small lighthouse with a red star —the emblem of the "Service des Phares et Balises" (Lighthouse and Buoyage Agency)— is above water, excepting a few rocks and sea-marks. The lighthouse indicates the safe channels for vessels approaching Portrieux, Binic or Saint-Brieuc. It was one of the first to be automated at the end of the 19th century. Just past the lighthouse a strange spot, three flat rocks protect a pool. This is called "le Secret" because it is very hard to see from outside. Traverse it, to the south-east is a paradise for rock-pooling and gathering shellfish. On spring tides a plateau, many tens of hectares in extent, emerges from the sea. It is sandy to the west and more rocky to the east.

The bay of Saint-Brieuc is a scallop fishery, with a strictly controlled season of only a few days between 1st October and 15 May. It lasts for the timetabled hours only, not a second more, not a second less. The fleet of fishing boats are surveyed from the air to make sure that no-one breaks the rules. The production from this bay is

Launching at Saint-Marc.

Around Paimpol

Low water, 12 metre tides at Harbour!

half the total production in France.

Explore at will in this vast area of sea and rocks. Slack water is the time to head back, paddle towards the north end of the harbour at Saint-Quay where there is a large beach backed by cliffs. As you approach, the Byzantine palace on the cliff, somewhat spoilt by the concrete holiday blocks built in the 1970s at its base, comes into view: bizarre. Even nearer, it looks as if a portion of the cliffs has detached itself: strange. High up, there is the "Kermoor Hôtel", facing the island of the Comtesse. An immense white staircase climbs the cliffs from the beach at the foot of the island. It belonged to an irascible countess, then someone who wanted to build a mansion with a garden (the origin of the walls), then Rimmel, of perfume fame lived nearby and grew scented flowers. It is now publicly owned and open to the public, so why not look around?

On the next headland the coastguard lookout of Saint-Quay, a hundred metres up, can survey the sea from Bréhat to Erquy. After this is the Casino beach, then the rural countryside takes over again all the way back to Saint-Marc. ■

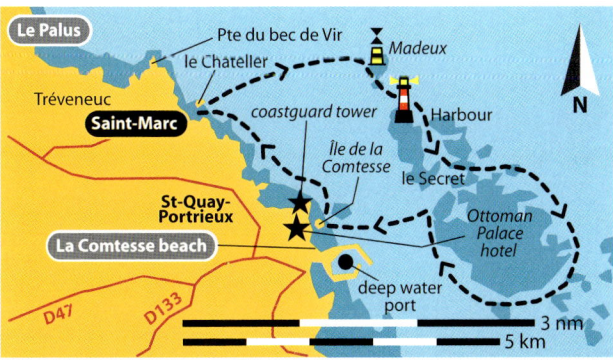

WEATHER, TIDE AND SAFETY

This is a good paddle for a spring tide, but take care ferry gliding across the tide. The general tidal flow is north from HW +1 and south from HW -5 (Paimpol), local streams can be quite strong (1.5kt) around the islands especially on the flood tide. Flows are weak inshore. The tide will be against you at the end of the return journey, but is weak inshore. Paddling either side of high water will make use of the tide, but there is less land to see.

Note that at mid-tide springs, the current at the entrance of Saint-Quay harbour can be very strong.

A piece of wood makes a simple spool and the paddle is held on a leash, Pierrot fishing at Trébeurden. Photo Y. Dodard

Learn more

by Yann Dodard

Kayak Fishing

Silent, at home on the sea, the sea kayak is an ideal platform for all sorts of angling. It can be a simple means of transport to good spots for gathering shellfish, snorkelling or line fishing. However, fishing from the kayak is becoming popular, either during a trip or on specific fishing expeditions. The kayaker can fish in hope of catching all of the species present in Brittany (i.e. mackerel, bass, pollack, wrasse and garfish), using lots of different techniques; trolling, jigging and lure fishing.

Trolling consists of trailing a line behind the kayak with one or several lures or feathers on the end. This can be with a handline (often only a piece of wood the line can be wound around), or with a short fishing rod designed for trolling. You can do this during a trip if conditions are suitable.

Jigging can be practised on the move, drifting with the tide, or stationary. It is effective in deep water and especially good at catching mackerel and pollack. The line is dangled vertically into the water and jerked up and down to give movement to the lure or feathers. It can be done with a handline or a rod, try at different heights in the water.

Lure fishing with a rod, where the lure or feathers is cast to cover a larger horizontal area of sea. Best practised in fishy spots such as rocky points or eddies, or where feeding terns indicate the presence of predatory fish driving small fry to the surface. This technique is best practised from the shore before trying it from a kayak.

The French regulations mean that an unregistered kayak, in theory, has only the fishing rights of an *engin de plage*, that is the use of a handline and not even a rod. A registered sea kayak becomes a leisure vessel with the legal right to many sorts of fishing; laying up to two crab pots, two floating trot lines, a 50m^2 gill net…

Never forget that a fishing kayaker is still a kayaker; what is going to happen if the hook snags the bottom in a strong current? Is there a knife to hand in the event of entanglement? How are you going to remove a hook that is caught in your clothing or hand? In the prevailing conditions, can I stop paddling for a few minutes to deal with a fish? Am I aware of the swell and breakers when getting in close after bass? Fishing in pairs with one fishing and one watching and helping works well.

Whatever technique is employed, early morning and evening around dusk are usually the best times. Avoid big spring or small neap tides especially in areas of strong tides.

Take care to kill the fish humanely and don't take more than you can eat. On a trip, if you can light a fire, cooking in aluminium foil or by hanging the fish vertically by its head over the fire work well. If not, pieces of fillet can be given a short cooking in boiling water, it may not look attractive, but it will taste good. You can experiment with marinading in lemon juice or dilute vinegar, fillets left in a plastic box for a few hours inside the hatch are ready at lunch time. ■

Catch a range of foods and obey the regulations.

On sandy beaches, cockles, clams and razor-fish can be raked or dug. A net will catch shrimps. Mussels, winkles and whelks can be collected by hand from rocks and oysters removed with a cold chisel. On spring tides, if it is allowed by local regulations, one can fish with a hook for ormers and also crabs, lobsters and crawfish. Collecting on foot is regulated by the by-laws relating to *la pêche à pied*. Snorkling from a kayak is regulated by those relating to *la pêche sous-marine*.

The size limits applicable in France are 20cm for mackerel, 30cm for pollack and 36 cm for bass, but a voluntary limit of 42 cm is often applied. Any fish taken by an amateur must immediately have the lower half of its tail removed. This is so that it cannot be sold. It is illegal to keep any fish not so marked.

280 | Sea Kayaking Guide **Brittany**

56 Cape Fréhel

Difficulty: ✗ ✗ ✗ / ✗ ✗ ✗

Distance: 10 nautical miles

Leaving and Arriving: Pléhérel beach, Vieux-Bourg

Maps:
SHOM 7155
Navicarte 536
IGN 1016ET

Cape Fréhel, la Cormorandière

The Emerald Coast

Cape Fréhel

Caves at Cape Fréhel. Photo D. Hottois

A VERY IMPOSING headland, Cape Fréhel, divides the bay of Saint-Brieuc to the west from the Emerald Coast to the east. Sea-birds make their home on the vertical cliffs of pink schist. The tide-swept bay of Sévignés leads on to the headland of La latte with its fort in silhouette. The cliffs are backed by a vast nature reserve of moorland and marsh.

Launching, Landing and Parking:

Pléhérel beach, Vieux-Bourg: slipway and large car park, the best launch site for the paddle.
La Fresnaye bay: 1) Saint-Géran harbour, west side of the bay, slipway and limited parking on the cliff top with impressive steps down. A difficult portage, a good place for a stop, but not to launch; 2) La Fresnaye beach at Saint-Cast, parking; 3) La Mare beach, limited parking, exposed to the west.
Saint-Cast harbour: 1) Slipway at the point of Saint-Cast; 2) Bay of la Vache, Canevez slipway, exposed to the wind and tide; 3) Slipway in the fishing harbour, priority given to commercial users.

Guillemot. Photo D. Collin

La Latte fort. Photo H. Le Flohic

Paddle east from the beach at Vieux-Bourg, leaving at HW -3 (Saint-Malo). The long and lovely beaches slowly give way to cliffs. The dark silhouette of the Cape with its two lighthouses, old and new, dominates the view along the coast.

The Roches de la Banche, spectacular detached portions of the cliffs near the headland of Jas set the scene. The caves at Jas, very high with sharply angled roofs, form tunnels through the headland, but the bends can be difficult to pass; think twice if there is a swell running.

Cape Fréhel is the next headland. During the breeding season, March to July, the bird calls and guano smells are everywhere. Razor-bills, guillemots, herring gulls, kittiwakes, fulmars and shags nest here. Guillemots lay their eggs on the bare rock, they are very pointed at one end, so they rotate rather than roll away if disturbed. The chicks jump into the sea at two weeks old and are fed on the water by their parents. The rock formation La Fauconnière forms a cleft in the cliff, don't paddle into it for fear of disturbing the birds, the rock itself, pink rock with horizontal ledges and vertical cracks is a veritable high-rise estate for the birds.

South of the headland of Château Renard, the Point of Sévignés, at the entry to the bay of the same name, allows landing. Fishermen have built cabins in niches in the cliff, a narrow pathway leads to them.

The Bay of Sévignés, with it curve of the cliffs, leading towards the impressive outline of the castle of La Latte, is swept by the tide. The castle was often attacked and besieged, but always held out because of its exceptional defensive position.

The Emerald Coast

Study the castle from all angles as you paddle around the headland. Behind it is a small beach with a footpath up the cliffs, a good place for a stop. You can enjoy the scent of the wild flowers, look at Le doigt de Gargantua (Gargantua's finger), a standing stone (Gargantua, a giant, was a creation of Rabelais, in a 16th century book, somewhat in the style of Gulliver's Travels), or visit the castle. This is one of the best preserved in Brittany, with an interesting oven for heating canon balls red hot before firing them so wooden ships would catch fire. Since the red hot cannon ball ended up very close to the gunpowder in the gun, it needed slick action to avoid accidents. There is a dungeon, a keep and of course panoramic views of all of your paddle. (It is open daily during the summer but only weekends and public holiday afternoons in winter).

Paddle back following the same route once the tide has turned. ∎

WEATHER, TIDE AND SAFETY

High cliffs, limited landing possibilities and the strong tides between Cape Fréhel and La Latte make this a committing paddle. Wind against tide can lead to a rough sea. Swell can make the rocks around La Banche tricky and entering the caves difficult and clapotis can necessitate staying well out to sea. A calm sea is needed to explore all of the caves. In calm weather at low water there are landing places on small beaches in the bay of Sévignés, but no way up the cliffs. There is a nice beach just east of Fort de la Latte. The tide runs eastbound from HW -6 and westbound from HW (Saint-Malo).

57 Saint-Briac and Les Hébihens Island

Difficulty: ✗ ✗ ✗

Distance: 10 nautical miles

Leaving and Arriving: Saint-Briac

Maps:
SHOM 7155
Navicarte 535
IGN 1016OT

At low water, the Hébihens are accessible on foot from Saint-Jacut.

The Emerald Coast

Saint-Briac

The south beach of the Hébihens is the most visited.

AN ARCHIPELAGO of contrasts protects a large bay. The island of Agot, a wild fortress; the gentle beaches of Hébihens; the Haches, facing the full force of the ocean: these islands offer a cocktail of sharp rocks and soft beaches. For the kayaker, rock-hopping can be coupled with a spot of surfing, bird watching or exploration on foot.

Launching, Landing and Parking:

Saint-Cast-le-Guildo: 1) Slipway at the point of Saint-Cast; 2) Bay of la Vache, Canevez slipway, exposed to the wind and tide; 3) Slipway in the fishing harbour, priority given to commercial users.
Saint-Cast-le-Guildo–Pointe de la Garde: slipway and parking.
Saint-Jacut-de-la-Mer: Houle-Causseul slipway, below the Yacht Club, get ready then drop off and return to the car park, portage, avoid low water.
Saint-Briac–Château du Nessay: the chateau is on a peninsula, leave from the beach, sea side (preferable) or inside. A long portage at low water, parking on the east side of the Boulevard du Bechay, congested in summer.
Saint-Briac–Port Hue: beach north of Saint-Briac, parking, congested in summer.

Nessay Chateau.

Passing the Haches en-route to the island of Agot.

Leave from the beach west of the Château du Nessay at HW -2 (Saint-Malo). Skirt the island of Perron (the summit gives a good view of the area), then on to the massive island of Agot. The flat top is the domain of the herring gull. To the east, the sea breaks on a reef of rock. Circumnavigate the island if the swell allows, then set off towards the necklace of rocks, the Haches (Axes), easily visible north of Hébihens.

The east side of the Haches is protected, the west less so. A series of channels and gulleys run between the rocks, fun to explore in all directions. The first rock, now an islet, was originally part of Hébihens and housed a village of Gauls from the Coriosolite tribe. Nowadays only a narrow band of sand, a tombolo, links it to Hébihens.

Cape Fréhel can be seen on the horizon to the west. Between the north coast of Hébihens and the island of La Nellière, sand and rock compete for space; beaches, ledges, tombolos, enormous masses of rock. Rock wins the day at high water, but as the tide drops the sand fights back. In good sunny weather there are some gorgeous beaches. This is a lovely place.

Further away, the island of La Colombière houses a tern colony, it is possible to go closer, but not too close, this is a bird reserve. The south side of Hébihens dries at mid-tide, so it might be difficult to get around without a portage. At low water, a vast expanse of sand links the island to the peninsula of Saint-Jacut, so a long portage (trolley desirable), or a wait for the tide to rise, are the two choices available. La Loge, one of the islets, has a salt-making oven dating from the Coriosolite Gauls.

The Emerald Coast

The beach to the south of Hébihens is a marvellous one, it is quite well known and busy in the season at low water. The island is private, but divided amongst many owners, you can land to have a look around. Green paint marks indicate a footpath leading towards the tower which dominates the island. One of Vauban's forts (see paddle 30) this was built at the same time as the forts of Saint-Malo, to prevent enemies making an easy landing on the beaches in this bay.

Follow the coast of Saint-Jacut as far as the funny little harbour of La Houle-Causseul, then head across the bay towards Lancieux, then north towards an islet topped with pine trees. It is private with landing discouraged, but a good landmark to aim for, shortly beyond this is our landing place.

Alternatives: 1) Paddle back directly from Hébihens; 2) Explore the estuary of Frémur with the tide. ∎

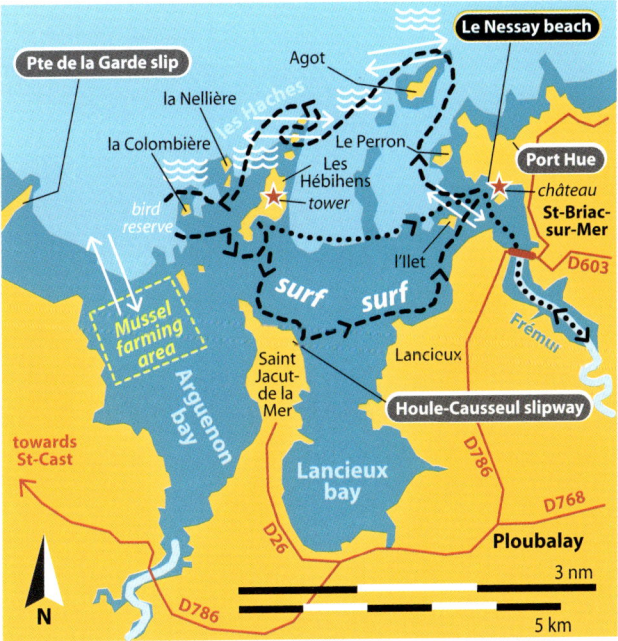

WEATHER, TIDE AND SAFETY

Swell hitting the mass of rocks and reefs north of Hébihens can give rise to a confused and dangerous sea with waves rising up from two directions, clapotis, breakers etc. The sea between Agot and Hébihens can also be rough in the same conditions. Near low water, a good swell can give excellent surfing conditions in front of Saint-Jacut and Saint-Briac.
In good conditions, the inshore area of sheltered water would be suitable for beginners.

58 The Tidal Rance

Difficulty: ✗ ✗ ✗ / ✗ ✗

Distance: 15 nautical miles

Leaving and Arriving: Saint-Suliac

Maps:
Navicarte 535
IGN 1116ET

The chateau of Chêne Vert.

The Emerald Coast

A square fishing cabin deep in the tidal Rance.

The dry dock at La Landriais.

THE LONG ESTUARY of the Rance, penetrating deep inland, favoured trade, but also the invasions of Vikings...and the English. A succession of small ports testifies to the strong maritime culture.

The Ille et Rance canal continues the waterway right across Brittany. The construction of the barrage and development of the tidal hydroelectric power station has changed both the ecology and the character of the estuary.

Launching, Landing and Parking:

Chateaubriand slipway: west bank, just above the barrage, large car park.

Slipway at the Pointe du Grouin and the beach la Passagère: east bank, parking along the access road, congested in summer, watch the current.

Saint-Suliac: slipway and beach: east bank, very difficult to park in summer, muddy at low water.

Saint-Jean harbour: slipway, east bank just above the two bridges, parking along the road.

Plouër-sur-Rance: slipway, west bank up a side creek, large car park.

Mordreuc: slipway, east bank, easy launching but limited parking.

Rounding Mont Gareau.

Read the note on the tides! Leave from Saint-Suliac and head north-west to look at the shipyards at La Landriais. The wooden dry-dock, recently restored, was used to repair *Terre-Neuvas* ships. These were sailing ships used for fishing off Newfoundland, at its peak around 1830, more than 10,000 French fishermen engaged in this every year and Saint-Malo was the main port. Over-fishing and the disappearance of the cod destroyed the industry. In 1930 Captain Charcot brought the *Pourquoi Pas ?* (Why Not?) into the dock, it was too big and was nearly wrecked.

Turn back and head upstream, Le Minihic is high on the west bank followed by a series of beaches. From time to time small side valleys create natural harbours. The valley sides draw in and two bridges come into sight. The most recent is the Chateaubriand bridge and the older one the Saint-Hubert bridge. Before these were built, boats were the only way across the Rance, the lowest bridge was at Dinan. Water was the main method of transport; wood from Mordreuc for the bakers ovens of Saint-Malo, fishing skiffs, heavy barges carrying building stone from Mont Gareau.

Continue to follow the main channel, passing the harbour of Plouër-sur-Rance and then having a chance to see the romantic, but mock, chateau of Chêne Vert, facing Mordreuc. Upstream the Rance narrows again, passing between wooded banks, the pretty hamlet of Moignerie, the working tide mill of Prat and the Rochefort mill which is now a holiday home.

The railway viaduct appears at the same time as various fishing cabins (*carrelets*). The latter built out on piles with a square drop-net on a makeshift derrick.

The Emerald Coast

They are put together with this and that, modestly claiming their spot in the muddy creeks. They are the equivalent of a vegetable garden for the owners. The lock at Chatelier marks the end of the tidal Rance.

On the way back, skirt the east bank, once having passed under the bridges, the 75m high Mont Gareau blocks the horizon. It has a monastery, quartz mines and Gargantua has lost a tooth! (a standing stone nicknamed "Gargantua's tooth" is also on top). At the head of the bay, south-east of the Mont, there are some walls hidden in the saltings... if the tide allows, thread your way into the north entry, if not land nearby and approach on foot. You are in a Viking camp, it was occupied between 900 and 950 AD and could have sheltered 18 long-boats.

Continue on around Mont Gareau and back to the start.

Alternatives: If the tide is high enough, but you do not want to go as far as Chatelier, take an inlet to the east above the bridges and paddle up the Coëtquen side stream, threading through the rushes as far as Pont-de-Cieux. ∎

WEATHER, TIDE AND SAFETY

The level in this part of the Rance is artificially maintained. It depends upon the demand for electricity from the tide turbines on the barrage. Predictions are made two days ahead and can be found online or in the newspaper *Ouest-France*, Saint-Malo edition or by telephone on 02 99 16 37 33. Levels are based on a zero datum at Saint-Suliac. Predictions are also displayed on notice boards on harbours and quays. The level can drop very fast once the sluices are open.

On the east bank just above the barrage, navigation is prohibited in a large area affected by the entry to the turbines with its strong currents and whirlpools. Mud banks are a hazard, stay in the main channels if the level is dropping.

59 The Forts of Saint-Malo

Sea Kayaking Guide — Brittany

Difficulty: ✗ ✗

Distance: 10 nautical miles

Leaving and Arriving: Saint-Malo

Maps:
SHOM 7155
Navicarte 535
IGN 1116ET

The walls of Saint-Malo from the Grand Bey at HW.

The Emerald Coast

Saint-Malo

Grand Jardin lighthouse.

HERE WE HAVE a paddle in the footsteps of the corsairs. It is a tour of the outlying fortifications that have served to protect the old walled town of Saint-Malo and control shipping since ancient times. We will go from the 14th century (Solidor Tower) to WW II. Towering walls, dungeons, turrets and a corsair's ship. Draw your sabres. . . up and at them!

Launching, Landing and Parking:

Dinard: slipway Port Nican a la Vicomté, accessible above mid-tide, limited parking. The slipway is near the gatekeeper's cottage for the Domaine de La Ronceraie.

Saint-Malo–Saint-Servan:
1) Naye, slipway in the Bas Sablons marina, near the ferry terminal. A sill blocks access at LW springs, large car park but congested in the summer; 2) Opposite, the slipway of Bas Sablons, parking and even unloading difficult; 3) Beaches either side of the Tour Solidor and slipway below the Tower, parking in the roads nearby, parking places can be hard to find at busy times.

The Petit Bey.

Le Renard *and* l'Istrec *in the bay of Saint-Malo. Photo E. Julé*

Leave from the Naye slipway a little before high water. Take care, this is a busy ferry port, the cross-channel ferries are travelling very fast compared to you! The marinas are also busy with leisure craft. After a few paddle strokes the massive walls of the old city come into view. The Malouins (inhabitants of Saint-Malo), famous for their seafaring skills, have an illustrious history and at times have formed a separate state, independent of both French and Breton authority. Inside the port, the sailing ship *Le Renard* (The Fox) is a replica of the ship sailed by Surcouf, the last and most famous Malouin corsair. By virtue of its speed and handling, he overtook, boarded and ransacked merchant ships sailing up the Channel as recently as the early 1800s.

Skirt the breakwater, watching out for fishing lines and head for the Grand (Large) Bey. Chateaubriand is buried here, continue along the ramparts to the Fort National, then cut back to the Petit (Small) Bey. All of these three islands can be reached on foot at low water. Look out to sea and then head for the La Conchée Fort. This is considered the best example of a fort built by Vauban and is now owned by a restoration society.

From La Conchée make a ferry glide across to Cézembre, it has the only south-facing beach in the area. The tide can run strongly in the channels. Cézembre is still riddled with unexploded munitions

La Conchée Fort.

The Emerald Coast

and only limited areas have public access, the rest is the haunt of gulls. There is a quay and a bar-restaurant, the "Repaire des Corsaires" (the "Corsairs Lair") above the beach.

Circumnavigate the island anti-clockwise, the outside coast is very rocky and swell swept, a great place to paddle, but one that demands some expertise. Consider staying on the inside if you met swell on the way over. The Grand Jardin (Great Garden) lighthouse was rebuilt in the 1950s in a contemporary classical style, it has a representation of Neptune just below the light. Cross the channel of La Petite Porte, this is the main shipping channel and can be busy, stay in a tight group, cross at right angles and keep a 360° watch. Once on the other side head for the last fort, that of Harbour Island, watch out for the numerous reefs. South of the fort are many sandbanks, one of these, Les Pourceaux, was a farm in the 15th century.

Skirt Dinard, with its kitsch skyline, these seaside villas were built as English holiday homes and boarding houses. The last obstacle is the current from the Rance Barrage power station, this can be strong and can change quickly, paddle against this as far as the Solidor Tower, then head back to the start point. ∎

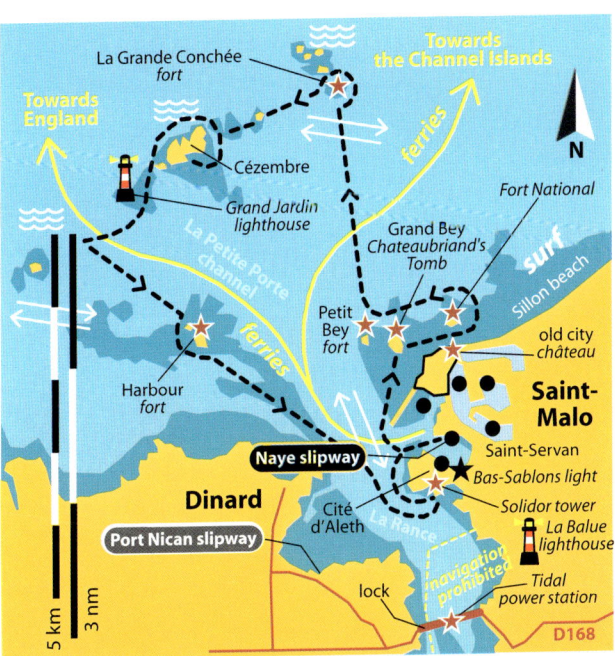

WEATHER, TIDE AND SAFETY

Heavy shipping traffic, keep a listening watch on channel 12. Strong tides, especially the flood tide, which runs from west to east from HW -5 (strongly HW -4 to HW -2) (Saint-Malo). The ebb flows west from HW. Water flowing out through the Rance power station can be strong inside the Rance and can also be felt in the shipping channel.

296 | Sea Kayaking Guide | **Brittany**

60 The Emerald Coast

Difficulty: ✖ ✖ ✖ / ✖ ✖ ✖

Distance: 19 nautical miles

Leaving: Saint-Malo — **Arriving:** Cancale

Maps:
SHOM 7155
Navicarte 535
IGN 1116ET

The Chevrets

The Emerald Coast

Cancale.

SALUTE TWO OF THE FORTS of Saint-Malo whilst paddling under the ramparts of the old city. Skirt the long golden curve of the beach. Tackle the sometimes capricious headland, La Varde. Wonder at the 300 granite carvings, cut by a deaf-mute priest, and now starting to blend back into the rock. Enjoy Rothéneuf harbour. Wander amongst the alternating black cliffs and sandy bays. Finally, get to grips with the Old River and its insane current.

A dolphin in front of the islands of Rimains and Chatelier.

Launching, Landing and Parking:

Launch from Saint-Malo: (see paddle 59) and organise a shuttle. For the full paddle this is a 20km drive.

To do the paddle in stages:
Rothéneuf harbour: 1) Chevrets beach, east of l'Île Besnard (a peninsula), at the end of the road, portage, sandy parking; 2) Eastern entry to Rothéneuf, beach inside the bay, limited parking but an interesting place, the sea goes out a long way, a bar can block the entry to the bay.

Further away: 1) Du Guesclin beach, facing the fort of the same name (out to sea), an interesting spot, parking; 2) Verger beach, parking, portage.
For the full shuttle, leave a car at Port-Pican (or Picain) north of Cancale (beside the youth hostel), pay parking in summer.

Other landing sites: 1) Port-Mer beach, congested parking, more parking higher up but a trolley essential; 2) Cancale harbour, many slipways, but difficult to park in summer.

Carved faces in the rock at Rothéneuf.

Leave Saint-Malo at HW +5, and say goodbye to the Solidor Tower. Keep an eye open for ferries as you cross in front of the terminal. You are paddling in the picture postcards of Saint-Malo; forts, ramparts, strongholds, the old city. You are following the footsteps of the corsairs of old. Carry on past the 19th century seafront of Sillon, opulent mansion vying with opulent mansion, bow-windows, turrets, carved and engraved stonework. The Pointe de la Varde can be choppy, take care.

Facing the rock of Bénétin take a break to look at the enigmatic work of Adolphe-Julien Fouéré (1839-1910), a deaf-mute priest, whose life's work was carving 300 sculptures in the living granite. They represent Breton rapscallions of old and who knows what. Weathering has only increased their mystery as they blend back into the rock.

Next up is Rothéneuf harbour, a vast flat sheltered area, a good place for another halt, but it is dry at low water. Between the headlands of Varde and Meinga, islets and rocks make for a confused sea, once beyond Meinga it is different again. Black cliffs are dissected with sandy bays. The beach at Touesse, behind the headland, is well sheltered from a nor'wester.

Pointe du Grouin, western coast.

The Emerald Coast

The beach of Guesclin is easily recognisable by an islet with a fort. It is here that Léo Ferré, lived with his chimpanzee Pépé (Ferré was a very respected singer and songwriter with a dark humour and a prominent anarchist). The broken cliffs hide fields of cabbages. After the Pointe du Nid, the tiny beach of Petit Port is a lovely spot, sheltered deep in a valley. This is followed by the bay of Verger with its popular beach.

The coast now leads out to the Pointe du Grouin, a mile away. Once past here the narrow channel between Île des Landes and the west side of the headland forms the famous Vieille Rivière (the Old River). The current will whisk you south. Before landing at Port Pican, take a look at the two islands of Chatelier and Rimains. Between Cancale and Pointe de la Chaîne are extensive oyster beds, spectacular at low-water and you can take a look at the harbour of La Houle and maybe even buy some oysters.

Alternative: On the flood tide, around mid-tide, the Old River is a play spot recommended for a strong party, good at rescues! You can make your way from rock to rock out to the Herpin lighthouse, playing all the way. ∎

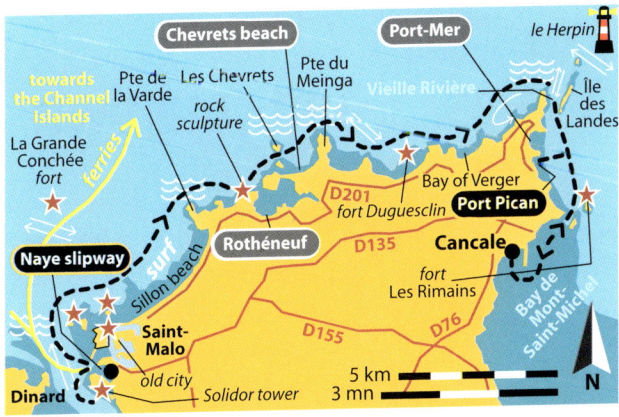

WEATHER, TIDE AND SAFETY

Passing through the Vieille Rivière near slack water will reduce the difficulty. Every headland, large or small can be tricky, especially with wind against tide conditions. Swell further complicates things. In a northerly wind, the beaches can have breakers, accentuated by the swell. The paddle could be made in the opposite direction. The most difficult places in bad conditions are the most interesting in good conditions. The flood tide runs eastbound from HW -6 (Saint-Malo) and is very strong at the Pointe du Grouin from HW -4 to HW -2. At HW -1 the tide is still pushing into the Bay on the outside, whilst eddying out through the Vieille Rivière. The ebb runs westbound from HW to HW +5, slack water HW +6.

Passing a mussel farmer's barge.

60 paddles… and your own

WE HAVE NOT INCLUDED Ushant and Sein amongst our paddles. Both can be reached by sea kayak in good conditions. The very strong tides (the infamous Fromveur, the Four channel and the Raz de Sein) coupled with the almost incessant ocean swell, make these suitable destinations for only the very experienced.

Our choice of what to include was subjective and there are lots of other good paddles to be had. On the other hand, many of the paddles in this book lay themselves open to be extended or combined.

Here are some suggestions: A comprehensive tour of a defined area, for example, the Gulf of Morbihan or Brest Harbour; a paddle down one estuary and up another for example Tréguier-Pontrieux or Quimperlé-Pont Aven; island hopping to complete a ring around a bay, example, Trévignon-Les Glénans-Loctudy-return along the coast; paddling around a peninsula with a shuttle back across the base, example, Ruaud slipway in the Gulf of Morbihan to Roaliguen outside the Gulf.

Longer trips of a week or so are equally feasible. Here are some classics developed by Guy Cloarec at Paimpol Youth Hostel sea kayaking centre: Le Croisic-Gulf de Morbihan; Gulf de Morbihan-Concarneau; Concarneau-Le Conquet, a hard one; Le Conquet-Roscoff; Roscoff-Paimpol; Paimpol-Mont Saint-Michel.

This is a guide to Brittany and limits itself to the Breton coast. This excluded a

Epilogue

Arriving at Mont Saint-Michel. Photo H. Le Flohic

classic paddle for local kayakers; Cancale-Mont Saint-Michel. Mont Saint-Michel is just inside Normandy and prior to being annexed by William I Duke of Normandy in 933 AD, would have been part of Brittany. We hope to bring out another guide to Normandy which will start from our finishing point of Cancale. It was also very tempting to include the Chausey archipelago, but no, that would have been greedy.

In any case, the multi-million Euro project currently under way to reconvert Mont Saint-Michel back into an island has complicated access and made it impossible to write a definitive guide. When the work is finished in 2014/15 it will be possible to investigate the best launching and landing sites near the Mount.

Part of the work is a tidal barrage to regulate flow in the Couesnon river so that silt will be swept away and not build up again. The plans include canoe ramps, which may help by making launching possible within a reasonable distance of the car parks. In the meantime there is still the tidal bore…for those who like that kind of thing. ∎

The Tour of Brittany for Everyone

Here are some examples: In 1980, Loïck Bourdon with some others paddled from Pénestin to Mont Saint-Michel in 26 days. Then in 1991 the Ponant Sea Kayaking Association completed the journey from Saint-Malo to Croisic in three weeks, (Ponant is an old French naval term for west and can refer to the assemblage of Atlantic and Channel coast islands) by island hopping without touching the mainland (Bréhat, the Sept Isles, Batz, L'Île Vierge, Ouessant (Ushant), Molène, Sein, Les Glénans, Groix, Belle-Île, Houat, Hoëdic). In 2005, Jean-Marc Janvier and Josée Conan circled Brittany in 24 days, leaving from Saint-Pol-de-Léon and returning via the Vilaine, canals, and the Rance.

Without going to these extreme lengths, paddling the entire coast in short sections over several years would be a good objective for the recreational paddler.

Paddling off Cap Fréhel in the fog. Photo D. Hottois

Beaufort Scale

Force	Wind Speed in Knots	English Term	French Term
0	1 or less	Calm	Calme
1	1–3	Light air	Très légère brise
2	4–6	Light breeze	Légère brise
3	7–10	Gentle breeze	Petite brise
4	11–16	Moderate breeze	Jolie brise
5	17–21	Fresh breeze	Bonne brise
6	22–27	Strong breeze	Vent frais
7	28–33	Near gale	Grand frais
8	34–40	Gale	Coup de vent
9	41–47	Strong gale	Fort coup de vent
10	48–55	Storm	Tempête

IN WINDS OF FORCE 2 or less a sea kayak will be able to maintain its cruising speed of about 3kt in any direction. A force 3 may not slow the kayak much, but will increase the effort required to make progress into the wind. At force 4 and above the wind will have an increasing effect. Force 6 is a kayaker's gale, progress into the wind will be slow. Some boats, especially those with weak weather-helm in light winds may develop lee-helm and be very hard to turn into the wind. Boat handling will be difficult. In force 8 and above, it may be impossible to make more than 100-200m upwind and most boats will tend to blow uncontrollably downwind.

Don't listen to the French kayaker with his saying: *"Qui écoute trop la météo, passe sa vie au bistro"* (He who pays too much attention to the weather forecast will waste away his life in the pub), if in doubt stay on shore. ∎

Addresses

Useful Addresses

HERE ARE SOME useful addresses for each of the 60 paddles. Nearby camp-sites can be useful as meeting up places, an overnight stay for an early morning launch, or as a base for exploring the area. The choice for inclusion was based on proximity to the paddle start location (paddle number in brackets after the name). There is a bias towards simple low cost camp-sites; municipal camp-sites, natural camp-sites and camping on the farm. The authors have not stayed on all of them and there are other good camp-sites available; the choice is yours. Use the internet or telephone to check on opening times and availability. Places of interest for bad weather or non-paddling partners are again a personal choice.

01 The Wild Coast of Croisic

Campsites

- *Camping Les Paludiers* (campéole) (01)
Rue Nicolas Appert
44740 Batz-sur-mer
tel. 02 40 23 85 84
Beginning of April to end Sept.
http://www.camping-atlantique.info/
- *Camping La Govelle* (01)
10, route de la Govelle
44740 Batz-sur-mer
tel. 02.40.23.91.63 or 02.35.92.18.36
http://www.ot-batzsurmer.fr

Places of Interest

- *Musée des marais salants* (salt marsh centre)
29 bis rue Pasteur
44740 Batz sur Mer
tel. 02 40 23 82 79
http://www.batzsurmer.com
- *Terre de Sel* (Visitor centre salt making)
Route des Marais Salants - Pradel
44350 Guérande
tel. 02.40.62.08.80
http://www.terredesel.com/
- *Ocearium du Croisic* (sea-life centre)
Avenue de St Goustan
44490 Le Croisic
tel. 02 40 23 02 44
http://www.ocearium-croisic.fr/

02 The Island of Dumet

Campsites

- *Camping de la baie* (02-03)
Ker Avelo
44 410 Assérac
tel. 02 40 01 71 16
Beginning of April to end Oct.
http://www.camping-delabaie.com/
- *Camping le Razay* (02)
Saint-Sébastien
44420 Piriac-sur-mer
tel. 02 40 23 56 80

Places of Interest

- *Musée « Maison de la Pêche »* (Museum of fishing)
44420 La Turballe
Visit the harbour to see fish auctions and learn about the species and their seasons and the fishing fleet.
tel. 02 40 11 71 31
http://musee-laturballe.fr

03 The Gold Mine

Campsites

- *Camping Loscolo* (03)
336 route de Lanchalle
56760 Pénestin
tel. 06 08 21 95 30
July to early Sept.
- *Camping de Kerlay* (03)
Kerlay - 56760 Pénestin
tel. 02 99 90 31 28
Beginning of June to mid-September
http://www.camping-de-kerlay.com/
- *Camping La Plage des Grange*s (03)
56190 Billiers
tel. 02 97 45 68 23 or 06 71 31 63 16
1st April to 31 Oct.
http://www.campingdelaplage.net

Places of Interest

- *La Maison de la Mytiliculture* (Exhibition in a lighthouse on mussel farming)
15 rue du Port-Tréhiguier
56760 Pénestin
tel. 02.99.90.33.11
or City-hall Pénestin, tél. 02 23 10 03 00
http://www.mairie-penestin.com
- *Musée de la Vilaine maritime*
Château des Basses-Fosses
56130 La Roche-Bernard
tel. 02 99 90 67 98
www.tourisme-pays-la-roche-bernard.fr

04 Boëd and Boëdic

Campsites

- *Camping municipal de Conleau* (04)
188 av. du Maréchal Juin
56000 Vannes
tel. 02 97 63 13 88
1st April to 30 Sept.
Launching is difficult at Conleau, use the slipway at the Chemin des Émigrés, north of the swing bridge on to the Vannes estuary.
http://www.tourisme-vannes.com
- *Camping Le Moulin de Cantizac* (04-06)
Rue de Cantizac
56860 Séné
tel. 02 98 92 53 52
6 April to 15 Oct.
camper vans throughout the year.
http://www.camping-vannes.com

Places of Interest

- *Aquarium océanographique et tropical de Vannes* (Marine aquarium and tropical fish)
21 rue Daniel Gilard
56000 Vannes
tel. 0 810 406 901
http://www.aquarium-du-golfe.com/
- *Footpath* the length of the river Vincin managed by the Coastal Conservancy.
http://www.conservatoire-du-littoral.fr
- *La Semaine du Golfe*
Held every other year (odd years) on Ascension weekend, a nautical festival with sailing regattas and traditional boats. The fifteen harbours and anchorages around the gulf take part in diverse activities.
http://www.semainedugolfe.asso.fr

Bistrot

- *Le Corlazo*, bar
Conleau
56000 Vannes
tel. 02 97 63 24 43
Start and finish of the famous *Bar to Bar* regatta from "Le Corlazo" to "La Trinquette" near Argol harbour and back.

05 A Tour of the Gulf

Campsites

- *Gîte d'étape du Moulin Vert* de Tumiac (05-06-07)
  22 r Jules César
  56640 Arzon (2km from Arzon).
  Gîte and camping, smart but not expensive.
  tel. 02 97 53 70 05.
  http://www.lemoulinvert.asso.fr
- *Camping de Bilouris* (05-06-07)
  Pointe de Kerners
  56640 Arzon
  tel. 02 97 53 70 55
  April-Nov.
  http://www.campingdebilouris.com
- *Camping municipal Le Tindio* (05-06-07)
  2 rue du Bilouri
  56640 Arzon
  tel. 02 97 53 75 59
  Mairie d'Arzon, service campings :
  tel. 02 97 53 44 60.
  1st April to beginning Nov.
  www.camping-arzon.fr
- *Île d'Arz - Camping municipal Les Tamaris* (04-05)
  tel. 02 97 44 33 97 or 02 97 44 31 14
  Space for 15 tents.
  Early April-15 Oct.
  http://mairie-iledarz.fr
- *Camping à la ferme du Menguen* (05-06-07)
  Route de Saint-Gildas-de-Rhuys
  56370 Sarzeau
  tel. 02 97 48 04 62 or 06.18.39.35.07
  www.camping-du-menguen.com/
- *Camping à la ferme L'Abri côtier* (05-06-07)
  Nathalie et Dominique Rio
  56730 Saint-Gildas-de-Rhuys
  tel. 02 97 45 27 42 or 06 11 97 31 76
  http://www.abri-cotier.com/
- *Camping mun. du Kerver* (05-06-07)
  Chemin du Kerver
  56730 Saint-Gildas-de-Rhuys
  tel. 02 97 45 21 21
  May-Oct.
  http://www.rhuys.com

Places of Interest

- *Footpath around Île d'Arz.*
- *Chantier du Guip* on Île aux Moines, traditional boat building.
  http://www.chantierduguip.com/

06 Towards the Island of Ilur

Camping

- *M. Mahé Daniel*, aire naturelle Birhit (06)
  Birhit - 56450 Noyalo
  tel. 02 97 43 02 12

Places of Interest

- *A guided walk of the salt marshes*, welcoming and informative host. Quiet area for bird watching.
- *Bird reserve*, Duer marshes on the Rhuys peninsula. Old saltings bordered by the coastal path, 2 observatories.
- *Nature reserve*, Séné marshes, east of Séné at Falguérec. A 410 ha. Reserve managed by Bretagne Vivante-SEPNB.
  tel. 02 97 66 92 76
  Numerous birds, free and paying access options.
  http://www.sene.com

photo C. Magré

07 The Mouth of the Golfe

Campsites
See paddles 05, 06 and 08.

Places of Interest

- *Numerous neolithic sites* on the Rhuys peninsula. Cesar and Bilouri free, Petit Mont entrance fee.
- *Cairn de l'île de Gavrinis*, access only by organised tours from Larmor-Baden, Pen-Lannic slipway; or from Port Navalo or Locmariaquer by *Passeur des Îles*.
  tel. 02 97 57 19 38

08 Up and down the Auray

Campsites

- *Camping municipal La Falaise* (08-07)
  LD Kerpenhir - Henri Ezan
  56740 Locmariaquer
  tel. 02 97 57 31 59
  mid-March to mid-Oct.
  www.campingmunicipallafalaise.com
- *Camping LannBrick* (08-07)
  56740 Locmariaquer
  tel. 02 97 57 32 79 or 06 07 58 47 10
  Open 1st April.
  http://www.camping-lannbrick.com
- *Camping Ker Eden* (08-07)
  Access direct from the beach, Locmiquel Bay near HW.
  56870 Larmor Baden
  tel. 02 97 57 05 23
  15th May-15th Sept.
  http://www.larmorbaden.com
- *Camping Le Diben* (08-07)
  Camping on the farm (May-Sept) Gite all year.
  56870 Larmor Baden
  tel. 02 97 57 29 12
  http://www.campinglediben.com/
- *Camping du Parc Lann* (08)
  Le Varquez - Rue Thiers
  56400 Le Bono
  1km from the harbour.
  tel. 02.97.57.93.93
  1st May to 30 Sept.
  http://campingduparclann.free.fr
- *Camping Le Fort Espagnol* (08)
  56950 Crac'h
  tel. 02 97 55 14 88
  http://www.fort-espagnol.com
- *Camping la fontaine du Hallate* (08)
  8 chemin de Poul fetan- Le Hallate
  56400 Plougoumelen
  tel. 06 16 30 08 33
  Mid-way between Vannes and Auray, Elizabeth and Claude welcome you to a "green" campsite.
  Open from the end of March.
  http://www.camping-en-morbihan.fr/

Places of Interest

- *Megalithic monument of Les Pierres-Plates*
  At Locmariaquer, the western end of Kerpenhir beach. Other impressive remains, but much visited.
- *Le Grand Menhir brisé* and the Table des Marchands cromlech (entrance fee) at Locmariaquer.
- *Explore Saint-Goustan* and the port of Le Bono on foot.
- *Grave of the famous yachtsman Bernard Moitessier at Bono*
  «You do not ask a tame seagull why it needs to disappear from time to time toward the open sea. It goes, that's all.»

09 The Crac'h Tidal River

Camping

- *Camping du Lac* (09)
  lieu-dit Lac
  56340 Carnac
  tel. 02 97 55 78 78
  http://www.lelac-carnac.com/

Places of Interest

- *Try some oysters* from one of the numerous oyster farmers along the river.

10 Belle-Île

Campsites

- *Camping Port Andro* (10)
  56360 Locmaria Belle-Île
  tel. 02 97 31 73 25 (in season)
  or 02 97 31 73 75
  50m from the beach.
  Mid-May to mid-Sept.
  http://www.belle-ile.com/tourisme
  http://www.locmaria-belle-ile.com/
- *Camping des Grands Sables* (10)
  56360 Locmaria Belle-Île
  tel. 02 97 31 84 46
  300m from the beach
  End April to end Sept.
  http://www.belle-ile.com/tourisme

Addresses

- *Camping de L'Océan* (10)
Rosboscer
56360 Le Palais
tel. 02 97 31 83 86 or 06 11 91 01 48
1st April to 30 Sept.
www.camping-ocean-belle-ile.com/
- *Auberge de Jeunesse* (10) (Youth Hostel)
tel. 02 97 31 81 33
Haute Boulogne
56360 Le Palais
http://www.belle-ile.com/tourisme
- *Camping municipal Pen Prad* (10)
Vallon du Port aux Plages
56360 Sauzon
tel. 02 97 31 64 82
or 02 97 31 62 79 (town hall)
April to early Nov.
http://www.sauzon.fr/
http://www.sauzon.fr/Lecamping.htm
- *Centre d'accueil l'Escale* (10)
Route de l'Apothicairie
56360 Sauzon
tel. 06 70 03 13 28 or 02 97 31 66 23
http://www.belle-ile.com/tourisme
- *Gîte communal de Lannivrec* (10)
Lannivrec
56360 Locmaria Belle-Île
tel. 02 97 31 70 92 or 02 97 31 73 75
April to mid-Nov.
http://www.locmaria-belle-ile.com/
- *Camping la Source* (10)
Vallon du Port aux Plages 56360 Sauzon
tel. 02 97 31 60 95 or 06 78 47 32 23
http://www.belleile-lasource.com
- *Camping de Bordeneo* (10)
56360 Le Palais - Belle-Île-en-mer
tel. 02 97 31 88 96
Landing on the beach at Port Fouquet. The bar owner is an ex-kayaker.
http://www.bordeneo.com

Places of Interest
- La Pointe des Poulains.
- A circuit of the island on foot in 3 days, very busy in the summer.
  At Le Palais
- The castle, the museum, the surroundings.
- *Maison de la nature* (CPIE)
Les Glacis, Le Palais
tel. 02 97 31 40 15
Guided walks throughout the year.
http://www.belle-ile.com/

11 Houat and Hoëdic
Campsites
- *Camping du Conguel* (11-12)
Bd de la Teignouse
56175 Quiberon
tel. 02 97 50 19 11
At the tip of the Quiberon peninsula, next to the sea, expensive in summer.
http://www.campingduconguel.com/
- *Camping de Houat* (11)
Visitors area, water and toilets.
tel. 02 97 30 68 04
- *Camping municipal d'Hoëdic* (11)
To the east of the village, looking out over the Lann-Vihan pond and Argol harbour.
Town hall of Hoëdic, tel. 02 97 52 48 88
Open during the summer.
http://www.hoedic.net/
- *Gîte d'étape Hoëdic* (11)
Gîte inside Fort Vauban
tel. 02 97 52 48 82
April to Nov.
http://www.hoedic.net/

Places of Interest
- *Houat - Plankton museum*, this was a lobster tank in the 1960s.
- *Hoëdic - Le Fort Vauban*
Gite and an ecomuseum open June-Sept. Free entry but they request a donation.

Bistrots
- *Bar La Trinquette* - Hoëdic
Above the harbour at Argol, one of the major stops during the *Bar to Bar* regatta from "Le Corlazo" at Conleau (Vannes).
- *Resto-librairie Chez Jean-Paul* - Hoëdic
Breakfast, lunch and dinner.

12 The Quiberon Peninsula
Campsites
- *Camping municipal de Kerné* (12)
On the wild coast, Kerné village
56 170 Quiberon
tel. in season: 02 97 50 05 07
tel. out of season: 02 97 30 24 00
End of June-end Aug.
http://www.ville-quiberon.fr
- *Camping municipal du Rohu* (12)
Chemin du Men Du
56510 Saint-Pierre-Quiberon
tel. 02.97.50.27.85
The Camp-site is near the National Sailing School, direct access to the beach.
April-beginning of Sept.
http://www.saintpierrequiberon.fr
- *Camping municipal de Kerhostin* (12)
Allée du Camping Kerhostin
56510 Saint-Pierre-Quiberon
tel. 02 97 30 95 25
End April to beginning of Sept.
http://www.saintpierrequiberon.fr
- *Camping municipal de Penthièvre* (12)
Rue Duquesne Penthièvre
56510 Saint-Pierre-Quiberon
tel. 02 97 52 33 86
Situated beside the beaches of Quiberon Bay. Access to Quiberon without using a car. At the pinch-point into Quiberon. Tourist railway.
Beginning of April to end Sept.
http://www.saintpierrequiberon.fr

Places of Interest
- *Footpath* la Côte Sauvage.

13–14 The Ria d'Étel
Campsites
- *Camping de Saint-Cado* (13-14)
56550 Belz
Beside the water.
tel. 02 97 55 31 98 or 06 17 20 27 71
1st April-30 Sept.
http://www.camping-saintcado.com
- *Camping municipal d'Étel* (13-14)
rue de la Barre
56410 Étel
tel. 02 97 55 33 79
Easter to end Sept.
http://www.campingdetel.fr/
- *Village de Gîtes Le Remoulin* (13)
Has a small beach suitable for a mid-tide launch.
56690 Nostang
tel. 02 97 65 64 42
www.gites-remoulin.com/fra/intro.htm

Places of Interest
- *Tuna Fishing Museum*
3, impasse Jean Bart - 56410 Étel
tel. 02 97 55 26 67
http://www.museedesthoniers.fr/
- *L'association Patron Émile Daniel*
A conservation group maintaining the historic lifeboat *Patron Émile Daniel* at the Étel lifeboat station, exhibition.
http://canotetel.free.fr

photo V. Dodard

15 The Blavet
Campsites
- *Camping municipal des Remparts* (15-16)
Rue des Récollets
56290 Port Louis
tel. 02 97 82 59 59 or 02 97 82 47 16
15 June-9 Sept.
mairie.ville-portlouis@wanadoo.fr
- *Camping municipal La Lande* (15)
Gavres peninsula
Contact: Town hall of Gavres, avenue des Sardiniers, 56680 Gavres
tel. 02 97 82 46 55
June to mid-Sept.
http://www.campinggavres.com/
- *Camping municipal des Joncs* (15)
tel. 02 97 82 46 88
June to mid-Sept.
http://www.gavres.fr

- *Camping municipal de Saint-Caradec* (15)
Saint-Caradec - 56700 Hennebont
tel. out of season 02 97 36 43 71
tel. 15 June/15 Sept. 02 97 36 21 73.
http://avironhennebontais.free.fr

Places of Interest
LORIENT
- The fishing port and market (the tourist office organises guides tours in summer). Fish market open every morning at Merville near the town hall, at the harbour. Stall 78 open to retail buyers Monday to Saturday, mornings 8-12.
- *CCSTI/Maison de la Mer*
(Centre de Culture Scientifique, Technique et Industrielle de Lorient)
Bd Adolphe Pierre (Quai de Rohan),
56100 Lorient.
tel. 02 97 84 87 37
Visits to the harbour and markets, conferences and exhibitions.
http://www.ccstilorient.org/
tel. 02 97 84 78 00
http://www.keroman.fr
- Base de sous-marins
Submarine base, the largest German U-boat base of WW II. Follow signs for « Base de sous-marins - Cité de la voile Éric Tabarly ».
tel. 02 97 02 23 29
http://www.uboat-bases.com
- *Cité de la voile Éric Tabarly*
Base de sous-marins de Keroman - 56623 Lorient
tel. 02 97 655 656
www.citevoile-tabarly.com
- *Theatre festival*, every year in the ship graveyard at Kerhevy, the last two weeks of July.
PORT LOUIS
The citadel houses two museums:
- *The East India company and a museum of art and history of Lorient*
Citadelle - 56290 Port-Louis
Ticket Office: tel. 02 97 82 56 72
http://musee.lorient.fr
- *The National Marine Museum*
Citadelle - 56290 Port-Louis
tel. 02 97 82 56 72
http://www.musee-marine.fr
RIANTEC
- *La Maison de l'île Kerner*
(museum of the inland sea of Gâvres)
Île de Kerner - 56670 Riantec
tel. 02 97 84 51 49
http://www.maison-kerner.fr/

Bistrots
- *Tavarn ar Roue Morvan*
1 pl Polig Monjarret
56100 Lorient
tel. 02 97 21 61 57
- *The Galway Inn* (pub)
18 rue de Belgique
56100 Lorient
tel. 02 97 64 50 77

- *The Quay Street Bar*
18 rue Poissonnière
56100 Lorient
tel. 02 97 64 38 48
- Transport Batobus
Water buses integrated with the bus network, linking: Lorient-Lociquelic etc. Information at the bus station: tel. 02 97 21 28 29
www.ctrl.fr

16 The Island of Groix
Campsites
- *Camping municipal* (16)
(fort du Méné, près de l'AJ)
Le Méné - 56590 Île de Groix
tel. 02 97 86 81 13 or 02 97 86 80 15
Accessible from the beach, sea views.
15 April to 30 Sept.
http://www.groix-tourisme.fr/
- *Camping des Sables Rouges* (16)
(close to Pointe des Chats)
Port Coustic - 56590 Île de Groix
tel. 02 97 86 81 32 or 02 99 64 13 14
1st May to 30 Sept.
www.campingdessablesrouges.com

Places of Interest
- *Groix Eco-museum*
Port Tudy
56590 Île de Groix
tel. 02 97 86 84 60
http://ecomusee.groix.free.fr/
- *Nature Reserve Visitor Centre "Francois Le Bail"*
Rue Maurice Gourong
Le Bourg - 56590 Île de Groix
tel. 02 97 86 55 97
www.bretagne-vivante.org
The only geological and mineralogical reserve in France; two places:
- Pen Men/Beg Melen: coast and bird cliffs.
- Locqueltas/Point des Chats: coastal geology.
- *International Island Film Festival*
2nd half of August, a competition for documentaries and films from all over the world.
http://www.filminsulaire.com

17 The Laïta
Campsites
- *Camping de Croas An Ter* (17-18)
Quelvez
29360 Clohars Carnoët
tel. 02 98 39 94 19
http://www.campingcroasanter.com
- *Camping Le vieux Four* (17-18)
rue des Grands Sables
29360 Clohars Carnoët
tel. 02 98 39 94 34
- *Aire de camping de La Laïta* (17-18)
Kerguilan (between Clohars-Carnoët and Le Pouldu)
29360 Clohars Carnoët
tel. 02 98 39 92 61 or 06 25 04 60 14
http://auvieuxmoulin.free.fr/
- *Camping Les Grands Sables* (17-18)
Le Pouldu
29360 Clohars-Carnoët
tel. 02 98 39 94 43
www.camping-lesgrandssables.com
- *Camping à la ferme - Au vieux Moulin* (17-18-19)
Kerguilan - 29360 Clohars-Carnoët
tel. 02 98 39 92 61 or 087-369-92-61 or 06 25 04 60 14
open from 15 April.
http://www.bretagnealaferme.com/

Places of Interest
- *Abbaye saint Maurice*
29 360 Clohars-Carnoët
Visit to the abbey and gardens, video link to the bat colony.
tel. 02 98 71 65 51
http://www.saintmaurice.clohars-carnoet.fr/
- *Carnoët forest*
This borders the west of La Laïta.

18 The Cliffs of Clohars-Carnoët
Campsites
- *Camping de l'Île Percée* (18-19)
Plage de Trénez - 29350 Moëlan-sur-mer
tel. 02 98 71 16 25
http://www.camping-ile-percee.fr
- *Camping Le Kergariou* (18)
Kervec, 29360 Clohars Carnoët
tel. 02 98 71 54 65
http://www.campinglekergariou.com/

19 The Aven and the Belon
Campsites
- *Camping Tal Ar Moor* (19-18)
Kerfany-Plage - 29350 Moëlan-sur-mer
tel. 02 98 71 11 98 or 06 73 90 66 36
Beginning of April to end Sept.
http://www.campingkerfanyplage.fr/
- *Camping des Chaumières* (19)
24 Hameau de Kérascoët - 29920 Nevez
tel. 02 98 06 73 06
www.camping-des-chaumieres.com

Addresses

Places of Interest
- *Pont-Aven fine arts museum*
 Place de l'Hôtel-de-Ville
 29930 Pont-Aven
 tel. 02 98 06 14 43
- *Try Belon oysters*

20 Concarneau Bay
Campsites
- *Camping la Plage Loc'h-Ven* (20)
 8 route du Camping - 29910 Trégunc
 tel. 02 98 50 26 20
 http://www.lochven.com
- *Camping Les Prés Verts* (20)
 Kernous-Plage - 29186 Concarneau
 tel. 02 98 97 09 74
 http://www.presverts.com
- *Auberge de Jeunesse Éthic étapes* (20)
 Quai de la Croix - 29181 Concarneau
 tel. 02 98 97 03 47
 http://www.ajconcarneau.com/
- *Camping de Kersentic* (20-21)
 Hent Kersentic
 29170 Fouesnant
 tel. 02.98.56.08.66
 http://www.camping-kersentic.com
- *Camping Leanou* (20-21-22)
 Natural camp-site
 Hent Kerler - 79170 Fouesnant
 tel. 02.98.56.15.32
 15 May-15 Sept.
 One km from the beach at Mousterlin;
 farm produce available according to season.
 http://www.camping-leanou.com

Places of Interest
- *Musée de la Pêche* (Museum of Fishing)
 3 rue Vauban - 29900 Concarneau
 tel. 02 98 97 10 20
 http://www.musee-peche.fr/
- *Le Marinarium* (Aquarium)
 Place de la Croix - 29900 Concarneau
 tel. 02 98 50 81 64
 http://concarneau.mnhn.fr/
- *Criée de Concarneau* (Fish market)
 5 impasse de Verdun
 29900 Concarneau.
 Open to visitors (entrance fee) from 06.30. Also access to the fish quay to watch the catch being landed.
 tel. 02.98.50.56.55
 http://www.bretagne.com

21 Glénan Islands
École des Glénans
8 pl. Philippe Vianney
29900 Concarneau
tel. 02 98 97 14 84
http://www.glenans.asso.fr/

Lodging
- *Sextant : le gîte de mer des Glénan* (21)
 Hent coz Kernanguel - 29170 Fouesnant
 tel. 02 98 56 10 16

or 9 rue Lamartine - 29900 Concarneau
tel. 02 98 97 89 48
http://www.sextant-glenan.org/

22 The Odet
Campsites
- *Camping Pors Keraign* (22)
 72 Vieille Route Pors Keraign
 29950 Gouesnac'h
 tel. 02 98 54 61 37
 www.camping-pors-keraign.com/
- *Camping municipal du bois du séminaire* (22)
 Avenue des Oiseaux - 29000 Quimper
 tel. 02 98 55 61 09
 http://www.quimper.fr

Places of Interest
- *Museum of fine arts*
 40 place Saint-Corentin
 29000 Quimper
 tel. 02 98 95 45 20
 http://www.mbaq.fr/

Bistrot
- *Poitin Still Irish Pub*
 2 avenue Libération
 29000 Quimper
 tel. 02 98 90 02 77

23 Towards Pont-L'Abbé
Campsites
- *Camping Kergall* (21-23)
 Boulevard Mer - 29750 Loctudy
 tel. 02 98 87 45 93 or 59 80
 or 06 98 25 78 33
 Easter to 30 Sept.
- *Camping Keraluic* (23 et 24)
 Coen & Tineke van Dorssen
 29120 Plomeur, France
 tel. 02 98 82 10 22
 1st May to 31 Oct.
 http://www.keraluic.fr/

Bistrot
- *À la descente des marins*
 19 rue du Port
 29740 Plobannalec Lesconil
 tel. 02 98 82 24 35

24 The Étocs
Campsites
- *Camping municipal Toul Ar Ster* (24)
 Toul Ar Ster - 29760 Penmarc'h
 tel. 02 98 58 86 88 or 02 98 58 60 19

Very close to Ster beach, accessible at HW.
- *Camping municipal de Kerguellec* (24)
 La Palue de Kerguellec
 29720 Tréguennec
 15 June to 15 Sept.
 Out of season: tel. 02 98 87 60 35 (town hall)
 from 15 June: tel. 02 98 82 67 85
 www.treguennec.fr/spip.php?article4
- *Camping Kerlaz* (24)
 Tréguennec
 tel. 02 98 87 76 79
 http://www.kerlaz.com

Places of Interest
- *Centre Haliotika – La cité de la pêche*
 A lovely exhibition on the life of the fishermen.
 Le Port - 29730 Le Guilvinec
 Above the market at Guilvinec.
 The return of the boats from 16.45 is worth seeing.
 tel. 02 98 58 28 38
 http://www.haliotika.com/
- *Eckmühl lighthouse*
 Open every day 10.30 to 18.00 April-Sept. (depending on the weather) might be combined with a visit to the Marine Discovery Centre to be found in the lighthouse at Penmarc'h.
 tel. 06 07 21 37 34 or 02 98 58 60 19
- *Association Papa Poydenot* (beside the lighthouse)
 The "Papa Poydenot" lifeboat (1901), a historic artefact.
 155, rue Edmond Michelet
 29760 Penmarc'h
 tel. 02 98 58 67 36 or 02 98 58 60 19
 http://www.papapoydenot.com/
- *Marine Discovery Centre*
 (in the lighthouse at Penmarc'h).
 tel. 02 98 58 72 87 or 02 98 58 60 19 (town hall)
- *Visit to the markets and harbours of* Guilvinec, St. Guénolé-Penmar'h, Lesconil, Loctudy, Plouhinec, Douarnenez. Organised at the tourist office during the arrival of the fishing boats.
 St. Guénolé-Penmarc'h, tel. 02 98 58 81 44
 Loctudy, tel. 02 98 87 53 78
 Plouhinec, tel. 02 98 70 74 55

Bistrot
- *Les Brisants*
 2 av. du Port
 29730 Lechiagat – Treffiagat
 tel. 02 98 58 18 36

25 The Pointe du Raz
Campsites
- *Camping à la Ferme de Kerguidy Izella* (25-26)
 Kerguidy Izella - 29770 Plogoff
 tel. 02 98 70 35 60
 http://locations29.com/hebergements/kerguidy-izella/index.php

- *Camping à la ferme du Goyen* (25-26-27)
Vigouroux Christian - Kersall
29790 Mahalon
tel. 02 98 70 40 20
Open all year
http://www.camping-du-goyen.com/
- *Camping de la Baie* (25)
Lescleden.
29770 Cleden-Cap-Sizun
tel. 02 98 70 64 28
- *Camping vert de Kéringard* (25-26)
Famille Briand – Scoarnec
Keringard
29770 Cleden-Cap-Sizun
tel. 06 49 22 87 37 or 02 98 70 41 71
http://keringard.free.fr/

Places of Interest
- Interesting walk: Pointe du Van–Pointe du Raz and back (3h).

26 The Bird Cliffs of Cap Sizun
Campsites
- *Camping Municipal de Kerros* (25-26)
29770 Goulien
tel. 02 98 70 06 04
1st July-31 August.
- *Camping de Pors Peron* (26-27)
Nikki and Graham Hatch
29790 Beuzec-Cap-Sizun
tel. 02 98 70 40 24
24 March-30 Sept.
www.campingporsperon.com

Places of Interest
- *La Maison du vent* (Windmill Visitor centre)
Association Cap sur les moulins
Maison du vent
29770 Goulien
tel. 02 98 70 04 09
www.moulinscapsizun.com/la-maison-du-vent/
- *Cap Sizun nature reserve*
Gestion Bretagne Vivante-SEPNB
Près de Goulien.
- *Kériolet water mill*
Nearby Pointe du Millier
tel. 02 98 70 04 09 or 02 98 70 53 99
http://www.moulinscapsizun.com/

27 Douarnenez
Campsites
- *Camping Indigo Le Bois d'Isis* (27)
Avenue du bois d'Isis
29000 Douarnenez
tel. 02 98 74 05 67
www.camping-indigo.com
- *Camping Croas Men* (27-26)
27 bis rue du Croas Men
29100 Douarnenez-Tréboul
tel. 02 98 74 00 18
http://croas.men.pagesperso-orange.fr/

- *Camping de Kerleyou* (27-26)
29100 Douarnenez-Tréboul
tel. 02 98 74 13 03
http://www.camping-kerleyou.com/

Places of Interest
- *Le Port-Musée* (Harbour museum)
Place de l'Enfer, 29100 Douarnenez
tel. 02 98 92 65 20
http://www.port-musee.org/
- *Douarnenez fish market*
See the market and fish landings.
Office du Tourisme du Pays de Douarnenez
tel. 02 98 92 13 35
www.douarnenez-tourisme.com
- *Ile Tristan, guided tours* (timed for low water)
For information : 1 rue du Docteur Mével - 29172 Douarnenez
tel. 02 98 92 13 35
http://www.douarnenez-tourisme.com
- *Les Plomarc'h*
Rue des Plomarc'h
29100 Douarnenez
An interesting conservation area, working farm, garden, Roman site and municipal gîte. Near the coast between Rosmeur and the east of the Ry bay.
Free entry.
tel. 02 98 92 75 41
http://www.douarnenez-tourisme.com

28 The Caves of Morgat
Campsites
- *Camping de l'Aber* (28-29-30)
Tala ar Groas
Route de l'Aber, 29160 Crozon
tel. 02 98 27 02 96 or 06 75 62 39 07
http://www.camping-aber.com
- *Gîte d'étape de Saint-Hernot* (28-29-30)
Presqu'île de Crozon, Jacqueline Le Guillou
Saint-Hernot - 29160 Crozon-Morgat
tel. 02 98 27 15 00 or 06 30 05 11 08
- *Camping Les Bruyères* (28-29-30)
Le Bouis - 29160 Crozon-Morgat
tel. 02 98 26 14 87 or 06 03 65 19 23
www.camping-bruyeres-crozon.com
- *Camping La Plage de Goulien* (28-29-30)
Kernavéno - 29160 Crozon-Morgat
tel. 06 08 43 49 32
http://www.camping-crozon-laplage-degoulien.com

- *Camping Pen Ar Ménez* (28-29-30)
Bd Pralognan 29160 Crozon-Morgat
tel. 02 98 27 12 36
Town camp site, open all the year.
http://www.camping-pen-ar-menez.fr

Places of Interest
- *Maison des Minéraux* (Geological visitor centre)
Route du Cap de la Chèvre - Saint-Hernot
29160 Crozon
tel. 02 98 27 19 73
Explains the geology of the Crozon peninsula and the Massive Armoricain.
http://www.maison-des-mineraux.org

29 The Tas de Pois
Campsites
- *Camping municipal du Lannic* (29-30)
Rue du Grouannoc'h - 29570 Camaret
tel. 02 98 27 91 31 or 02 98 27 94 22
http://www.camaret-sur-mer.com/le-camping-municipal.php
- *Camping de Trez Rouz* (29-30)
Camping Plage de Trez Rouz
Route de camaret à Roscanvel
29160 Crozon
tel. 02 98 27 93 96
http://www.trezrouz.com/

Places of Interest
- *Vauban tower*
A UNESCO heritage site, near the Chapel of Notre-Dame de Rocamadour.
Tourist office Camaret-sur-mer
tel. 02 98 27 93 60
http://www.camaret-sur-mer.com
- *Lagatjar megalithic alignments*
About a 100 stones between Camaret and Toulinguet, along the road out to Pen-Hir.
http://www.camaret-sur-mer.com

30 Islands of Île des Morts and Trébéron
Campsites
- *Camping municipal de Roscanvel* (30-29)
29570 Roscanvel
800 m from the town.
tel. 02 98 27 43 23
Town hall : tel. 02 98 27 48 51
roscanvel.fr/-Camping-Municipal-
- *Camping Les Pieds Dans l'eau* (30-29)
Saint-Fiacre - 29160 Crozon
tel. 02 98 27 62 43
http://lespiedsdansleau.free.fr

Places of Interest
A tour of the forts
In the Roscanvel commune. By car or on foot to see the forts and admire the Goulet and Brest Harbour from high vantage points.

Addresses

31 Brest Harbour–The Aulne

Campsites

- *Camping au bord de l'Aulne et petit gîte d'étape* (31)
  Information at the town hall
  29560 Landévennec
  tel. 02 98 27 72 65
  http://www.inet-bretagne.fr/com/landevennec/

- *Camping de Gouelet Ker* (31)
  Gouelet Ker
  29460 Logonna-Daoulas
  tel. 02 98 20 64 52
  Open all year.
  http://www.camping-goueletker.com/

- *Camping Le Roz* (31)
  M. Thierry Olu
  Route Anse Du Roze
  29460 Logonna Daoulas
  tel. 09 81 92 67 86
  http://www.camping-du-roz.com

Places of Interest

- *Landévennec Abbey museum*
  29560 Landévennec
  tel. 02 98 27 35 90
  Beautiful displays.
  www.musee-abbaye-landevennec.fr/

- *Landévennec belvedere* offers an exceptional panorama of the Aulne.

- *Daoulas Abbey*
  Chemins du patrimoine en Finistère
  21 rue de l'église - 29460 Daoulas
  tel. 02 98 25 84 39
  A cultural centre with seasonal prestigeous international exhibitions. Also houses a botanic and physic garden.
  http://www.cdp29.fr/daoulas-lab-bayeenbref.html

Bistrot

- *Aulne, right bank*
  Bar-Resto, L'Ermitage,
  pas Terenez - 29590 Rosnoën
  tel. 02 98 81 93 61

32 The Headland of St. Mathieu

Campsites

- *Camping municipal de la plage de Portez* (32-33-34)
  29280 Locmaria-Plouzané
  tel. 02 98 48 49 85
  http://www.locmaria-plouzane.fr/

- *Chambres d'hôtes et camping à la ferme de Kériel* (32-33)
  Kéryel - Kérinou
  29217 Plougonvelin
  tel. 02 98 48 33 35 or 06 62 06 33 35
  1st May to 30 Sept.
  http://keryel.pagesperso-orange.fr/keryel.html

- *Camping et gîte accueil paysan* (32-33)
  Marie-Claire and Yves Jégou
  3, Kerivin - 29280 Plouzané
  tel. 02 98 45 82 32 or 06 84 16 74 88
  http://accueil-paysan-bretagne.fr

Places of Interest

- *Océanopolis*
  Port de Plaisance du Moulin blanc
  29210 Brest
  tel. 02 98 34 40 40
  Oceanic exhibition centre, 8000m^2 of exhibitions, aquariums and activities. The temperate house examines the seas off Brittany, there are also tropical and polar houses.
  http://www.oceanopolis.com/

- *Musée national de la Marine de Brest*
  (Brest National Marine museum)
  Château de Brest - 29200 Brest
  tel. 02 98 22 12 39
  Exhibitions on the maritime culture of France.
  http://www.musee-marine.fr/

- *St.Mathieu lighthouse*
  Inside the ruins of an old abbey, visit to the lighthouse and panoramic views.
  Office de tourisme - 29217 Plougonvelin
  tel. 02 98 48 30 18
  http://www.plougonvelin.fr

- *Fort de Bertheaume*
  Exhibition on the history and architecture of the fort. Night-time visits in summer.
  Office de tourisme - 29217 Plougonvelin
  tel. 02 98 48 30 18
  http://www.plougonvelin.fr

- *Corsen Coastguard lookout (CROSS)*
  Ten km north of Conquet, the theoretical boundary between the Atlantic and the Channel, the most westerly point on the mainland of France.

- *Les Tonnerres de Brest* – International marine festival
  A gathering of traditional boats, yachts and other vessels, sea-planes, kayaks etc.
  http://www.lestonnerresdebrest.fr

Bistrots

- *Bar Pub Les Quatre Vents*
  18 quai de la Douane
  29200 Brest
  tel. 02 98 44 42 84

- *Bar Les Mouettes*
  30 quai de la Douane
  29200 Brest
  tel. 02 98 44 33 21

- *The Dubliners*
  28 rue Mathieu Donnart
  29200 Brest
  tel. 02 98 46 04 98

- *The Tara Inn*
  1, rue Blaveau
  29200 Brest
  tel. 02 98 80 36 07

- *Le Tour du Monde*
  (Kersauzon bistrot)
  Moulin Blanc Harbour - Brest
  tel. 02 98 41 93 65
  http://www.tourdum.fr

33 Molène Archipelago

Campsites

- *Camping Les Blancs Sablons* (32-33)
  29217 Le Conquet
  tel. 02 98 36 07 91
  http://www.les-blancs-sablons.com

- *Camping municipal de Molène* (33)
  29259 Île de Molène
  Information from the town hall/
  tel. 02 98 07 39 05
  http://molene.fr

- *Quéménès Island farm guest house*
  29259 Archipel de Molène.
  Soizic and David's.
  tel. 06 63 02 15 08
  http://iledequemenes.hautetfort.com/

Places of Interest

- *Drummond Castle Museum*
  Bourg de Molène
  Famous British shipwreck in 1896, the survivors were rescued by the people of Molène.
  tel. 02 98 07 38 41
  http://molene.fr

- *Maison de l'Environnement Insulaire*
  (Island Life Visitor Centre)
  The natural history and culture of Molène.
  tel. 02 98 07 38 92
  http://molene.fr

34 Aber Ildut to Portsall

Campsites

- *Camping municipal de Porsevigné* (34)
  tel. 02 98 89 69 16 or 02 98 89 60 07
  29810 Plouarzel
  http://www.plouarzel.fr/

- *Camping municipal de Porscuidic* (34)
  Rue des mouettes
  29810 Plouarzel
  tel. 02 98 84 08 52 or 02 98 89 60 07
  15 May-15 Sept.
  http://www.plouarzel.fr/

- *Camping municipal de Ruscumunoc* (34)
  Ruscumunoc
  29810 Plouarzel
  tel. 02 98 89 63 49 (or out of season 02 98 89 60 07) or 06 24 42 67 85
  15 May-15 Sept.
  http://www.plouarzel.fr/

- *Camping municipal de Saint-Gonvel* (34)
Saint-Gonvel, Argenton
29840 Landunvez
tel. 02 98 89 91 00
http://www.landunvez.fr/
- *Ferme de Lanniouarn* (34)
Mme et Mr Joseph L'Hostis
Caletour - 29810 Plouarzel
tel. 02 98 89 60 44
http://www.bretagnealaferme.com

Places of Interest
- *La maison de l'algue* (Seaweed visitor centre)
Port de Lanildut
tel. 02 98 48 12 88 or 02 98 04 31 62
- *L'Ancre « An Eor », Port of Portsall.*
An exhibition about the tragedy of the Amoco Cadiz shipwreck. Named after the ship's anchor in front of it.
- *Kerglonou Quarries, aber Ildut*
Visitor trail exploring the history of the quarrying.
http://www.geodiversite.net/tag315

35 The Aber Benoît
Campsites
- *Camping municipal des Dunes* (35-34)
Le Vourc'h
29830 Lampaul-Ploudalmezeau
tel. 02 98 48 14 29 or 02 98 48 11 28
- *Camping de l'Aber Benoît* (35-34)
89 rue de Corn ar Gazel
29830 Saint-Pabu
tel. 02 98 89 76 25
Easter-end Sept.
www.camping-aber-benoit.com/

Speciality
- *Oysters and seafood at Prat Ar Coum*
Prat Ar Coum - 29870 Lannilis
tel. 02 98 04 00 12

36 Aber Wrac'h and Île Vierge
Campsites
- *Camping municipal de Penn-Enez* (35-36)
Presqu'île Sainte-Marguerite
551 Lieu-dit Penn Enez
29870 Landeda
A lovely spot beside the sea.
April to end Sept.
tel. 02.98.04.99.82
http://www.camping-penn-enez.com/

Places of Interest
- *La Vierge lighthouse*
Open April-Oct.
Entrance fee euro 2.50. Visits are organised by the Plouguerneau Ecomusee. To join a group visit contact: 02 98 37 13 35.
On large spring tides access on foot is possible from Lilia (45 minutes walk and 2 hour visit).
http://www.abers-tourisme.com

- *Île Wrach lighthouse*
Temporary exhibitions.
Accessible on foot at low water from Saint-Cava beach.
tel. 02 98 04 70 93 (Tourist office des Abers)
- *L'Écomusée de Plouguerneau*
(Seaweed and Goémonier Museum) offers courses in cooking seaweeds.
Route de Saint-Michel
29880 Plouguerneau
tel. 02 98 37 13 35
www.ecomusee-plouguerneau.com/
- *Festivals to celebrate the Goémoniers*
In August at Koréjou, Plouguerneau, August 15th at Memham, Keriouan and every other year (odd years) in summer at Kerurus, Plounéour-Trez.

37 The Pagan Coast
Campsites
Camping du Phare (de Pontusval) (37)
Route du Phare
29890 Brignogan-Plage
tel. 02 98 83 45 06
http://www.camping-du-phare.com
- *Camping de la Côte des Légendes* (37)
Rue Douar ar pont
29890 Brignogan-Plage
tel. 02 98 83 41 65
www.campingcotedeslegendes.com
- *Camping municipal de Rudoloc* (37)
Rudoloc
29890 Kerlouan
tel. 02 98 83 94 48 or 02 98 83 93 13
http://www.tourisme-lesneven-cote-deslegendes.fr
- *Camping de Neiz Vran* (37)
Pointe de Neiz Vran
29890 Kerlouan
tel. 02 98 25 63 11 or 02 98 83 93 13
15 March-15 Nov.
http://www.camping-bretagne-kerlouan.com/
- *Aire naturelle de Kerallloret* (37)
Kerallloret
29880 Guissény
tel. 02 98 25 60 37
http://www.keralloret.com/
- *Gîte du village de Ménez-Ham* (37)
3.5km north of Keriouan village, nice atmosphere.
Françoise Lyvinec, tel. 06 43 38 16 03
http://www.gite-meneham.fr/
http://www.tourisme-lesneven-cote-deslegendes.fr/

Places of Interest
- *Tour of Menez-Ham*
Beautiful, but touristy old village, fishermen, farmers and goemoniers, artists workshops.
tel. 02 98 83 95 63 or 02 98 83 92 87

38 The Dunes of Keremma
Campsites
- *Camping municipal de Keremma* (38)
La sablière - 29430 Tréflez
tel. 02 98 61 62 79 or 02 98 61 45 72 (town hall)
Mid June to end August.
- *Camping municipal de Poulfoën* (38-39)
Poulfoën - 29430 Plouescat
tel. 02 98 69 81 80 (in season) or 02 98 69 62 18 (out of season)
Mid June to mid Sept.
http://www.tourisme-plouescat.com/
- *Camping de la Baie du Kernic* (38)
Rue de Pen an Theven, au lieu-dit Pors Guen - 29430 Plouescat
tel. 0825 002 030 or 02 98 69 86 60 (in season)
Beginning April-mid Sept.
http://www.paysduleon.com
- *Camping municipal de Poulennou* (38-39)
Poulennou - 29233 Cléder
Close to Kervaliou beach.
1st July-31 August: tel. 02 98 69 48 37
out of season: tel. 02 98 69 40 09
http://www.camping-poulennou.fr/
- *Camping de Kérurus* (38-37)
Rue de Beg Kuleren
29890 Plounéour Trez
tel. 02 98 83 41 87
1st April-30 Sept.
http://www.camping-kerurus.com/
- *Camping municipal d'Ode Vraz* (38)
300m from bay of Kernic.
tel. 02 98 61 65 17
Mid June-mid Sept.
Contact: town hall Plounévez-Lochrist
- *Aire naturelle de camping Goulven* (38)
Ty Poas
29890 Goulven
tel. 02 98 83 40 69 or 06 64 63 94 07
http://campinggoulven.free.fr/
http://www.tourisme-lesneven-cote-deslegendes.fr
- *Camping village de Roguennic* (38-39)
Roguennic - 29233 Cleder
tel. 02 98 69 63 88
Open all year.
www.campingvillageroguennic.com/

Places of Interest
- *Maison des Dunes et de la Randonnée* (visitor centre and trail, exhibitions etc.)
Route de Goulven
29430 Tréflez
tel. 02 98 61 69 69
http://www.maisondesdunes.org

39 The Island of Siec
Campsites
- *Camping municipal des Dunes* (39-40)
590 rue du Theven Bras, Le Dossen
29250 Santec
tel. 02 98 29 75 34

Addresses

A lovely site in the dunes, direct access to the beach, and handy for Roscoff ferry port.
http://www.santec.fr
- *Camping municipal du Bois de la Palud* (39)
Le bois de la Palud - 29250 Plougoulm
tel. 02 98 29 81 82
tel. 02 98 29 90 76 (town hall)
15 June-5 Sept.
A nice site in the Guillec valley, 5km from Saint-Pol-de-Léon and 8km from Roscoff.
http://www.paysduleon.com
- *Camping Le Theven* (39)
Moguériec 29250 - Sibiril
tel. 02 98 29 96 86
Open all year.
http://camping.theven.29.pagesperso-orange.fr/
- *Camping Ar Roc'h*
Moguériec - 29250 Sibiril
tel. 02 98 29 97 14
15 june-15 Sept.
http://www.paysduleon.com

40 The Island of Batz
Campsites
- *Terrain d'hébergement de plein air* - Île de Batz (40-39)
29253 Île de Batz
On the SW of the island, beside the beach.
tel. 02 98 61 75 70 or 02 98 61 77 76
http://www.iledebatz.com
- *Camping « Aux Quatre Saisons »* (40-39)
Perharidy, Le Ruguel - 29680 Roscoff
tel. 02 98 69 70 86
tel. 06 07 41 28 53 (out of season)
April-Oct.
www.camping-aux4saisons.com/

Places of Interest
- *Batz lighthouse*
Open everyday in July and August and weekends and public holidays. Superb views of the island.
- *Georges Delaselle Garden*
Penn Batz
Entrance fee.
tel. 02 98 61 75 65
1st April-1st Nov.
http://www.jardin-georgesdelaselle.fr/
- *Roscoff fishmarket*
port du Bloscon
Exhibitions on fish and fishing, activities for children.
tel. 02 98 62 39 26
http://www.roscoff-tourisme.com
http://www.morlaix.cci.fr
- *La Maison des Johnnies et de l'Oignon de Roscoff* (Onion museum and Annual Onion Festival)
History of the French onion seller and his bicycle.
48, rue Brizeux - 29680 Roscoff.
tel. 02 98 61 25 48
http://www.roscoff-tourisme.com/index.php/content/view/full/17593/

41 The Bay of Morlaix
Campsites
- *Aire naturelle les Hortensias* (41)
Kermen
29660 Carantec
tel. 02 98 67 08 63
Organic vegetables available from "Ferme de Kermen".
http://www.leshortensias.fr/
- *Camping municipal de la Mer* (41-42)
15 route de Karreg An Ty
Primel - Trégastel
29630 Plougasnou
tel. 02 98 67 30 06
http://www.mairie-plougasnou.fr/
- *Camping Tal Ar Mor* (41)
Kerlaudy
Pont de la Corde
29420 Plouénan
tel. 02 98 15 89 35
On the banks of the river Penzé.
http://campingtalarmor.com/
- *Camping de la Baie de Térenez* (41-42)
Térénez
29252 Plouezoc'h
tel. 02 98 67 26 80
www.campingbaiedeterenez.com/
- *Camping de Trologot* (41)
Grève du Man - 29250 Saint-Pol-de-Léon
tel. 02 98 69 06 26 or 06 62 18 39 30
http://www.camping-trologot.com/
- *La Maison de Kerdiès* (41-42)
(Gite and restaurant)
5, route de Pérherel - Saint-Samson
29630 Plougasnou
tel. 02 98 72 40 66
http://maison.kerdies.free.fr
- *Gîte de l'île Louet à Carantec* (41)
An unusual spot that can welcome 10 persons
30 March-31 Oct.
Very successful, advance booking necessary (internet):
http://tourisme.morlaix.fr
- *Camping municipal de Kérilis* (41)
Menec Izella - 29670 Henvic
tel. 02 98 62 82 10 or 02 98 62 81 11
or 02 98 62 81 56
Possible accommodation out of season
tel. 02 98 62 81 11
http://tourisme.morlaix.fr

Places of Interest
- *Baranez megalithic site*
29252 Plouezoc'h
tel. 02 98 67 24 73
or 02 98 79 51 58
barnenez.monuments-nationaux.fr/
- *Taureau Castle*
Information: 02 98 62 29 73
http://www.chateaudutaureau.com/

42 Primel
Campsites
- *Camping municipal du fond de la baie* (42)
Route de Plestin-les-Grèves
29241 Locquirec
tel. out of season: Mairie 02 98 67 42 20
tel. in season : 02 98 67 40 85
www.mairie-locquirec.com
- *Camping municipal de Pont Ar Gler* (42)
Pont Ar Gler
29630 Saint-Jean-du-Doigt
tel. 02 98 67 32 15 or 02 98 67 34 07
or 02 98 67 84 64
- *Camping Municipal de Saint-Efflam* (42)
Rue Lan Carré - Saint-Efflam
22310 Plestin-les-Grèves
tel. 02 96 35 62 15
http://www.camping-municipal-bretagne.com/
- *Camping de Kerven* (42)
1 impasse de Kerven
29630 Plougasnou
tel. 02 98 72 41 22 or 06 09 42 13 89
http://campingkerven.free.fr
- *Camping du Rugunay* (42)
7 rue Rugunay - 29241 Locquirec
tel. 02 98 67 41 06 or 06 30 04 73 18
http://www.campinglerugunay.com/

Bistrot
- *Caplan and Co*
Poul Rodou - 29620 Guimaëc
tel. 02 98 67 58 98
Cafe, book shop, pubisher and Greek specialities, near the beach.
http://www.caplanandco.fr/

43 Trébeurden and Île Grande
Campsites
- *Camping municipal du Dourlin* (43-44)
By the sea on Île Grande.
End April to end Sept.
tel. 02 96 91 92 41
http://www.pleumeur-bodou.com
- *Auberge de Jeunesse du Toëno* (43)
(Youth Hostel)
60, corniche de Goas Treiz
22560 Trébeurden
Facing the sea.
tel. 02 96 23 52 22
1st March-31 Oct. and all year for groups

with prior booking, 55 beds, 20 camping places.
http://www.fuaj.org/
• **Auberge de Jeunesse de Beg Léguer** (43) (Youth Hostel)
Plage de Goas Lagorn - Beg Léguer, 22300 Lannion
tel. 02 96 47 24 86
http://www.fuaj.org
http://www.ot-lannion.fr
• **Gîtes d'étape de l'île Milliau** (43)
Information and reservations : Office de Tourisme
Place Crec'h Hery - BP 49
22560 Trébeurden
tel. 02 96 23 51 64
http://www.tourisme-trebeurden.com
• **Camping municipal de Landrellec** (43-44)
2 Karrhent Bringwiller
Presqu'île de Landrellec
22560 Pleumeur-Bodou
tel. 02 96 23 87 92
tel. 02 96 23 91 47 (out of season)
1st May-mid Sept.
http://www.pleumeur-bodou.com

Places of Interest
• *Quellen marshes*
Near the beach of Goas triez. A marked path allows access to grazing Camargue horses. Guided tours of the horses and the wildlife in July and August.
• *Le Toëno*
Natural salt marshes, a menhir in the middle is covered by the sea at HW.
• *Notenno marshes*
Terra Maris organises outings "ancient stones and salt marsh plants". Guided tours in July and August.
Information and reservations at the tourist office: 02.96.23.51.64
http://www.tourisme-trebeurden.com
• *Le Parc du Radôme* (Radar Dome)
22560 Pleumeur-Bodou
Science, astronomy, history, archaeology, natural history, family activities…
http://www.parcduradome.com/
1) Planetarium
tel. 02 96 15 80 30
Info 24h/24: 02 96 15 80 32
http://www.planetarium-bretagne.fr/
2) "Cité des Télécoms" (telecomunication exhibition).
3) Breton culture and technology, exhibitions, activities, tours.
4) Village of Gauls.

44 Trégastel
Campsites
• *Camping Ferme de Kerangloff* (43-44-45-46)
Aire naturelle de camping.
Barnabanec
22700 Perros Guirec
tel. 02 96 23 28 67

• *Camping Tourony* (44-45-46)
105 rue de Poul Palud
22730 Trégastel
tel. 02 96 23 86 61
Beginning April-end Sept.
http://camping-tourony.com/

Places of Interest
• *Aquarium Marin de Trégastel* (Marine aquarium)
Boulevard du Coz-Pors
22730 Trégastel
tel. 02 96 23 48 58
Beach walks, seaweed identification.
http://www.aquarium-tregastel.com

photo Y. Dodard

45 Pink Granite
46 The Sept Îles
Campsites
• *Camping municipal des Deux Rives* (43-44-45-46)
Rue du Moulin du Duc
22300 Lannion
tel. 02 96 46 31 40 or 06 13 22 97 86
Open all year.
http://www.ville-lannion.fr

47 The Islands of Port Blanc
Campsites
• *Camping des Dunes* (47)
Rue de Crec'h Avel
Port-Blanc
22710 Penvénan
tel. 02 96 92 63 42
tel. 02 96 92 67 59 (out of season)
Mid May-Mid Sept.
http://www.ville-penvenan.com
http://www.tregor-cotedajoncs-tourisme.com/
• *Camping de Buguélès* (47-48)
Crec'h Kerdouaré
Buguélès
22710 Penvénan
Near Bilo beach.
tel. 02 96 92 87 83 or 02 96 92 67 59
Beginning July-end August
http://www.ville-penvenan.com
• *Camping Les Mouettes* (48)
22660 Trévou-Tréguignec
Simple and friendly, direct access to the sea (trolley at LW).
tel. 02 98 67 02 46

Bistrot
• *Gwenojenn Bar-Expo*
50 rue du Royau 22660 Trévou Tréguignec
tel. 02 96 23 71 36
http://gwenojenn.Brittanyinfo.org/

48 The Island of Er
Campsites
• *Camping municipal de Beg Ar Vilin* (48)
Beg Ar Vilin - 22820 Plougrecsant
tel. 02 96 92 56 15
Adjacent to a slipway.
Mid June-mid Sept.
http://www.plougrescant.fr/camping
• *Camping Le Varlen* (48)
4 Pors Hir 22820 Plougrescant
tel. 02 96 92 52 15 or 06 03 96 64 11
1st April-beginning Nov.
http://www.levarlen.com/
• *Ferme du Syet* (47-48)
Natural camp site.
Le Syet - 22220 Minihy-Tréguier
tel. 02 96 92 31 79 or 02 96 92 14 38 or 06 73 39 43 91
1st May-30 Sept.
http://www.la-ferme-du-syet.com/
• *Camping du Gouffre* (47-48)
Hent Crec'h kermorvan
22820 Pougrescant
tel. 02 96 92 02 95 or 02 96 92 52 99 or 06 89 60 10 19
1st April-30 Sept.
http://www.camping-gouffre.com/
• *Camping à la ferme des Hortensias* (47-48-52)
Odile et Alain Connan
Lestivoan Bras
22450 Pommerit-Jaudy
tel. 02 96 91 33 31 or 02 96 91 50 00 or 06 71 30 27 82
Open all year.
www.campingalaferme-leshortensias.com
• *Camping de Port la Chaîne* (48)
22610 Pleubian
tel. 02 96 22 92 38
April-mid Sept.
http://www.portlachaine.com/

Places of Interest
• *La maison du littoral* (Coastal visitor centre)
Castel Meur - 22820 Plougrescant
Information and activities on the coastal environment.
tel. 02 96 92 58 35
• *Coper Marine* (bits and pieces)
Pont Canada
22220 Trédarzec
tel. 02 96 92 35 72
An Aladdin's cave for all those who like the sea.
http://www.coper-marine.com/

Addresses

Bistrot
- *Café Pesked*
La Roche Jaune - 22220 Plouguiel
Left bank of the Jaudy between Treguier and Beg ar Vilin.
tel. 02 96 92 01 82

49 The Sillon de Talbert
50 The Rocky Bréhat
Campsite
- *Camping Municipal Le Ouern* (Gouern Bay) (49-50-52)
Loguivy (750m due south-east of Loguivy harbour).
tel. 02 96 55 80 36
22620 Ploubazlanec

Bistrot
- *Café Chez Gaud*
Port de Loguivy
Unmissable.

51 Circumnavigating Bréhat
Campsites
- *Camping Panorama du Rohou* (50-51-52-53)
5 chemin du Rohou, Pointe de l'Arcouest
22620 Ploubazlanec
tel. 02 96 55 87 22
Open all year.
http://www.campingpanorama.com/
- *Le camping municipal de Bréhat* (50-51)
On the south-west point of the island at Goareva, just above Port-Clos
1st June-12 Sept (busy in mid season).
tel. 02 96 20 00 36 (town hall).
Goareva: 02 96 20 02 46
http://www.iledebrehat.fr

Places of Interest
- *Le musée de la Mer de Paimpol* (Museum of the sea)
Rue de Labenne
22500 Paimpol
tel. 02 96 22 02 19
http://www.museemerpaimpol.com/
- *Birlot mill* (association)
22870 Île de Bréhat
tel. 02 96 20 02 83
http://www.bretagnenet.com/moulin_brehat/
- *Les Verreries de Bréhat* (Bréhat glassworks) Fort de Bréhat
22870 Île de Bréhat
tel. 02 96 20 09 09
http://www.verreriesdebrehat.com/
- *St-Michel chapel*, panoramic viewpoint.
- *Le Paon lighthouse*
A good objective for a walk.
- *Festival du chant de marin* (sea shanty and world music festival)
August every other year.
http://www.paimpol-2013.com/

52 The Trieux Estuary
Campsites
- *Camping municipal de Kermarquer* (52)
23 rue de Kermarquer
22740 Lézardrieux
tel. 02 96 20 17 22 (in season)
tel. 02 96 20 10 20 (out of season)
Access to a small beach.
15 June-15 Sept.
http://www.tourismebretagne.com
- *Camping municipal du Bois d'Amour* (52)
At the imit of the maritime Trieux, short trolley to the Kerblouc'h slipway.
tel. 02 96 95 62 62 (Quemper town hall) 22260 Guézennec)
http://www.quemper-guezennec.com/
- *Gîtes Du-zé* (52)
Lieu dit Ar C'hadiou
22740 Pleumeur Gautier
tel. 06 84 55 14 61 or 02 96 22 18 37
http://www.gites-duce.com/

Places of Interest
- *La Vapeur du Trieux* (Steam railway)
Explore the valley between Paimpol and Pontrieux by steam.
tel. 0 892 391 427
http://www.vapeurdutrieux.com/
- *Château de la Roche Jagu*
22260 Ploëzal
Magnificent gardens and exhibitions in the chateau.
tel. 02 96 95 62 35
http://www.larochejagu.fr/
- *Maison de l'Estuaire de Traou-Nez*
22860 Plourivo
In the ancient farmstead of Traou-Nez, site of the infamous Seznec murder.
tel. 02 96 55 96 79
http://www.plourivo.fr

53 Porz Even
Places of Interest
- *Le mur des disparus en mer*
At the Ploubazlanec cemetery, an emotive hommage to those who lost their lives fishing on the high seas.
- *Le musée « Mémoire d'Islande »*
Museum of the Newfoundland and Icelandic cod fisheries.
Ploubazlanec, place de la Mairie
tel. 02 96 55 84 62 or 02 96 55 82 16

54 The Cliffs of Bréhec
Campsites
- *Camping de Cruckin* (49 to 54)
Rue de Cruckin, Kérity
22500 Paimpol
tel. 02 96 20 78 47
tel. 02 96 55 31 70 (out of season)
http://www.camping-paimpol.com/
- *Camping municipal La Pépinière* (54-55)
Rue René Cassin
22470 Plouézec
tel. 02 96 20 68 78
tel. 02 96 20 64 90 (out of season)
15 June-15 Sept.
http://www.tourismebretagne.com
- *Camping Le Varquez-sur-mer* (54-55)
5 route de la Corniche Bréhec-plage
22580 Plouha
tel. 02 96 22 34 43
http://www.camping-le-varquez.com/
- *Camping du Cap Horn* (54-55)
Cap des îles
Port Lazo - 22470 Plouézec
tel. 02 96 20 64 28
31 March-30 Sept.
http://www.lecaphorn.com

Places of Interest
- *Abbaye Maritime de Beauport* (Beauport Marine Abbey)
Kérity - 22500 Paimpol
tel. 02 96 55 18 58 or 02 96 55 18 55
http://www.abbaye-beauport.com/

55 The Islands of Saint-Quay
Campsites
- *La Ferme de Kerogel* (54-55)
Laurent and Christine Le Faucheur
22290 Goudelin
tel. 02 96 70 03 15 (evenings)
or 06 75 89 89 47
http://www.kerogel.com
- *Camping municipal Les Fauvettes* (55)
13 rue des Fauvettes
22520 Binic
tel. 02 96 73 60 83
tel. 02 96 73 39 90 (out of season)
http://www.ville-binic.fr

56 Cape Fréhel
Campsites
- *Cidrerie de la Baie* (56)
Home brewed cider, camping, donkey hire; Jean-Marc Camus and Corinne Rousseau (kayakers).
Saint-Plestan - 22400 Plancuenoual
tel. 06 71 19 35 29
or 02 96 93 89 82
April-Sept.
http://www.cidrerie-delabaie.com/
- *Camping Municipal du Pont de l'Étang* (56)
Pléhérel-Plage - 22240 Fréhel
tel. 02 96 41 40 45
1st April-30 Sept.
http://www.camping.frehel.info
Out of season contact the town hall
tel. 02 96 41 40 12
- *Camping municipal Saint-Michel*
Rue Saint-Michel - Les Hôpitaux
22430 Erquy
tel. 02 96 72 37 67
tel. 02 96 63 64 64 (out of season)
2 April-30 Sept.
http://www.ville-erquy.com

- *Camping municipal Le Guen*
  23, Avenue Léon Hamonet - 22430 Erquy.
  tel. 02 96 72 07 05 (in season)
  tel. 02 96 63 64 64 (out of season)
  Mid-June to mid Sept.
  http://www.ville-erquy.com

Places of Interest
- *Phare du Cap Fréhel* (lighthouse)
  Open to the public from April.
  http://www.plevenon.fr
- *Fort La Latte*
  tel. 02 99 30 38 84
  http://www.casteland.com
- *Visite de la criée d'Erquy* (fish market)
  Tourist office Erquy
  tel. 02 96 72 30 12
  http://www.erquy-tourisme.com
- *Donkey hire* by the half-day, day or week.
  tel. 06 71 19 35 29 or 02 96 93 89 82
  http://www.korrig-ane.com

57 Saint-Briac–Les Hébihens
Campsite
- *Camping municipal Les Mielles* (57)
  Rue Jules Jeunet
  22770 Lancieux
  tel. 02 96 86 22 98 or 06 20 00 69 46
  1st April-30 Sept.
  http://www.mairie-lancieux.fr/

58 The Tidal Rance
Campsites
- *Camping municipal le Rivage* (58)
  Mont rivage
  35870 Le Minihic-sur-Rance
  tel. 02 99 88 56 15 or 02 99 88 59 10
- *Camping municipal de Saint-Suliac* (58)
  35430 Saint-Suliac
  Bord de Rance.
  tel. 02 99 58 41 98 (town hall)
  tel. 06 07 80 48 51 (in season)
  1st April-31 Oct. (camping)
  http://www.saint-suliac.fr

Places of Interest
- *Usine marémotrice de la Rance* (tidal power station)
  Visit: tourist office Dinard tel. 02 99 16 37 14
  http://www.ot-dinard.com

- *Moulin à marée du Prat* (Prat tide mill)
  Le Prat - 22690 La Vicomté-sur-Rance
  Exhibition, demonstrations of mills and milling on the Rance. This mill has been restored to original working order.
  tel. 02 96 83 21 41 (town hall)
- *La Maison de la Rance* (visitor centre)
  Quai Talard, port de Dinan-Lanvallay
  22100 Lanvallay
  tel. 02 96 87 00 40
  www.codi.fr/la-maison-de-la-rance

Bistrot
- *Bistrot Jersey Lillie*
  Typical English pub, easy access by kayak. Left bank of the Rance, slipway.
  51 rue de la Cale de Jouvente
  35730 Pleurtuit
  tel. 02 99 88 51 80
  http://www.jerseylilliejouvente.com/

59 The forts of Saint-Malo
Campsites
- *Camping municipal de la Cité d'Alet* (58-59-60)
  Allée Gaston Buy
  35400 Saint-Malo
  tel. 02 99 81 60 91 (in season)
  tel. 02 99 21 92 64 (out of season)
  End April-end Sept.
  http://www.ville-saint-malo.fr/tourisme/les-campings/
- *Camping municipal Les Nielles* (58-59-60)
  Avenue John Kennedy
  35400 Saint-Malo
  tel. 02 99 40 26 35 (in season)
  tel. 02 99 21 92 64 (out of season)
  July-August.
  http://www.ville-saint-malo.fr/tourisme/les-campings/
- *Camping municipal Le Nicet* (59-60)
  Avenue de la Varde
  35400 Saint-Malo
  tel. 02 99 40 26 32 (in season)
  tel. 02 99 21 92 64 (out of season)
  July-August.
  http://www.ville-saint-malo.fr/tourisme/les-campings/

Places of Interest
- *Le fort national*
  Historic monument built by Vauban. Facing the Saint-Thomas gate.
  tel. 06 72 46 66 26
  When the flag is flying it is open. Access on foot at low water.
  http://www.fortnational.com/
- *L'île du Grand-Bey*
  Chateaubriand's tomb, access on foot at low water.
  http://www.saint-malo-tourisme.com
- *Le fort du Petit-Bey*
  Exhibition on Vauban and the military history of Saint-Malo. When the flag is flying it is open, Access on foot at low water.

  tel. 06 08 27 51 20
  http://www.petit-be.com/
- *Le grand aquarium de Saint-Malo* (aquarium) Avenue du Général Patton
  35402 Saint-Malo
  tel. 02 99 21 19 00
  http://www.aquarium-st-malo.com/
- *Musée d'Histoire (Château et Tour Solidor)*
  - History of Saint-Malo (the Chateau)
  - Windjammers and tall ships (Solidor Tower)
  tel. 02 99 40 71 58
  http://www.ville-saint-malo.fr

Bistrots
- *Cunningham's Bar*
  2 rue des Hauts Sablons
  (In front of Bas-Sablons harbour)
  tel. 02 99 81 48 08
- *Le Repaire des Corsaires* (The Corsair's Lair), Île Cézembre
  tel. 02 99 56 78 22
  End March-end October.
  Best out of season.

60 The Emerald Coast
Campsites
- *La ferme de la Briantais* (58-59-60)
  Chantal Cadiou
  35430 St. Jouan-des-Guerets
  (5 minutes from Saint-Malo) space for 6 tents, open thoughout the year.
  http://www.bretagnealaferme.com
- *Auberge de Jeunesse de Port Picain* (youth hostel) Port Picain
  35260 Cancale
  Close to the beach.
  tel. 02 99 89 62 62 or 02 99 89 78 79
  http://www.fuaj.org/cancale-baie-de-saint-michel

Places of Interest
- *Boat trips on « La Cancalaise »* a traditional gaff rigged sailing boat
  information; Halle aux marées
  35260 Cancale
  tel. 02 99 89 77 87
  http://www.lacancalaise.org
- *Hike along the lovely coastal path* from Cancale to Grouin headland.
- *La ferme marine de Cancale*
  Oyster farming and sea shells.
  tel. 02 99 89 69 99
  http://www.ferme-marine.com
- *La Maison de la Baie du Vivier-sur-mer*
  Visitor centre and guided tours, mussel farming, shrimping and use of traditional fish traps in the Bay of Mont Saint-Michel.
  Port Le Vivier / Cherrueix
  35960 Le Vivier-sur-mer
  tel. 02 99 48 84 38
  Open all year.
  http://www.maison-baie.com/ ∎

Addresses

Useful websites

THE MORE FRENCH you understand the more useful they will be...

Kayaking organisations

Pagayeurs Marins, Fédération de la Plaisance en Kayak de Mer. This association is very active in lobbying for kayakers' rights and responsibilities when paddling on the sea. The back issues of their magazine *Pagaie Salée* are available on the website and make fascinating reading.
www.pagayeursmarins.org/

Comité Régional de Bretagne de Canoë-Kayak (CRBCK). Regional branch of the Fédération Française de Canoë-Kayak (FFCK), official competition programme, but also useful links to weather and tides for the sea paddler.
www.canoe-kayak-bretagne.fr/

Connaissance du Kayak de Mer (CK/mer). Newsletter, trips and a training programme. Organises a biennial gathering which is well worth attending. English and Catalan/Spanish spoken as well as French.
www.ckmer.org/

« ***kayakdemer.eu*** ». Internet forum, organised trips and a biennial gathering (alternates with CK/mer). Non-French can sign up, but contact the site for a working alternative to the departmental code which you need to put after your forename.
www.kayakdemer.eu/

Kayakalo. Details including, maps, photos and GPS co-ordinates, for all the launch points in this guide and many more.
www.kayakalo.fr

Magazines

Carnets d'Aventures. Online magazine and forum on non-motorised travel and expeditions, on foot, bike, horse...and kayak. Useful articles on short and long expeditions and equipment reviews.
http://www.expemag.com/

Canoë Kayak Magazine. Covers all kayaking and canoeing disciplines, free online content.
www.canoekayakmagazine.com/

Institutions

Mer et Littoral (Sea and seashore). Government site with regulations and advice.
http://www.mer.equipement.gouv.fr
http://www.developpement-durable.gouv.fr/Kayaks-et-avirons-de-mer.html

SHOM (Service Hydrographique et Océanographique de la Marine). Charts, tides and weather.
http://www.shom.fr/

L'Almanach du marin breton. Links to ports and anchorages, weather and safety, and much more; including sea kayaking. The maritime maxims at the top of the page are an opportunity to practice your French, here is a good one for the kayaker in Brittany; *Le pire des défauts, c'est le découragement: mais il est inconnu du marin breton.*
http://www.marinbreton.com/

Société Nationale de Sauvetage en Mer (SNSM).
http://www.snsm.org

La Bretagne et la mer (Brittany and the Sea). Developing a sustainable Breton coast.
http://www.labretagneetlamer.fr/

IFREMER - Marine scientific research, English website.
http://wwz.ifremer.fr/institut_eng

Conservatoire du littoral (Coastal conservancy). Details of sites of managed by the conservancy.
http://www.conservatoire-du-littoral.fr

Bretagne Vivante (SEPNB) (Living Brittany). Details of nature reserves etc.
http://www.bretagne-vivante.org/

Ligue pour la Protection des Oiseaux (LPO) (League for the protection of birds).
http://www.lpo.fr/

Eau et Rivières de Bretagne. Pressure group for cleaner rivers and coastal waters.
http://www.eau-et-rivieres.asso.fr/

Gateway to tourist information.
http://www.tourismebretagne.com

Lexicon

English	French
aground	échoué
back rest	dosseret (m)
bail / bailer	écoper (verb) / écope (noun) (f)
beach (sandy) (shingle etc.)	plage (f) (grève) (f)
beam	maître bau, largeur
bilge	fond (m) de cale
boil (in an eddy)	marmite (f)
bow / bow-stem	proue (f) / étrave (f)
brace high brace low	appui en suspension appui en poussée
break, a rest to break something	repos (m) casser
breaker	brisant (m)
broach	aborder
bulkhead	cloison (f)
buoy (cardinal / lateral)	bouée (f) (cardinale / latérale)
capsize (noun) capsize (verb)	chavirage / dessalage dessaler / chavirer
change course go about	virer virer bord pour bord
chine (hard chine) (soft chine)	bouchain (m) (bouchain vif) (bouchain adouci, en forme, arrondi)
clapotis	ressac
cleat	taquet (m)
cliff	falaise (f)
coaming	hiloire (f)
compass	compas
deck (fore-deck / aft-deck) (deck-line)	pont (pont avant / pont arrière) (ligne de vie)
dimensions (length / beam / depth)	gabarit (longueur / largeur / profondeur)
dive (bow or stern plunging under water)	enfourner
draft	tirant d'eau
draw stroke	appel
dry bag	sac étanche
dry suit	combinaison étanche
dry top	anorak étanche

English	French
ebb (tide)	jusant (m), marée descendante
eddy	contre-courant
edge / edging	gîte / avec gîte
feathered paddle (no feather)	pales croisées (pales décroisées)
ferryglide to ferryglide	bac (m) faire un bac
flare (i.e. of a bow)	élancement
flood (tide)	flot (m), marée montante
foot rest foot pegs	appuis pieds, cale-pieds pédales
free board	franc-bord
gunwale	plat-bord
hatch (hatch cover) (watertight compartment)	trappe (couvercle de trappe) (caisson)
heading	cap (m)
helmet	casque (m)
help	secours, sauvetage (dial 112 not 999)
hull (hull below the waterline) (superstructure)	coque (f) (carène) (f) (fardage) (m)
keel	quille
kit (all your equipment) kit (useful bits and pieces)	équipement accastillage
knee brace (hip brace / thigh brace)	cale-genou (cale-hanche / cale-cuisse)
knot	nœud (m)
land, go aground, anchor	atterrir, accoster
landmark	amer
launch	mettre à l'eau
leeway / make leeway	dérive (f) / dériver (verb)
moor / mooring	amarrer / amarrage (m)
mud (estuary mud)	vase (f)
outfitting (to customise the cockpit fit)	calage
paddle (wing paddle) (greenland paddle) (blade) (splits)	pagaie (f) (pagaie creuse) (pagaie groenlandaise) (pale) (f) (pagaie démontable)
painter (bow line)	bosse
PFD / buoyancy aid	VFI (veste de flottaison individuelle) / gilet
pin (against an object)	cravate, coincement
portage	portage

English	French
pry	écart
rapid (water feature)	rapide (m), torrent (m)
reef	récif (m), écueil (m)
rescue (bow or paddle presentation) ("T" rescue)	récupération (à l'esquimaude) (récupération en "T")
rip, riptide	baïne (f)
rock-hopping	rase-cailloux
rocker rockered	giron (m), ligne de quille (f) gironné, banané
eskimo roll to roll	esquimautage esquimauter
rudder	gouvernail (m)
seat	siège
scull (for support) (sculling draw)	godille (appui en godille) (appel en godille)
seam	soudure, plan de joint
shuttle	navette
skeg	dérive (f)
slackwater (tide) slack above a rapid in a river	étale bief, planiol
spraydeck (grab loop) (tube)	jupe (f), jupette (f), pontage (m) (sangle d'évacuation, tirette) (col)
stern	poupe (f)
sweep stroke	balayage (m)
swell	houle (f)
tide (low tide / high tide) (tidal range) (spring tide / neap tide)	marée (f) (basse mer / pleine mer) (marnage) (grande marée, vives-eaux / mortes-eaux)
toggle	poignée (f), cabillot
touch (a rock whilst rock-hopping)	talonner
tow	remorquage
track (maintain a heading)	garder un cap
trolley	chariot (m)
vee (smooth water down the centre of a rapid)	veine d'eau
volume	volume
wake	sillage (m)
waterline	ligne de flottaison
wave	vague, onde
whirlpool	tourbillon
whitewater	eau vive

Lexicon

English	French
directions	
north / south	nord / sud
east / west	est / ouest
port / starboard	bâbord / tribord
windward / leeward	au vent / sous le vent
upstream / downstream	en amont / en aval
sea animals	
basking shark	requin pèlerin
dolphin	dauphin
porpoise	marsouin
seal	phoque
coastal birds	
black-backed gull	goéland brun
black-headed gull	mouette rieuse
chough	crave à bec rouge
common gull	goéland cendré
cormorant	grand cormoran
curlew	courlis
fulmar	pétrel fulmar
gannet	fou de Bassan
greater black-backed gull	goéland marin
guillemot	guillemot de Troïl
herring gull	goéland
kittiwake	mouette tridactyle
manx shearwater	puffin des Anglais
marsh harrier	busard des roseaux
osprey	balbuzard pêcheur
oyster catcher	huîtrier pie
peregrine	faucon pèlerin
puffin	macareux
razorbill	pingouin torda, petit pingouin
shag	cormoran huppé
skua	labbe
tern	sterne

Also available from Le Canotier

- **Guide Kayak de Mer Méditerranée**
  50 itinéraires sur la côte méditerranéenne : 38 de Banyuls à Menton, incluant les étangs languedociens, et 12 pour tout le littoral corse.

- **La Loire vue du fleuve**
  Guide de randonnée nautique du Puy-en-Velay à St. Nazaire. Très détaillé pour la navigation, il fourmille d'informations pour découvrir au plus près le fleuve royal.

- **Construire et utiliser les kayaks de l'Arctique**
  Manuel qui vous permettra de fabriquer votre kayak en bois et toile, sa pagaie, et qui vous enseignera leur maîtrise.

  And many other titles…

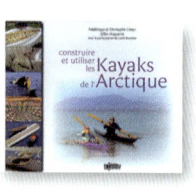 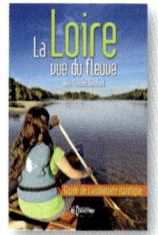

Le Canotier is also an online bookshop specialising in sea kayaking and other paddle sports. Charts, maps and guides for many countries, kayaking and canoeing related books etc.

See the entire catalogue:

www.canotier.com

The SNSM (Société Nationale de Sauvetage en Mer) is the French equivalent of the British RNLI, the Dutch KNRM or the German DGzRS. A charity dedicated to offering a rescue service to all those in peril on the sea. Sea kayakers like all other mariners hope that they will never need their services, but it is very comforting to know that they are there.
To help support them, for each copy of this book sold,
1 euro will be donated to the SNSM.
www.snsm.org

 FOREST STEWARDSHIP COUNCIL

Printed and bound in France in April 2013 by Imprimerie France Quercy - Mercuès (Lot).